A COMMUNITY IN THE ANDES

PROBLEMS AND PROGRESS IN MUQUIYAUYO

The American Ethnological Society
Verne F. Ray, Editor

A COMMUNITY IN THE ANDES
Problems and Progress in Muquiyauyo

BY *RICHARD N. ADAMS*

1959 · University of Washington Press · Seattle

In Memory of

Randolph Greenfield Adams

and

Wendell Clark Bennett

CONTENTS

Part Three: Culture Change in Muquiyauyo

ILLUSTRATIONS

MAPS

FIGURES

INTRODUCTION

THIS BOOK is the result of a field study carried on in the town of Muquiyauyo, department of Huancayo, Peru, in the period from August, 1949, until May, 1950. The original object of the study was to explore the nature of the progressivism that had been reported by various students as characterizing the community.[1] Muquiyauyo was brought to the writer's attention by the late Dr. Wendell Bennett, and the original plan of study, as well as the doctoral dissertation which resulted, was done with his expert and sympathetic aid.[2] The study was financed by a Research Training Fellowship of the Social Science Research Council.

It was originally hoped that an exploration into the materials of local history, as well as into the ethnology of the community, would reveal why Muquiyauyo had manifested various traits that were called "progressive" by other students. It was also hoped that delineation of these traits, besides providing a general account of the life in a Peruvian mountain community, might help solve problems faced in applied anthropology and provide a test for hypotheses in anthropological theory.[3]

With respect to the first goal, there are recounted in the pages to follow many events that played a role in this "progressiveness." The history of the problems faced and solved by the community and its leaders is traced. However, a single ultimate and sufficient explanation of the fact that Muquiyauyo, and not some other town, manifested such progressive activity did not develop. The research involved in this study suggests that to ask a question of this kind is to set up a false issue. There is, after all, no logical reason to think that a simple series of processes can "explain" why one town and not another seems progressive. Certain factors can be selected and emphasized, but the same factors may be present elsewhere and the same events will not take place. This follows from the in-

evitable fact that a community is a unique event; it is a product of
a peculiar local history which in turn is made up of minute strands
of life and action which are impossible completely to reproduce
through historical analysis.

The research carried out in Muquiyauyo led back through some
seventy years of community, district, and *cuartel* records; reports
of sessions were read with care, and the events of the past thus revealed were discussed with informants who had frequently participated in them. During my months of residence in Muquiyauyo, I visited and collected information on the contemporary life of the Muquiyauyino. These data, which are woven into Part I and comprise most
of Part II of the present book, were at the time a side issue; the major effort was devoted to the written and oral reports of local history. After my visit in Muquiyauyo I worked in Central America. It
was not until 1953 that I again turned my attention to the Muquiyauyo
study, which was completed in its present form in 1954. The time
spent on other studies permitted a new approach to the Peruvian
data. Most of the material in chapter 2 was worked out at this time,
and the entire orientation of Part II is new. Even Part I, as it now
appears, could not have been written in 1950; it required the inter-
im period for me to clear my mind of some of the dust of the field.

The book in its present form has two goals: first, to provide a
description of the life of a Central Sierran mestizo and Indian community, since other studies made in this geographical region are
not readily available; and second, to show through the recent history of this community how local history is directed through the
presence of a few pressing unsolved problems, how each generation makes new attempts to solve these problems and in so doing
brings drastic cultural and social change into the community. Often in the course of reworking the materials I found that the only
apparent explanation for the appearance of some trait or the occurrence of some event was that the people faced a problem and
solved it according to methods within their experience. As more
and more problems and solutions were studied, a number of things
became apparent. One was that there were very few original solutions; when a new problem arose, the immediate reaction was to
follow some solution which had been tried before. This, of course,
is not new; psychologists of learning theory have long reported
such behavior. The Muquiyauyo data, however, provide perfectly
clear evidence that history, at least on the local level, can be
analyzed in part through psychological concepts.

Of perhaps even greater interest and importance in the Muquiyauyo material is the fact that many of the problems that were

faced were very old problems that had been growing increasingly
serious in spite of numerous attempts on the part of the townspeople to solve them. From these half-successful solutions often
came new problems, and they were answered by solutions which
in turn served to bring some new element into the culture of the
community. Thus the community changed, some old problems remained, and new problems were constantly being created.

This book is, then, an attempt to tell the story of how the problems faced by the people of Muquiyauyo have shaped the events
which, in turn, have made up the history that we study. It is perhaps inevitable in research of this kind, where documentation is
slim at best and the memory of individuals must be depended upon
to a degree that is often unwise, that there are many leads which
cannot be followed up; there are others that, because the information is available, can be pursued back three or four hundred years.
Thus the reason we dwell on some subjects and not on others is
not always because we think them to be the most important subjects. At times, they are the only subjects that can tell us anything. In this way the data, and not the writer, have often been the
principal selective factor in what was studied.

No piece of work is done alone: friends, colleagues, and even customs agents can make or break a study. The original planning of the
present study was accomplished with the aid of Wendell Bennett
and Gabriel Escobar. In Lima, Dr. Jorge Muelle, Dr. Luis E.
Valcarcel, Sr. José Matos, Sr. Hernando de Lavalle and family,
Dr. and Mrs. Ozzie Simmons, Mr. and Mrs. Cloyce Tippitt, Mr.
and Mrs. Homer Diman, and Dr. Clifford Pease all shared in pav-
ing the way leading to Muquiyauyo. In Tingo Maria Dr. and Mrs.
Howard Allard kindly offered their hospitality; in Huarón, a very
pleasant visit was made possible through the courtesy of the administrator of the mines, M. Louis Charbonneau, and the Muquiyauyinos resident at the mine. In La Oroyo, Dr. and Mrs. Knute E.
Berger, Mr. Egbert M. Robinson, and Mr. Charles Dasso of the
Cerro de Pasco Corporation offered their hospitality and kindness
during periods when I was ill.

In Muquiyauyo, I was fortunate enough to have the assistance of
three persons from time to time. During the first month and a half,
Sr. Alfonso Trujillo, then student in the Faculty of Geography of the
University of San Marcos, collaborated with me in the field and
helped me over the hurdle of initial unfamiliarity with Spanish.
During February and March, 1950, Mr. Edward Bernard, of Ver-
mont, then a student in the University of San Marcos, joined me
and made a study of the religious *cofradías* in the town. During

much of the same period, Sr. Erberto Dávila, a patient at the Jauja
sanatorium, came twice a week to collect excellent material on
the fiestas in Muquiyauyo; the descriptive data on religious celebrations herein are largely the results of the work of Messrs. Davila
and Bernard. Also in Muquiyauyo, of course, the Muquiyauyinos
provided the essential help which made the study possible. It is
not possible to list here by name all the informants who provided
materials and information, and permitted me to visit their homes
and participate in their fiestas with them. With very few exceptions,
everyone with whom I came into contact in the town provided help
in one way or another. One Muquiyauyino, however, gave so much
of his time, and so much of the present work depends upon his constant cooperation and goodwill, that he must be especially thanked.
Sr. Pedro Bustamante, a second-generation Muquiyauyino, has
been one of the leaders in the public works of the community and
has long interested himself in the history of the community. Sr.
Bustamante contributed countless hours and invaluable knowledge
to the writer; without his aid, this study could not have been accomplished.

The patience and help of my wife, Betty H. Adams, has made
possible the reworking of the original materials. The base maps
used for the study are based upon those made by a Muquiyauyino,
Teófilo Moreno, in 1937 and supplemented by Sr. Trujillo. The edi-
tors of *Human Organization and Social Forces* have kindly granted
permission to reproduce in chapter 5 some materials that appeared
originally in their journals.

To all these people I owe a debt of gratitude; the form and content of the final product is entirely my own responsibility.

The two men to whom this study is dedicated are in great part responsible for the accomplishment of the work. My father, Randolph
G. Adams, led me into the paths of history; my teacher, Wendell
Bennett, directed me to Latin America. I sincerely hope that this
effort, which owes to them whatever merits it may have, will in
some measure honor their memory.

Richard N. Adams

PART ONE

EXPLORING MUQUIYAUYO HISTORY

THE SETTING TODAY

THE JAUJA Valley in Peru, located in the highlands above the modern national capital of Lima, first stepped into the current of western history with the arrival of Pizarro in 1533. It was in this valley that Pizarro first met strong armed resistance from the Inca forces and it was here that he first planned to establish his capital in the New World. As W. H. Prescott later wrote, "It was a favorable position for holding the Indian mountaineers in check, while, at the same time, it offered an easy communication with the seacoast."[1] The town of Atunxauxa, or Jauja as it is known today, was located at the northern end of an eleven thousand-foot-high intermountain valley which was originally formed by the Mantaro River. The river, arising some one hundred kilometers northwest of Jauja, cuts through the mountains just south of the town and enters the wide flat plain that spreads for fifty kilometers southeast to the town of Huancayo.

When Pizarro visited the valley and the first Spaniards camped near the town of Jauja, buildings of stone and mortar, usually round, and plastered inside, lined the sides of the mountains that jut up sharply from the valley floor. These structures were without windows, and the doors were only two or three feet high, requiring that a person stoop to enter or leave. They were grouped at intervals along the slopes, and many seem to have had little planning as to location. Others, however, were so arranged that the structures formed a single wall facing the valley. The local Indians who lived in this region went under the name of Huanca, although there were scattered among them groups of colonists (mitimaes) brought by the Incas from other parts of Peru. These people, natives and colonists alike, tilled the floor of the valley and pastured their llamas and vicuñas in the puna[2] or high land in the broken hills behind the towns. During this period few of the towns which now

dot the valley floor existed. Most of the present population centers
were formed later as a part of the Spanish policy of *reducción*,
whereby the Indians were brought together and settled in the flat
lands of the valley. Ancestors of the present Muquiyauyinos were
among those brought together in this manner.

Today the Jauja Valley presents a very different picture from that
seen by Pizarro and his companions when they arrived four centuries ago. Instead of open fields, there are large growths of eucalyptus trees partially hiding many of the towns which are set
back from both banks of the Mantaro River. Most of these towns
have retained names which stem from the days of the Huanca: Paca,
Jauja, Huaripampa, Muquiyauyo, Pacamarca, Ataura, Huamalí,
Pucucho, Apata, Sincos, Matahuasi, Mito, Aco, Orcotuna, Sicaya,
Chupaca, and Huancayo, the modern departmental capital. Both the
streets of the towns and the fields surrounding them are laid in rectangular patterns, and stretching out from some of the towns here
and there are long eucalyptus alamedas.

The architecture in all these towns is very uniform. Houses of
adobe brick or rammed earth with red or orange-red tile roofs line
the streets around the center plaza or park, and are scattered along
the outlying streets. Most of the houses are of one story, frequently
with high roofs, although around the plaza there may be a number
of two-story buildings. From numerous empty lots sprout small
corn patches and eucalyptus trees, and through some of the towns
run irrigation canals. Each town has its church, which may be
old, and each district capital has its municipal building. Set off
to one side of each town is a walled-in cemetery.

Muquiyauyo lies on the valley floor to the west of the river about
seven kilometers south of Jauja. The main road running through
the valley is on the east side of the river, so the road to Muquiyauyo is important primarily for local commerce and travel. Even
the bridge spanning the Mantaro at the time the study was made
had been built by local people; not until 1950 did the national government start work on a new bridge to replace the one built by the
people of Muquiyauyo eighteen years earlier.

Long-distance travel in the valley or to and from outside regions is mainly by bus or truck. The railroad is used as well, but
buses run more frequently, especially on fair days, and are cheaper. For shorter distances donkeys and less frequently horses may
be used, but most often people go on foot. Aside from a few wheel-
barrows or rare complex introduced articles such as motor vehi-
cles and bicycles, the wheel is not prevalent in this region. Although oxen are used in plowing, there are no oxcarts. Except be-

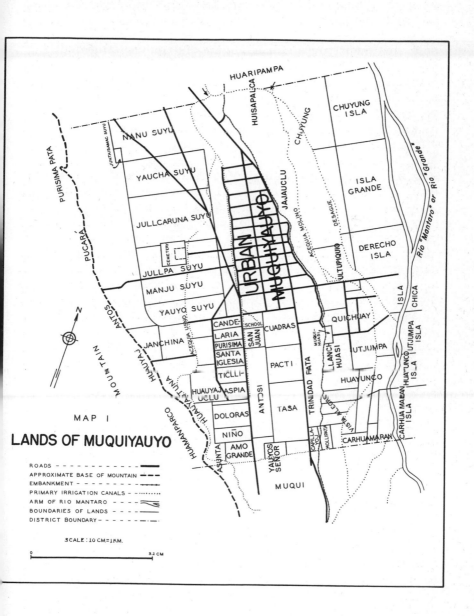

MAP I

LANDS OF MUQUIYAUYO

ROADS - - - - - - - - - -
APPROXIMATE BASE OF MOUNTAIN - - -
EMBANKMENT - - - - - - - - -
PRIMARY IRRIGATION CANALS - - - - - - - -
ARM OF RIO MANTARO - - - - -
BOUNDARIES OF LANDS - - - -
DISTRICT BOUNDARY - - - - - - - -

SCALE : 10 CM=1KM.

0   3.2 CM

tween the major towns of Jauja, Huancayo, and Oroya, the roads
frequently become impassable in the rainy season.

Just to the north of Muquiyauyo, closely bordering the town itself, lies Huaripampa, formerly the district capital and still the
parish center for Muquiyauyo. To the south, in the district of Muquiyauyo, is the town of Muqui. The district of Muquiyauyo ex-
tends from the center of the river west across the mountains and
borders in the *puna* on the hacienda of Llacuarí. In addition to
Muquiyauyo and the smaller center of Muqui, there is within the
district a small village called Los Andes, located in the hills behind the town.

In its general appearance, Muquiyauyo looks very much like
other settlements in the valley. The streets are straight now and
in some places on or close to the plaza there are paved sidewalks.
The center of the town is the plaza, on which are located the old
church; a park with paved walks, benches, and large trees; the
municipalidad or district government building; stores; and houses.
Just off the plaza to the west is the girls' school, and on the southern edge of town is the new boys' school. Along most of the streets
near the center of town are adobe walls, forming part of a house
or surrounding a *chacra*, a small cultivated plot of land. *Chacras*
within the town are usually irrigated from the town's canal system, and are planted in corn, broad beans, or potatoes. There
are still a number of old houses in Muquiyauyo, some dating back
to early in the nineteenth century. Houses are usually built bit by
bit as the owner can afford to pay for them, so the compounds are
often mixtures of old and new, and walls awaiting roofs. Ruins of
some of the old houses give the town something of a dilapidated
appearance. Except on the main streets and near the plaza the
houses are seldom built immediately adjacent to each other.

Down the center of most streets running east and west are small
banked canals, carrying water for irrigation, washing, drinking,
and, although not so planned, refuse. The western limit of the urban section is the large upper canal, Acequia Alta; the eastern
limit is formed generally by an embankment dropping some eight
meters. To the south the houses stop at the last cross street, Avenida Escuela, on which is located the boys' school; and to the north,
houses string out irregularly along the road to Huaripampa. There
are a few homes west of the Acequia Alta and east of the embankment. To the southeast is a small section called Quichuay, referred
to as a barrio, or ward, by the people living in the town. No social
or political factors distinguish the inhabitants of Quichuay from
those of the rest of the town.

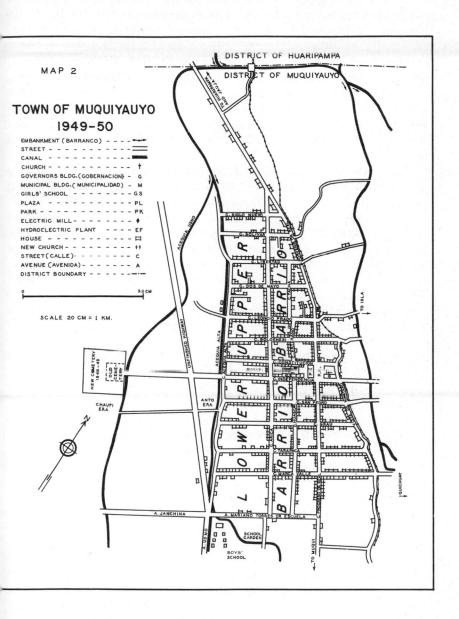

MAP 2

TOWN OF MUQUIYAUYO
1949-50

EMBANKMENT (BARRANCO) - - - - ⊣
STREET - - - - - - - - - - -
CANAL - - - - - - - - - - ▬
CHURCH - - - - - - - - - - †
GOVERNORS BLDG.(GOBERNACION) - G
MUNICIPAL BLDG.(MUNICIPALIDAD) - M
GIRLS' SCHOOL - - - - - - - GS
PLAZA - - - - - - - - - - PL
PARK - - - - - - - - - - PK
ELECTRIC MILL - - - - - - - ⚡
HYDROELECTRIC PLANT - - - EF
HOUSE - - - - - - - - - - ▢
NEW CHURCH - - - - - - - ††
STREET(CALLE) - - - - - - - C
AVENUE (AVENIDA) - - - - - - A
DISTRICT BOUNDARY - - - - ⊷

0   3.2 CM

SCALE 20 CM = 1 KM.

DISTRICT OF HUARIPAMPA

DISTRICT OF MUQUIYAUYO

The main street in Muquiyauyo is that coming in from Huari-pampa. It is called Calle Real and is divided into two parts, Calle Porvenir north of the plaza and Calle Progreso south of the plaza. Actually, all three terms are used almost interchangeably. This street enters along the top of the embankment north of the plaza, then turns south, perpendicular to the east-west streets, reaching the plaza slightly to one side of the center. From the other side of the plaza it goes directly to Muqui. This and the next street west are the only ones adequately prepared for automobile travel, since all the others have the center canal and each cross street has an unbridged canal.

The landscape surrounding the town presents two particularly impressive features. One is the sharp incline of the mountain wall that rises behind the town and provides a year-round gray-brown backdrop for the people living in the valley below. The other is the valley floor itself, which is in alternate patches of green and brown, depending upon the time of the year and the particular pieces of land cultivated. In the rainy summer months, most of the valley floor turns green with wheat, barley, corn, and other crops. The mountains, on the other hand, never lose their brown cast. Almost all the farmers of the towns along the river have some holdings in the mountain lands above, and most of the districts control a certain amount of this land.

The flat, valley land of Muquiyauyo is agriculturally divided into two distinct regions, the irrigated and the unirrigated. Unlike some towns in the valley, which are without irrigation, Muquiyauyo has had water brought to the town for almost eighty years. The construction of the first canal is attributed to Román Amanzo, who, because of this and other works, has assumed almost legendary status in the town. The unirrigated lands are called *temporales,* while those which have access to water are called *riegos.* While the valley land appears rich and fertile initially, a closer look shows it to be poor in many places. The mountain lands have outcroppings of bedrock and the irregular topsoil is full of small angular stones. Along the sides of the mountains are numerous *quebradas,* small and medium-sized canyons, which cut their way out to the valley floor. The sides of the mountains are often steep, and many sections are composed of a soft shale which breaks underfoot and is unfit for any agricultural or livestock industry. Other sections of the mountain sides are sandy or contain clay deposits, some of sufficiently good quality to be used as a source of adobe for building. These deposits vary in composition and utility; the darker clays are used for the heavy adobe construction, while almost pure white or cream-colored clays are extracted for the *tierra blanca,* or white earth, a plaster finish applied to many of the house walls. The mountain slopes provide occasional pasturage for the animals of the townspeople, and a few small foothills provide some level land for cultivation.

Between the base of the mountain slope and the westernmost canal are the most important of the unirrigated lands. There the soil is predominantly clayey, and although rocks are present they provide no great barrier to cultivation. These lands are divided into long rectangular sections called *suyus,* separated by low mounds of earth, or *surcos.* The irrigated lands begin to the east of the Acequia Usno, the uppermost canal. Irrigated plots are very often surrounded by tall eucalyptus trees, a hedge of scrub bush, or a wall of adobe.

In the embankment that limits the main part of the settled portion of the town to the east, it is possible to see the stratum of large water-worn pebbles which, covered with a topsoil varying in depth from a third of a meter to a meter, forms the land on which the agriculture above the embankment is based. Below the embankment the soil could doubtless compete with rocky New England. The rocks, all rounded, are of little use in construction and must be constantly removed from the fields. In this area the dividing lines between the fields are most commonly long rows of these rocks piled together. Occasionally they are cemented with a clay mortar. In general, farming is more difficult below the embankment than above, increasing in difficulty with proximity to the river. The region between the town and the river is mostly without irrigation water and is used for pasturage. This particular area is called Isla (island), a most appropriate name because over the years the river has chosen numerous channels and the entire region has been under water at one time or another. The problems of land ownership here have been solved by maintaining most of the Isla land as communal property to be used by the community members when and where the river permits.

The Muquiyauyinos racially are in general mestizo, the same mixture of Indian and white that characterizes a large portion of Peruvians and other Latin Americans. No measurements or systematic observation of physical characteristics were made during the study. Some Muquiyauyinos appear to be predominantly Indian and some are predominantly white. The people are generally short, the men standing on the average about five feet four or five inches, and the women slightly shorter. The blending of Spanish and Indian has now been going on for at least three hundred years in Muquiyauyo, so, except for the few recent migrants, the entire population may be considered mixed.

While everyone speaks Spanish, most of the older generation and about half of the younger also speak Quechua, or Huanca, as it is called locally. This is equally true among those who are regarded as mestizos as among those regarded as Indian. The Quechua language is mainly retained by the women and by those who seldom venture out of the valley. There was only one person in town at the time of the study, an elderly woman, who spoke only Quechua. The use of Quechua is also retained by some of the masked dancers in the Christmas and New Year fiestas. Spanish is without question now the dominant language. It is used by all men, taught in the schools, and used in all dealings with outsiders. Doubtless Quechua will linger for many years to come, continuing to be used only as a second language.

LAND AND POPULATION

THE PEOPLE of Muquiyauyo have always been farmers, and their main activity is gaining a living through the production of crops. Sufficient land for the people of the town, therefore, is always a matter of concern. The relation between land and population has set the stage for much of what has happened in the recent history of the town.

I found no record of the exact date when Muquiyauyo as a town was founded nor of its size in the early colonial days. The earliest figures on the population are for 1742; they are provided in a document which lists the number of Indian *tributarios* of the town. For the ancient province of Jauja, however, we have figures going back to 1525,[1] and from these we can trace the decline and rise of the population within the province as a whole. This "province," it should be noted, is not the present-day province of Jauja, but includes the modern provinces of Jauja and Huancayo. While the boundaries do not coincide exactly for some of the figures available, they are close enough to reveal the general trend of population growth through most of the postconquest history.

John Rowe estimates that the Inca province of Jauja had a population of 135,000 in 1525. By 1571 this population had declined to about 36,000,[2] and by 1754 it had dropped to a little over 21,000.[3] At about this time the population started to rise again. When the census of 1940 was taken, it had reached over 258,000, and by 1950 it was probably in the neighborhood of 280,000. In approximately two hundred years, then, between 1754 and 1950, the population of the colonial province of Jauja increased over thirteen times to a figure which is probably twice as high as it was in pre-Spanish times. It is probable that never before in its history has this region had to support such a large population.

Our first estimates for the population of Muquiyauyo come from

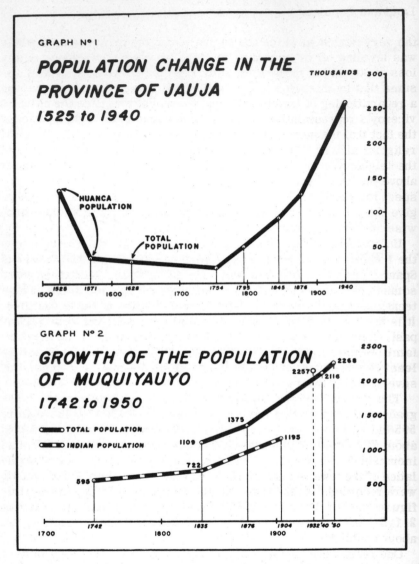

1. Population change in the province of Jauja (1940 provinces of Jauja and Huancayo), 1525 to 1940. Sources: 1525, 1571--Rowe, 1947, Table 1; 1628, 1754--Kubler, 1947, Table 2; 1795, 1845-46, 1876, 1940--Kubler, 1952, Table 9.

2. Growth of the population of Muquiyauyo, 1742 to 1950. Sources: 1742--Doc.-A-17, factor of 5/family; 1835--Kubler, 1952; 1876--Doc.-A-18; 1904--Doc.-A-20, factor of 4.2/family; 1932--census by P. Bustamante; 1940--national population census, 1940; 1950--writer's census, 540 families, factor of 4.2/family.

the very period in which the population of the province as a whole was leveling off or beginning to rise. We have no evidence of any loss of population in the town after 1742 and so we may as well assume that by this time it was beginning to rise. In 1742 there was a repartitioning of land in Muquiyauyo, and at that time the colonial viceroy's representative in charge of dividing up the land mentioned the fact that the people of Muquiyauyo were all participating in local religious affairs. This was important because many of the people of the neighboring town of Huaripampa were in the *puna*, the highlands above the town, and were reluctant to come in and show proper respect for the church. As a result, the representative decided to give the people of Muquiyauyo some of the land which would otherwise have been given to the Huaripampiños.

Unfortunately, figures on the population at this date include only the *tributarios*, the Indians, and there are no data on the number of Spanish and mestizo people who were in the town. That there were some is certain, since existing documents dating back to the seventeenth century concern the land claims of some of these families. It is known that prior to this time and even until the very recent past, some mestizos moved into Muquiyauyo. Most of the mestizo families in the town claim some antiquity, however, and one at least is composed of the descendants of the man who made the seventeenth-century land claims.

The population figures for Muquiyauyo indicate a much more gradual curve than that for the entire province. In 1742 there were 595 Indian *tributarios* in the town;[4] by 1835 they had increased to about 722,[5] and by 1904 the number of persons called Indian had increased to almost 1,200.[6] The earliest figure for the entire population of the town is that for 1835, at which time about 1,100 people were recorded.[7] At the time that the census of 1876 was taken, this figure had increased to 1,375,[8] and by 1940 it was recorded as 2,116.[9] In the century between 1835 and 1940 the population just about doubled.

One reason that the Muquiyauyo population does not seem to have risen so rapidly as that of the province as a whole is emigration. The problem of overpopulation in Muquiyauyo has regularly been at least partially solved in this way. In 1932, for example, Pedro Bustamante took a census of Muquiyauyinos, including in it some who were away from the town at the time working in the mines. He obtained a figure of 2,257. Comparing this with the 1940 census figure of 2,116, we can see that perhaps 250 of the people whom he recorded as Muquiyauyinos were not actually living in the town at that time, and would not have been included in an official census.

The Muquiyauyinos were early aware of the fact that their population was growing. One of a series of documents concerning an issue between the town and the parish in 1819 and 1820 states that the population of the town had tripled since the repartitioning of land in 1742. The figures we have do not sustain this claim, since the total population figures for 1835 are not even twice as large as those for Indians alone in 1742, but there is no doubt that there had been some growth. Besides a natural growth, probably of greater importance was the immigration of mestizos and Spaniards into the town. From our figures it would seem likely that a strain on the land resources began to be felt early in the nineteenth century and became more serious as the century wore on.

It is not known precisely how the land was divided up at the time of the conquest. It is likely that many people lived on the hillsides around the valley, as the remains of structures there today testify. Sometime after the conquest, the *reducción* movement displaced the Indian social groupings known as *ayllus*, and among the first *ayllus* to form what is today Muquiyauyo were those of the Muqui and the Yauyos. The Muqui were a Huanca community, and the Yauyos were a group from a neighboring tribe of the same name, which the Incas had moved into the region. Tradition has it that the Yauyo *ayllu* was moved into the section of the present district known as Molli and the Muqui were moved into the section around Muquihausi. In a seventeenth-century land claim document it is mentioned that the land known as Tasa (near Molli) belonged to the cacique, or leader, of the Yauyo *ayllu*;[10] this tends to confirm the tradition.

That these early settlements of land were soon disturbed by the arrival of Spaniards is indicated by the seventeenth-century documents. In 1661 a Spaniard, Juan Martínez Franco, claimed a series of pieces of land which included two known as Muqui and Guansey; these two were doubtless the section known today as Muquihausi, the same originally given to the Muqui *ayllu*. The Spaniard evidently made good his claim, but by 1728 his descendants felt the land was being encroached upon by the Indians and started another claim to revalidate their title. In documents concerning this issue it is said that their ancestor, Juan Martínez Franco, was the founder of Muquiyauyo; while we have no positive evidence to support this, we do know that Vázquez de Espinosa in his journey through the valley in the early part of the seventeenth century does not mention Muquiyauyo as a town;[11] he does mention a population of "Yauyus" living near Jauja and thus implies that Muquiyauyo did not exist as a town at that time. So while we may tentatively accept

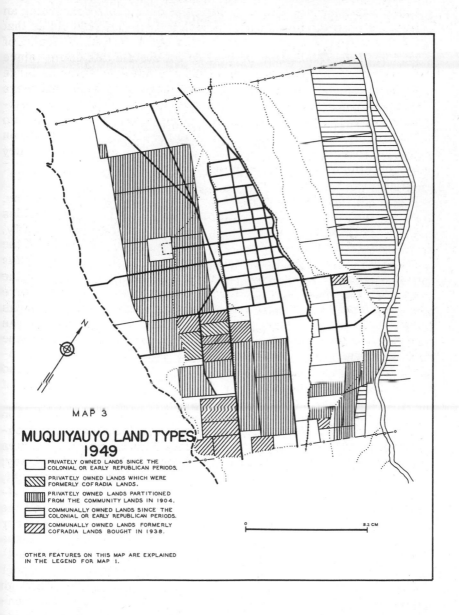

MAP 3

MUQUIYAUYO LAND TYPES
1949

PRIVATELY OWNED LANDS SINCE THE
COLONIAL OR EARLY REPUBLICAN PERIODS.

PRIVATELY OWNED LANDS WHICH WERE
FORMERLY COFRADIA LANDS.

PRIVATELY OWNED LANDS PARTITIONED
FROM THE COMMUNITY LANDS IN 1904.

COMMUNALLY OWNED LANDS SINCE THE
COLONIAL OR EARLY REPUBLICAN PERIODS.

COMMUNALLY OWNED LANDS FORMERLY
COFRADIA LANDS BOUGHT IN 1938.

OTHER FEATURES ON THIS MAP ARE EXPLAINED
IN THE LEGEND FOR MAP 1.

0   3.2 CM

the claim of the Martínez descendants that their ancestor was the first Muquiyauyino, we are also assured that he established himself as the first Spanish citizen of Muquiyauyo by taking the land that must originally have been assigned to some of the local Indians. The 1728 documents also state that the Muqui lived at this time in an area now occupied by the town of Muqui, then in the jurisdiction of the neighboring town to the south, Sincos.

The first information indicating with any certainty the amount of land in the hands of the Indians of Muquiyauyo is contained in a document dated 1742.[12] In that year Pedro de Valenzuela y Rios, a representative of the Court of Measurement, Sale, and Adjustment of Lands (Juzgado de Remensura, Venta y Composición de Tierras), partitioned the lands of Muquiyauyo and Huaripampa. This was presumably not the first time that such a partition had been made. Since the sixteenth century, the crown had been ordering that towns be created in the colony and that the lands be divided; and the general rule, established by Viceroy Toledo, was that the lands should be reapportioned every three years to be sure that every person had enough. The first adjustment was begun in 1591 and continued until 1604. A second was made between 1642 and 1666. It may well have been this second adjustment of land which stirred Juan Martínez Franco to make his claim in 1662. Early in the eighteenth century the Court of Measurement, Sale, and Adjustment of Lands was established in Lima,[13] and between 1722 and 1725 a review was made of all claims. Hence while the original plan was to reapportion the lands frequently it was actually done fairly infrequently.

The 1742 division of the Muquiyauyo and Huaripampa lands was the last such repartition for which we have any evidence during the colonial period. There is every reason to believe that the adjuster recognized the claims of the local Spanish-mestizo population with respect to their private titles, since there is neither record nor memory of any ensuing disputes; in addition, most of the lands claimed by Martínez' descendants in 1735 were still in private hands in 1949, and were recognized as the lands over which the family had established rights. Such rights, therefore, were doubtless validated by de Valenzuela y Rios.

Among the lands which were apportioned in 1742 were five cofradía, or religious brotherhood, lands. Cofradía lands were established to provide income for religious activities. The cofradías themselves had been established before this time. It is not possible to say whether the 1742 allotments were merely a recognition of lands already assigned to cofradías, whether they added more to those already established, or whether they reduced an

Law and Status among the Kiowa Indians. Jane Richardson. (Monograph I) 1940. 142 pages, bibliography. Out of print

Rank and Warfare among the Plains Indians. Bernard Mishkin. (Monograph III) 1940. 73 pages, bibliography. Out of print

Disease, Religion and Society in the Fiji Islands. Dorothy M. Spencer. (Monograph II) 1941. 92 pages, chart. Out of print

An Analysis of Inca Militarism. Joseph Bram. (Monograph IV) 1941. 93 pages, bibliography. $1.50

A Primitive Mexican Economy. George M. Foster. (Monograph V) 1942. 123 pages, plates, maps, bibliography. Out of print

The Effects of White Contact upon Blackfoot Culture, with Special Reference to the Role of the Fur Trade. Oscar Lewis. (Monograph VI) 1942. 79 pages, maps, bibliography. $1.50

Arapesh. R. F. Fortune. (Publication XIX) 1942. 243 pages. $5.00

Prayer: The Compulsive Word. Gladys A. Reichard. (Monograph VII) 1944. 121 pages, figures, bibliography. $2.50

Changing Configurations in the Social Organization of a Blackfoot Tribe during the Reserve Period (The Blood of Alberta, Canada). Esther S. Goldfrank. (Monograph VIII, bound with IX) 1945. 81 pages, plates, bibliography. $2.50

Observations on Northern Blackfoot Kinship. L. M. Hanks, Jr., and Jane Richardson. (Monograph IX, bound with VIII) 1945. 37 pages, figures. $2.50

Map of North American Indian Languages. Compiled and drawn by C. F. Voegelin and E. W. Voegelin. (Publication XX) 1945. Wall size, color. $2.00

The Influence of Islam on a Sudanese Religion. Joseph Greenberg. (Monograph X) 1946. 83 pages, figures, map, bibliography. $2.50

Alaskan Eskimo Ceremonialism. Margaret Lantis. (Monograph XI) 1947. 143 pages, maps, bibliography. $2.75

Economics of the Mount Hagen Tribes, New Guinea. Abraham L. Gitlow. (Monograph XII) 1947. 122 pages, plates, figures, maps, bibliography. $2.75

Ceremonial Patterns in the Greater Southwest. Ruth M. Underhill. (Monograph XIII, bound with XIV) 1948. 74 pages, bibliography, index. $2.50

Factionalism in Isleta Pueblo. David H. French. (Monograph XIV, bound with XIII) 1948. 54 pages, bibliography. $2.50

The Negro in Northern Brazil: A Study in Acculturation. Octavio da Costa Eduardo. (Monograph XV) 1948. 139 pages, map, bibliography. $2.75

Bali: Rangda and Barong. Jane Belo. (Monograph XVI) 1949. 71 pages, plates, figures, bibliography. $2.75

The Rubber-Ball Games of the Americas. Theodore Stern. (Monograph XVII) 1950. 129 pages, plate, maps, bibliography. $2.50

Fighting with Property: A Study of Kwakiutl Potlatching and Warfare 1792-1930. Helen Codere. With Tribal and Linguistic Map of Vancouver Island and Adjacent Territory, drawn and compiled by Vincent F. Kotschar. (Monograph XVIII) 1950. 143 pages, figures, maps, charts, bibliography. $3.00

The Cheyenne in Plains Indian Trade Relations 1795-1840. Joseph Jablow. (Monograph XIX) 1951. 110 pages, maps, bibliography, index. $2.50

The Tsimshian: Their Arts and Music. The Tsimshian and Their Neighbors, by Viola E. Garfield; Tsimshian Sculpture, by Paul S. Wingert; Tsimshian Songs, by Marius Barbeau. (Publication XVIII) 1951. 302 pages, plates, figures, maps, music, bibliography, index. $6.00

Navaho Grammar. Gladys A. Reichard. (Publication XXI) 1951. 407 pages, bibliography. $7.00

Buzios Island: A Caiçara Community in Southern Brazil. Emilio Willems in cooperation with Gioconda Mussolini. (Monograph XX) 1952. 124 pages, figures, maps, bibliography. $2.75

Chichicastenango: A Guatemalan Village. Ruth Bunzel. (Publication XXII) 1952. 464 pages, figures, bibiliography. $7.00

Changing Military Patterns on the Great Plains (17th Century through Early 19th Century). Frank Raymond Secoy. (Monograph XXI) 1953. 120 pages, maps, bibliography. $2.75

Bali: Temple Festival. Jane Belo. (Monograph XXII) 1953. 78 pages, plates, chart, bibliography. $2.75

Hungarian and Vogul Mythology. Géza Róheim. With appendixes by John Lotz. (Monograph XXIII) 1954. 96 pages, map, bibliography. $2.75

The Trumaí Indians of Central Brazil. Robert F. Murphy and Buell Quain. (Monograph XXIV) 1955. 120 pages, plates, map, bibliography. $2.75

The Deeply Rooted: A Study of a Drents Community in the Netherlands. John Y. Keur and Dorothy L. Keur. (Monograph XXV) 1955. 208 pages, plates, maps, bibliography. $3.00

The Tlingit Indians: Results of a Trip to the Northwest Coast of America and the Bering Straits. Aurel Krause. Translated by Erna Gunther. 1956. 320 pages, plates, figures, map, bibliography, index. $4.50

Village and Plantation Life in Northeastern Brazil. Harry William Hutchinson. 1957. 209 pages, plates, maps, charts, bibliography, index. $3.50

Malaya. Norton Ginsburg and Chester F. Roberts, Jr. 1958. 547 pages, maps, charts, bibliography, index. $6.00

Social Stratification in Polynesia. Marshall D. Sahlins. 1958. 306 pages, figures, bibliography. $4.50

Status Terminology and the Social Structure of North American Indians. Munro S. Edmonson. 1958. 92 pages, charts, bibliography. $3.00

A Community in the Andes: Problems and Progress in Muquiyauyo. Richard N. Adams. 1959. 265 pages, maps, figures, bibliography, index. $4.75

earlier amount. The last possibility seems very remote, since
the church was strongly established in the colonial regime and
it is most likely that by this date the *cofradías* were as important to the local population as they were to the colonial administration. Tradition has it that the five *cofradías* were San Juan Bautista (the patron saint of the town), Asunción, Yauyos Señor, Purísima, and Amo Grande (called Nuestro Amo at that time).
The repartition of 1742 divided the lands as follows:

114 *tributarios*, each to receive
    10 *topos* of land . . . . 1,140 *topos*
50 widows and old persons, each to
    receive 5 *topos* of land 250
70 single men and women, each to
    receive 4 *topos* of land 280
5 *cofradías* to receive a total of 56
5 caciques, each to receive 5
    topos of land 25
The community to receive 20

Any extra land was to revert to the community; the document
stated that there was quite a bit of land that would be communal.
The document specified that the *topo* was to be 70 x 40 *varas*, that
is, 2,800 square *varas* or approximately 1,950 square meters.

Three questions arise in any attempt to understand the development of land problems in Muquiyauyo. First, what was the actual
usufruct of the various lands of the town? Second, where did these
lands lie? And finally, of what area were the lands? In order to
answer these questions, we must draw inferences from information taken from various periods in the town's history.

During the colonial period, the principal concepts of land ownership were based upon the idea that all land pertained to the crown.
Grants were made from these holdings to Spaniards, to the church,
and to communities of Indians. Under the original *encomienda*
system, a Spaniard was granted the right to exploit a given area
of land together with the *repartimientos*, or groups of Indians resident on the land. He was not given the land as private property,
however, and it theoretically reverted to the crown after two or
three generations. During the seventeenth century, the *corregimiento* system gradually replaced the *encomienda* system; in prin-
ciple the *encomiendas* came to an end and the land once more came
under the control of the crown. During this period, however, actual grants of property were evidently made to Spaniards, especially to those appointed as caciques or those who assumed such a

position. The rest of the land was not actually granted to individual Indians, but to an Indian community; a certain part of this community land was then allotted to an Indian for his use. Thus, as Kubler has pointed out, while the Spanish were on the one hand trying to foster a sense of the responsibility of private property in the population, they effectively kept the Indians from gaining such an attitude by calculating tribute on a community basis instead of an individual basis. While an Indian was allotted a piece of land from his community by the *corregidor*, cacique, or some other colonial agent, he was not given this land as permanent private property. The only Indians who came near actually receiving property in the Spanish sense were the caciques. This policy continued up to the time of the wars of independence. The documents from the dispute in 1819 state clearly that from the point of view of the crown officials, the lands in these towns did not belong to the towns but rather to the crown, and that they were to be redivided whenever the crown's representative felt they should be.

Historians have perhaps placed too much emphasis upon the Peruvian Indian's tendency to regard his land as a communal matter and not as private property. The Spanish colonial government seems to have encouraged this concept in the Indian by never permitting him to own any land privately. Through the centuries of colonial rule, the lands remained communal; after one century of republican rule, in which many of the colonial policies were continued in fact if not by law, the Muquiyauyinos abandoned the large communal land holdings, repartitioning them as private property in 1904. The maintenance of land under control of the crown was quickly ended at the time of the independence; one of the first measures decreed by both San Martín and Bolívar was the distribution of lands which had been kept communal under colonial authority.

At the time of the land partitioning in Muquiyauyo in 1742, three basic types of landholdings existed:

1. Crown lands
    a. Allotted to Indian *tributarios*
    b. Allotted to widows and old people
    c. Allotted to single people
    d. Allotted to caciques
    e. Allotted to the community
2. Church lands
    a. Owned for use by the church
    b. Held by *cofradías*
3. Private lands, held by Spanish, creoles, mestizos, etc.

With the coming of independence, the formal allotting of lands by colonial authorities ceased; the national government did not try to take over the position of the crown as landowner. The new policy, although not always realized, was that the lands should once and for all be divided as private property. In fact, the lands which had formerly been allotted by the crown authority to Indian *tributarios*, widows and old people, single people, and the community, now fell into a general category of communal property of the Indian community. During the succeeding years, many fraudulent claims to these lands were produced on behalf of mestizos, creoles, or Spaniards; but the original grants had not been to these people, and early documents could not be produced.

Between the 1742 repartition of the Muquiyauyo lands and the end of the colonial rule, however, the Indians of the town evidently lost control of much of the land which had been assigned to them. The Indians, excluding the caciques, had received 1, 690 *topos* or about 3, 295, 000 square meters (329. 5 hectares) of land in 1742. When the Indian communal lands were finally divided up into private property in 1904, only some 1, 091, 000 square meters (109. 1 hectares) were left. In other words, between 1742 and 1904 the Indian and communal lands decreased to one-third their original size. It is not known how this occurred, but there is some suggestion that this land left the control of the Indians before the end of the colonial epoch.

If the data we have collected on the growth of the Muquiyauyo population are correct, there was probably an increase of only about one hundred Indians in the period between 1742 and 1819. At the latter date, however, the Indians of the town complained that because their population had tripled there were now only about three *topos* of land per individual family head instead of the ten originally assigned in 1742. It is possible that the statements of the Indians at this time were simply gross exaggerations of the facts. On the other hand, the situation may be interpreted in another way. Since there is no reason to believe that the Indians had access to population data of 1742 when they discussed this matter in 1819, they cannot be expected to have known how much their population had increased in the intervening period. They probably did know, however, through tradition, that each man had received ten *topos* originally; and they could observe that each had only about three in 1819. From this they might have calculated that their population had tripled; from this we can also calculate that they had lost somewhere between two-thirds and one-half of their land in this period. The conclusion that the Indians had lost most of their

lands before the end of the colonial period is supported by data on
the *cofradías*; in chapter 4 we shall see that there is good evidence
that the *cofradía* lands expanded during this same period.

It will be recalled that there are three geographically distinct
areas of land in the district of Muquiyauyo: the lands between the
river and the embankment; those between the embankment and the
foot of the mountains; and those in the mountains. The history of
the land problem is concerned mainly with the first two of these.
It is mostly in recent years, as the pressure of the population has
grown, that the mountain lands have played an important role in
the community. For the moment, then, we shall concern ourselves
with the two types of valley lands. They will be referred to as the
lower and *upper* valley lands.

The total area of the valley lands of Muquiyauyo includes about
700 hectares;[14] of these, about 423 hectares are upper lands and
277 are lower lands. Of the 277 hectares of lower lands, about 125
hectares comprise the area known as Isla, that region which is
periodically being changed in surface area owing to the wanderings
of the Mantaro River. While this land is very good for pasturage,
it is difficult to assign individual titles in the region. Sometime
in the past the community decided to keep much of this land as a
communal holding to avoid disputes which might arise from rival
claims when the river changed its course. These Isla lands were
evidently not part of the lands specified in the 1742 allotments, but
were probably part of the "extra" land not so included and which
therefore reverted to the community.

At the time of the completion of the 1742 allotments, the arrangement of valley land in Muquiyauyo was as follows:

	Hectares	Per Cent
Total valley land	700	100
Assigned to Indians and the Indian community	329.5	47.1
Assigned to *cofradías*	10.9	1.5
Isla lands (probably communal)	125.0	17.9
Remainder, probably private lands of mestizos, Spaniards, and caciques	234.6	33.5

The next date for which we can fix any information on the relative
distribution of lands is 1819 (using the 1904 figure for the amount
of Indian land); by this time the situation had changed as follows:

	Hectares	Per Cent
Assigned to Indians and the Indian community	109.1	15.6
Church and *cofradía* lands	36.4	5.2
Isla lands	125.0	17.9
Private lands of mestizos, Spaniards, etc.	429.5	61.3

The implications of these figures are clear. Between 1742 and 1819, the lands available to the Indians were cut by two-thirds; the *cofradía* lands more than tripled, and the private lands increased by over 80 per cent.

The distribution in 1819 in terms of upper and lower lands was as follows:

	Upper		Lower	
	Hectares	Per Cent	Hectares	Per Cent
Indian lands	101.1	23.9	8.0	2.9
Cofradía and church	34.9	8.3	1.5	0.5
Isla	0	0	125.0	45.1
Private	287.0	67.8	142.5	51.5
Total lands	423.0	100.0	277.0	100.0

Of the different kinds of land:

	Per Cent in Upper	Per Cent in Lower
Indian lands	92.7	7.3
Cofradía and church	96.0	4.0
Isla	0	100.0
Private	66.9	33.1
Total lands	60.4	39.6

It will be seen from the above that the private property holders had a majority of both upper and lower lands. The Indians and the *cofradías*, however, were almost entirely located in upper lands, while the private property holders were distributed fairly evenly between the two.

Between 1819 and 1904, the principal change in landholdings involved the purchase of a large area of *puna* land in the mountains behind the town, called Tunancancha. This land was located south and southwest of the urban section, about five kilometers away. It was bought at a very low price from a hacienda owner who planned to live in Muquiyauyo; it was agreed that the people of Muquiyauyo would help him build his house in the town. This land, it should be noted, was not purchased by the Indian community, but by the town of Muquiyauyo as a whole.

The next two major changes in land ownership occurred in 1904, when the communal lands of the Indians were divided up into private property, and in 1937, when the town bought the *cofradía* lands from the church. Each of these events fits better into another aspect of the history of the town, and will be taken up in later chapters.

To review the land and population picture: we can assume that the town of Muquiyauyo was founded at least by the beginning of the eighteenth century. At that time, there were some Spaniards in the town who had already assumed title to certain lands which had previously been assigned to some of the Indian *ayllus*. In 1742 the land was reallotted in such a way that the Indians were given approximately one-half the lands on the valley floor, a little was set aside for the *cofradías,* and about one-third was in the hands of the Spanish. During the second half of the century, the population gradually expanded, but at the same time the amount of land in the hands of the Indians was reduced from 47 per cent to under 16 per cent. A little of this became *cofradía* land, but the great majority was taken over by Spaniards and mestizos. This suggests that during this period there may have been an influx of non-Indians into the community. By the time of independence, the land-owning relationships were established, but the population was also beginning to grow at a greater rate, increasing between 1835 and 1940 from about 1,100 to 2,100. In 1904, the remaining communal lands were redivided among the family heads of the Indian community. Through intermarriage and the fact that some Indians were beginning to become wealthy, some of the land which had formerly belonged to Spaniards was being sold to people of more recent Indian descent.

The first mention we have of a consciousness of the restriction of available land is in the 1819 document, and from the evidence available it must have been due at least as much to an influx of mestizos and Spaniards as to growth within the Indian population. The greatest population growth was in the period after 1835, evidently after the Indians had lost most of their lands. The increasing pressure did not bother the non-Indian population greatly until the close of the nineteenth century. Then, to help alleviate this situation, the town purchased the Tunancancha lands, and later, under encouragement from the non-Indians, the members of the Indian community repartitioned their remaining lands. Still later, the *cofradía* lands were officially taken over from the church.

Such is the general picture of the population growth and the developing land problem in Muquiyauyo. It is already obvious that the solutions proposed by the townspeople did not begin to answer the pressing need for more land as the population grew. There was no other free land in the valley itself, since the whole valley floor was under cultivation or being used by the expanding populations of the numerous other valley towns. In the following chapters we shall see how attempts to solve this basic problem of population growth led to changes in the political, religious, and social life of the inhabitants of Muquiyauyo. The pressure of growing population is not the only factor in the culture change in Muquiyauyo, but it is by far the most important.

POLITICAL AND ADMINISTRATIVE DEVELOPMENT

TO OBTAIN a broad picture of the development of the political history of Muquiyauyo we must go back to the period of the conquest.
The population of the Jauja province during the last years of Inca
rule was not equaled in numbers again until about 1880, and in
1880 we know that population pressure was being felt by the Muquiyauyinos. Between these two periods the population of the entire
region declined and rose again, but the new increase came with a
markedly different political organization.

The Huanca, once presumably an independent or semi-independ-
ent tribe living in the present region of the Jauja Valley, were
conquered by Capac Yupanqui, a general of the Inca Pachacuiti,
sometime between 1438 and 1463.[1] By the time of the arrival of
the Spaniards in the 1530's, the Huanca region had long been con-
solidated as a part of the Inca Empire. The Incas established the
Huanca as a separate province and, as elsewhere, placed an imperial governor over it. Under the governor, there were several
officials generally called *curacas.*[2] The position of *curaca* was
hereditary, providing the Inca emperor approved. The *curaca* was
the head of an *ayllu*, and the importance of any particular *curaca*
depended upon the size of the *ayllu* or *ayllus* responsible to him.

John Rowe, to whom we are indebted for these notes on Inca organization, has concluded that the *ayllu* was

> . . . a kin group with theoretical endogamy, with descent in the
> male line, and without totemism. It was, therefore, not a clan
> in the classical sense at all. . . . The ayllu owned a definite
> territory, and each married couple cultivated as much of it as
> they needed for their support. . . . The ayllus of each province
> were grouped by the *Inca* Emperors into two or three sections
> (SAYA).[3]

The Inca organization was a hierarchical system, with the Inca in Cuzco at the top, the imperial governor in the provincial capital of Jauja, and under him the *curacas* controlling specific *ayllus*. The structure was considerably more complex than has been indicated here, but when the Spanish set up their colonial system, the principal elements that they perpetuated were the provinces, sometimes the subdivisions, the *ayllus,* and the *curacas.* The conquest destroyed the upper levels of the Inca structure and substituted the Spanish colonial system, which affected the importance and functions of the surviving Inca elements.

George Kubler has pointed out that "the conversion of the individual Indian from the status of an Inca subject into a Colonial *Quechua* was achieved by means of the Spanish grants known as encomiendas."[4] The *encomienda* system gave white colonists the right for a few generations to be the trustees of crown lands and certain groups of Indians *(repartimientos).* "The encomendero (or colonist) owned no title to the land on which the Indians of his repartimiento worked and lived, although he was entitled to a fixed share of the fruits of their labor."[5] The Spanish colonial law concerning the *encomienda* system forbade the *encomendero* to visit or demand hospitality of the Indians in his *repartimiento.* Although this rule was frequently broken, as Kubler notes, it nonetheless served to extend the use of the *curacas,* who collected tribute for the *encomenderos.* Under the Inca Empire the curacas had been strictly controlled and supervised in order to avoid malpractices, but the Spanish destruction of the Inca imperial system destroyed this control. In addition to this, according to Kubler, *encomenderos* often interfered in the appointment of the *curacas,* and the *encomendero's* object was to choose a foreman dependent upon his patron's favor rather than one concerned for the welfare of the Indians. "In general . . . with the decapitation of the Inca state, and with the assistance of the encomendero, the status of each local curaca received a vast increment of power."[6]

The *encomiendas* attained their greatest power at the end of the sixteenth century. The abuses had reached such proportions and the number of *encomenderos* had grown so large that the crown instituted a new policy of royal control called the *corregimiento,* initiated in Peru by Toledo during the last part of the sixteenth century. As Kubler points out, the *corregidores,* or crown officials in charge of a *corregimiento,* were so badly paid that they did not correct abuses but simply replaced the *encomenderos* in the exploitation and abuse of the Indians. The *corregimiento* system reduced the number of Indian officials in the local political

structure and replaced them from the gradually growing population
of Spanish and mestizos.

At the same time, Toledo furthered another crown policy, that
of the *reducción*, which was designed to bring the Indians in from
their scattered settlements and establish them in colonial towns,
thereby facilitating political administration, religious indoctrina-
tion, and the collection of tribute. It is likely that Muquiyauyo was
first formed into a town as part of the *reducción* policy.

During the period of the Inca Empire, the Huanca region included
roughly the Jauja Valley and the adjacent Yanamarca Valley; to the
west it was bordered by the territory of the Yauyos, another sub-
dued tribe, and to the east the region extended indefinitely into the
montaña. The Huanca province had been subdivided by the Incas into
three territorial subdivisions, Hanan Wanca, Lurinhuanca, and
Atunjauja.[7] The northwestern and southeastern boundaries of the
present province of Jauja are roughly the same as those of Atunjauja and Lurinhuanca. The present area of the district of Muquiyauyo
was at that time divided between the area of Huaripampa in Atunjauja, and of Sincos in Lurinhuanca. The dividing line between these
two subprovinces remains today a social barrier within the district of Muquiyauyo, dividing the town of Muquiyauyo and the town
of Muqui.

With the establishment of Spanish colonial control, Huaripampa
was made parish headquarters, and its jurisdiction included approximately the present townships of Huaripampa, Muquiyauyo (not
including Muqui), Llocllapampa, Paccha, and Parco. These divisions later served as a basis for the creation of the districts of
the republic, but Muquiyauyo has remained in the parish of Huaripampa.

The precise date of the establishment of Muquiyauyo as a town
is not now known. Vázquez de Espinosa, who traveled in Peru in
the second decade of the seventeenth century, mentions that in the
priory of Jauja there were two towns, Guaripampa and Yauyus,
the latter taking its name from the group of colonists brought in
by the Incas under their policy of breaking up the old tribal groups.
They lived in what is now the area of the town of Muquiyauyo.[8]

In the papers concerning the Martínez claim in 1662,[9] Muquiyauyo
is mentioned as being a town between Huaripampa and Sincos. Since
Vázquez de Espinosa mentioned both Sincos (spelling it "Cincos")
and Huaripampa, but not Muquiyauyo, it seems reasonable to conclude that Muquiyauyo was formed sometime during the period between 1620 and 1660. In the 1662 documents, it is stated specifically that the Muqui *ayllu* belonged to the town of Sincos, but no

other Muquiyauyo *ayllu* is mentioned. The governing officials referred to in these papers include a *cacique principal, segunda persona* of the *repartimiento* of "Atun Jauja," a *principal* of Muquiyauyo, a cacique of the Muqui *ayllu* of the town of Sincos, the *cacique principal* of the *repartimiento* of Lurinhuanca, and scribes of the towns of Huaripampa and Muquiyauyo. All these officials were Indians, with combined Spanish and Indian names such as Pedro Milachami, Pedro Ticsepicho, Juan Cristóbal Paucarcicsa, Pedro Pircacunyas, Pedro Mandujano, and Julio Guachovilca. It seems likely, then, that in 1662 there were very few Spaniards or creoles in Muquiyauyo.

We have a much clearer picture from the land claims of 1728-35.[10] Specifically mentioned are a number of *ayllus*, each with a cacique: Ayllu Celpa with cacique Martín Miranda, Ayllu Mamayaucho with cacique Andres Carrillo, and Ayllu Celcaruna with cacique Juan Cuyubamba. Another cacique, Pedro Flores, is referred to, but the name of his *ayllu* is not specified. Also mentioned is an Ayllu Yauyo, the first specific mention of the Yauyos since the visit of Vázquez de Espinosa. Since in the 1742 land partition papers five caciques arc discussed, it seems reasonable to conclude that there was an additional *ayllu*, and that it was Ayllu Muqui. These *ayllu* names survive in the names of the *suyus* just to the west of the town: Yauyo Suyu, Jullpa Suyu (Celpa *ayllu*), Jullcaruna Suyu (Celcaruna *ayllu*), and Yaucha Suyu (Mamayaucho *ayllu*). The other *suyu* land in this group was said by informants to have belonged to the Muqui *ayllu* and is called today Manju Suyu.

Among the other Indian officials mentioned at this period are: an *alcalde ordinario,* Francisco Pizarro; an *alcalde de campo; regidores; mandones;* an *indio principal del pueblo y mandón del pueblo,* Pedro Ibaniz Yacxa Guaringa; and a scribe of the *cabila de los naturales de Muquiyauyo*. It is not certain whether the term *cabila* is that which was taken from Morocco, meaning tribe, or whether it is a slip in the spelling of *cabildo,* meaning municipal council. In any case, the scribe was for the *"naturales"* of Indians of Muquiyauyo.

The papers from which this information is taken mention two families of Spanish derivation, the Sotomayers, granddaughters of the Juan Martínez Franco of the 1662 papers, and a Terreros, who married one of these granddaughters.

It is of interest to note that by 1735 a majority of the Indian caciques and officials had Spanish surnames: Pizarro, Miranda, Carrillo, and Flores are Spanish, while Cuyubamba and Yacxa Guaringa are Indian. In the municipal record books of the twentieth century, all these names except Yacxa and Pizarro occur with some frequency, and are all registered as being Indian, not mestizo. Evidently the Indian caciques had by the middle of the eighteenth century taken Spanish names in preference to Indian names. It is mentioned specifically that Pedro Ibanez Yacxa Guaringa is *ladino en la lengua castellana*. The term *ladino* is no longer used in Peru but survives in Central America as a term designating a person who speaks the Spanish language. In this earlier period it meant an Indian who had the ability to speak Spanish and was therefore "latinized." None of the other officials mentioned is described as able to speak Spanish.

About the middle of the eighteenth century, then, the Indian population of the town was clearly divided into five *ayllus*, each with a cacique, and there were in addition several Indian officials for the entire Indian town. There was, furthermore, an increasing number of Spanish persons, but whether peninsular-born or creole we do not know.

The next information on the political and social organization of Muquiyauyo comes from a dispute between Muquiyauyo and Huaripampa in 1819-20.[11] The documents on this issue give essentially the same picture of official structure as that found in 1735: there were five caciques, three *indios principales*, an *alcalde ordinario*, an *alcalde de campo*, and *regidores;* and in addition are mentioned *alguaciles*. Only five of the fourteen named Indian officials of this date, however, have Indian names: Juan and José Yaulimango, Antonio Vilcas, Miguel Guaringa, and Juan de Mata Camac. The rest have names considered today in Muquiyauyo to be held by Indian (as opposed to mestizo) families, but which are of Spanish origin: Sobero, Carrillo, Palomares, Leonardo, Jurado, Salcedo, Landeo, Ramón, and Soto.

The population of Spanish extraction had grown considerably during this period. Seven different family names are mentioned in 1819; four of these are called *"vecinos principales,"* literally "important residents" of the town, while three others are named as the legal representatives of the "mestizo residents and creoles of Muquiyauyo." The distinction is clearly made throughout these documents between the Indians, or *naturales*, on the one hand, and the Spanish, mestizos, and creoles, on the other. They had different legal representatives, although both groups were joined in the dispute against Huaripampa.

In the development of the political organization, it is of interest to note that the caciques at this time are mentioned only as a group, and never by name as they were in the eighteenth-century documents. In contrast, the alcaldes, *principales, regidores,* and other hierarchical officials of the Indian community are named many times. This doubtless reflects the declining importance of the caciques, and probably a simultaneous decline in the distinction between the *ayllus.* At the same time, the other officials, established on a purely Spanish colonial pattern and with no Inca counterparts, became more important. This process was doubtless influenced by the growing creole and mestizo population. These people, who were not a part of the Indian community, had many dealings with their Indian neighbors. It was much more convenient for them to deal with a single series of officials, such as the alcaldes and subordinates who were in charge of the entire Indian population, rather than with several caciques each of whom was in charge of a separate *ayllu.*

To follow the next step in the political history of Muquiyauyo, we must return briefly to the earlier picture of Peru's political organization. From the time of their establishment at about 1570 until 1784, the *corregimientos* were the principal political as well as economic divisions of Peru. Within the *corregimientos,* the *ayllu* social groups, led by the caciques, retained considerable importance. Even with the establishment of various towns during the *reducción,* the town governments did not immediately replace the caciques. During this period Jauja was a *corregimiento* in the diocese of Lima. In 1784 Peru was politically reorganized, and the delineation of *corregimientos* in terms of church diocese was changed. The new divisions were *intendencias* and *partidos.* In that year, the area that had previously been the diocese of Lima was split up into the *intendencia* of Lima and the *intendencia* of Tarma. Jauja was made a *partido* in the latter division. The *partidos,* therefore, corresponded more or less to the former *corregimientos.*

With the coming of independence, San Martín formed *departamentos* out of the *intendencias.* The departmental subdivisions followed in some confusion. The constitution of November 12, 1823, stated that the departments would be composed of provinces and districts, the latter formed in accordance with existing church parishes. In general, this meant that the colonial *partidos* were formed into provinces, and the parishes served as the basis for the creation of districts. Tarazona, [12] who studied this subject in some detail, reports that he knows of no law or decree which directed such demarcation, but it subsequently evolved in just this manner.

With the establishment of independence or shortly thereafter,

Huaripampa, which had been a parish center, also became a
district, and Muquiyauyo came under its political as well as religious jurisdiction. The Muquiyauyinos' discontent with their
subordination to the officials of Huaripampa gradually increased.
Ill feeling between these two towns had been developing for some
time and had manifested itself openly in the dispute of parish
jurisdiction and use of lands in 1819, but it was not until 1876
that the bitterness of the Muquiyauyinos grew to such proportions
that they decided to take the reins of political control out of the
hands of Huaripampa.[13]. On August 16 of that year, during the fiesta of the Vírgen Asunta, a group of twelve Muquiyauyo mestizos formed the Sociedad del Porvenir, or "Society of the Future," with the object of examining the possibilities and undertaking the task of gaining political independence from Huaripampa. On the following fourth of October they sent to the congress in
Lima a petition:

> The undersigned residents of the town of Muquiyauyo, of the
> Province of Jauja, before the National Representatives, in
> use of the right conceded by Article 30 of the Constitution,
> respectfully say: That the said (Huaripampa) district of the
> said province has for its capital the town of Huaripampa, not-
> withstanding that it lacks all the conditions necessary to oc-
> cupy the category of capital of a district, and furthermore it
> is a place devoid of population, unequipped with means of com-
> munication and the resources most indispensable for life,
> and its topographic situation makes it unsatisfactory for oc-
> cupying the position it now holds.
>
> Furthermore, excellent gentlemen: The town of Muquiyauyo
> is twice as big and counts all types of appropriate resources
> incomparably superior; because of its easy lines of communi-
> cation, it is in close contact with all towns of the district as
> well as with the capital of the province; that with all the income
> produced by the bridge [a bridge built over the Mantaro by the
> Muquiyauyinos, and on which they charged toll], a mill which
> belongs to the commune, and other goods, there is sufficient
> to cover the public costs, and so, for many other reasons
> which we will not enumerate, it ought to be the capital of the
> district. . . .

Although the Huaripampiños were hardly pleased with the description of their town and fought the demand made by the Muquiyauyinos, a committee was formed in congress the following year
and brought back a recommendation in favor of Muquiyauyo. The

committee noted that in the census of the previous year, Muquiyauyo had 1,375 inhabitants while Huaripampa had but 798, and
felt that Muquiyauyo should be made a district capital. But it felt
that since the contemporary district of Huaripampa was so large
anyway, it would be wiser to make two separate districts. In this
way, they avoided the insufferable insult to Huaripampa of putting
it under the jurisdiction of Muquiyauyo. However, after the recommendation of the committee, the Huaripampiños attempted to
put off the actual change, and in 1879 the war with Chile stopped
all such administrative changes.

In 1886, when the war was over and congress was once again
active, another note was sent to Lima asking for action on the recommendation the committee had made nine years earlier. A little
over a month later, on October 26, 1886, a new district was established with Muquiyauyo as its capital. The new district included
Muquiyauyo and the towns of Paccha, Canchapunco, Canchaillo,
Viscas, and Muqui. In taking Muqui from the jurisdiction of Sincos
and placing it in the Muquiyauyo district, the administrators finally
eliminated the division between Atunjauja and Lurinhuanca which
had existed since the time of the Incas. The boundaries of the Muquiyauyo district remained as now established until October, 1896,
when a new district of Llocllapampa was created, and Muquiyauyo lost the towns of Paccha, Canchapunco, Canchaillo, and
Viscas. [14]

Between the establishment of independence in 1821 and the establishment of Muquiyauyo as a separate district in 1886, the general
political structure of Muquiyauyo was completely subordinate to
Huaripampa. The municipal officials were all men of Huaripampa,
and the Muquiyauyinos had little to say in municipal government.
In Muquiyauyo itself were a few mestizo officials, a lieutenant governor and a municipal agent, appointed by the governor and the
alcalde in Huaripampa as their agents in Muquiyauyo. There was
also a justice of the peace, but it is not clear whether he was appointed in Huaripampa or Jauja.

At the same time, the Indian community continued and retained its own officials. During the first fifty years of the republic, however, the Indians' positions declined in importance,
and many of the posts were dropped. By 1886, the position of cacique had disappeared entirely and with it the last vestige of Inca
officialdom; only the posts of the Spanish colonial hierarchy survived.

There is some disagreement among informants as to the composition of the late nineteenth-century Indian political organiza-

tion. The main Indian official was the *alcalde auxiliar* or *alcalde de vara*. Under him there were, according to different informants, two *regidores* and four *campos*, or just two *campos*. The *campos* were evidently descended from the former *alcalde de campos*, while the *alcalde auxiliar* or *alcalde de vara* was the carryover of the *alcalde ordinario*.

One informant described the functions and interrelation of the various officials as follows:

> The municipal agent and the lieutenant governor received orders only from the district (in Huaripampa) and then passed on the orders to the *alcalde auxiliar;* the latter then called the people together in a meeting. These meetings, called *convocatorios,* were usually held after Mass on Sunday, around seven or eight o'clock in the morning. Everything was done verbally and no session books were kept. They usually met in a circle in the plaza; the *alcalde auxiliar* would say that such-and-such was needed, and the group, which was composed of all [Indian] men who had reached majority, would agree or disagree. If there was agreement, then a date and time would be set if there was something to be done.
>
> The *alcalde auxiliar* was named by the *comunidad* on the first of January of each year. A man would be named and the group would either accept him or not. The new *alcalde auxiliar* took up his position on January 6, Dia del Pascua de Reyes. The *alcalde auxiliar* carried a baton or *vara;* his helpers, the *campos,* had charge of keeping order and carried smaller batons.

Another informant adds, concerning the other officials, "The *regidores* were assistants to the *alcalde auxiliar,* and were elected annually as he was, by the Indians. The *campos* acted as authorities of the third order, and were also elected."

Another element of communal organization had become established by the time of the creation of the Muquiyauyo district; this was the set of four *cuarteles,* or four subdivisions of the members of the community for purposes of direction and control. The status of the *cuarteles* at this period is not entirely clear. It is said that they were each composed of one-quarter of the Indian community, and their boundaries were primarily territorial. Muquiyauyo at that time had ten parallel streets running east and west. The people living on the two southernmost streets composed the first *cuartel;* those on the next two were in the second *cuartel,* as were presumably those who lived on the fifth street, which bordered the southern edge of the plaza. However, since most of the residents this close to the plaza were mestizos, the fifth and sixth streets may not have had many *cuartel* members. The third *cuartel* included possibly the people who lived on the street bordering the plaza to the north, and certainly those on the next two streets; and the fourth *cuartel* consisted of the people who lived on the last two streets.

We have no clear picture as to exactly how the *cuarteles* were established or when. The Book of Regulations for the first *cuartel*, published in 1938, states that the *cuartel* was founded in 1897; the regulations for the second *cuartel*, published in 1948, state that it was founded in 1892. It seems likely, however, that these formal founding dates refer to the time when the organizations were crystallized; probably they existed before and these dates reflect some phase of the formalization of their organization.

There was in each *cuartel* a *comisionado* whose responsibility was to notify people in his *cuartel* of coming events, collect money to cover expenses for work, keep track of who was present and who was absent at work sessions, and make a list of the defaulters for the *alcalde auxiliar*, who gave them to the *agente municipal*. The *comisionado* also collected fines. The *comisionado* was always an Indian and continued to be until the post ceased to exist in the 1930's.

Moisés Sáenz states that the *cuartel* came into existence at the same time as the towns created by the policy of the *reducciónes*, and that they were subdivisions planned by colonial policy to further the control of the population. [18] If this is the case, it seems odd that there is no mention of them in the Muquiyauyo colonial documents at our disposal. Furthermore, if they were established in the colonial period in a predominantly Indian town such as Muquiyauyo, it seems inevitable that they would have duplicated the function of the distinct *ayllus*. It seems more likely in the case of Muquiyauyo that the *cuarteles* were established, or at least became important, after the *ayllu* structure had broken down. With the establishment of the republic, the position of cacique, which had been on the decline anyway, lost all meaning. The *ayllus*, if they retained any social unity, must have been very weak. It seems reasonable to suppose that sometime during the first few decades of the republic, the growing mestizo population of Muquiyauyo instituted the *cuarteles* to provide more efficient control of the Indian population by the Indian officials. There is no evidence to support the idea that the *cuarteles* were direct outgrowths of the *ayllus* themselves. There are four *cuarteles*, while there were five *ayllus*, and there is no tradition of such a relationship in the town.

With the establishment of Muquiyauyo as a district, all of the Inca elements of sociopolitical organization which had been carried over into the colonial period were finally eliminated. The *ayllus* were gone, with no evident survival, and with them the caciques. The entire municipal structure of alcalde, *regidores*, and so forth was a colonial innovation and had no counterpart in the Inca organization; the very existence of a town community with district officials was a colonial policy. The Indian community was also basically the result of colonial policy, and the existence of the mestizo-Indian caste distinction grew out of the colonial situation. Even the traditional dislike for Huaripampa and Jauja, a resentment kept alive in Muquiyauyo today, appeared first as a result of colonial policy, which placed people originally of the Muqui *ayllu* and the Yauyos, from an entirely different tribe, under the control of the Atunjauja subprovince.

Only in territorial demarcations can the preconquest divisions still be recognized today. The contemporary provinces of Huancayo and Jauja comprise the territory which was formerly that of the Huanca Indians.

The social and political organization of Muquiyauyo in 1890 was a republican reworking of a colonial inheritance, and it reflected Many of the conflicts implicit in the colonial establishment as well as three-quarters of a century of neglect of the Indian population. The formation of a district government of mestizos in 1886 underscored the division between Indians and mestizos, a social caste distinction which had developed with the Spanish colonial policy. There existed two separate political organizations, the Indian community and the municipality; the realms of authority of the two soon came into conflict.

It is of some importance that the Indian organization of the nineteenth century indicates some degree of autonomy on the part of the Indians. Even though they were ordered about by the mestizo-controlled district organization, they met and decided whether they would in fact do what was ordered and when and where they would do it. The retention of communal lands by the Indians provided them with some security in their actions; these lands could not be easily threatened by the mestizos. In addition, there is strong evidence of considerable solidarity in the nineteenth century between Muquiyauyo mestizos and Indians which evidently stemmed in part from their common interest in being freed from the control of the Huaripampa district and church authorities. The

1819 documents reflect considerable unity of action in the dispute with the church in Huaripampa, and the creation of the district of Muquiyauyo certainly was to be of common benefit to both groups.

The stealing of Indian communal lands, which was a hallmark of Indian-mestizo relations in many parts of Peru during the nineteenth century, evidently did not occur extensively in Muquiyauyo. There the usurpation of the Indian lands took place in the eighteenth century under the colonial system, and the creation of the republic tended to bring this to a halt. As a result, the nineteenth century was a time during which Indians and mestizos grew closer together in their interests. Both groups would benefit by political and religious independence from Huaripampa; no conflict-creating activities were being conducted by the mestizos; the Indians had maintained a certain degree of independence of action within their communal organization; and both were beginning to feel the pressure of growing population. This century set the stage for the two to join in trying to solve the problem of population growth.

Some of the political terms being used should be clarified at this point. The Peruvian district, or *distrito*, is roughly equivalent to the Anglo-American county; it is a piece of territory in which may be located both rural and urban populations. The district government is the local level of the national government; it is as if the American county had a mayor who was appointed by the state governor, and the state governor, in turn, was appointed by the president. In Peru, a group of districts compose a unit known as the province, and a group of provinces compose a department. Peru itself is made up of a group of departments. Within a district there may be one or more urban settlements, places divided into blocks and in which people live in close proximity. One of these towns will be the district capital, and in it will be located the district, or municipal, officers and building. As the district officers have responsibility for the entire district there is usually no specific government in the American sense for the town itself; there is, as it were, a mayor for the county but none for the town. The Indian community with which we have been dealing refers to the Indians who lived in the town of Muquiyauyo, not necessarily all the Indians in the district. Thus during much of the nineteenth century, the town of Muquiyauyo had its district officers in Huaripampa, but the Indian community of the town of Muquiyauyo had its own officers. It was the Indian community which had title to the Indian communal lands; but it was the town of Muquiyauyo as a whole (not the district) which bought the Tunancancha lands and which had title to the Isla lands.

The district administration that was set up when Muquiyauyo became a separate district consisted of an alcalde, *teniente alcalde,*
sindico de gastos, sindico de rentas, and three *regidores.* The entire group made up the district *consejo* or council. In 1887, the
first council took office and with some irregularities has been succeeded by another every two years ever since. In addition to the
council, a *gobernador* was appointed for the town in 1889. Muquiyauyo had justices of the peace before it became a district; and,
at least by 1905, it had two. In essence, this structure has remained the same until today. The most significant changes have
involved the number of *regidores.*

Since 1919 the administrative officers of the district have been
installed by decree, although at times there has been some disagreement as to whose decree should be taken as final. The office
of *gobernador* requires appointment by the prefect of the department upon the recommendation of the subprefect of the province,
and has always been filled by a Muquiyauyino. To assist the *gober-*
nador in his functions, there are a *tentiente gobernador* from Muquiyauyo and another from Muqui. The duties of the governor consist principally of keeping the peace and carrying out whatever police activities are needed. The governor retains office for no specified length of time; he keeps his position as long as he, the district,
and the subprefect are satisfied. If he leaves the town for more
than a few days for any reason he may be replaced. The machinery
of government is sufficiently slow, however, that it may be some
time before a replacement is named. In one case over a month
and a half passed before the subprefect appointed a new governor.

There is usually one justice of the peace for every thousand inhabitants. There were at the time of the study two justices in Muquiyauyo. They were distinguished as the "Justice of the First
Nomination" and the "Justice of the Second Nomination." Justices
have regularly been appointed by the departmental superior court
on the recommendation of the provincial "Judge of the First Instance." The usual procedure is for the district council to submit
a list of recommended names, called the *turno,* and from this list
the superior court selects the names of two to be justices. The
court does not have to use the list in making its selection, but respect for the local recommendations is usually shown. The justices
are responsible for settling local disputes over land and other minor civil complaints. Any dispute that is not settled to the satisfac-
tion of the parties concerned is taken to the court in Jauja, the
provincial capital.

The district council members are perhaps the most active of the district officers. The alcalde acts as the chief of the council, and the *teniente alcalde* acts as his assistant and replacement if he cannot be present at council meetings. The *sindicos* are responsible for the funds which pass through the council's hands. The *sindico de rentas* is in charge of incoming monies, while the *sindico de gastos* is responsible for expenditures. The two *sindicos* thus act as a check on each other. The *regidores,* or aldermen, act as councilmen and usually hold at least one of the inspectorships of canals, roads, public health, markets, fiestas, and so on. The number of inspectorships is large and is dictated by the national government; except where the collection of taxes is concerned, they tend to be merely nominal positions. There have been as many as seven aldermen and as few as two.

The council is supposed to hold meetings monthly. The frequency of meetings varies in fact from two to three times a year to every two or three days over a period of a month. Formerly the posts were elective by all men of the district; actually the town population determined the vote because it has always been the main population center. Since the elections were stopped in 1919, the council has been set by decree.

When the first council was established in 1887, one of the seven members was an Indian. The four following councils were composed entirely of mestizos, and it was not until 1907 that the Indians began to receive more than one or two posts. From 1913 on, of the twenty-five councils for which we have the membership lists, Indians have been in the majority seven times. Of the thirty-five councils established since 1887 for which we have data (there were no council lists available for the 1899-1901 and the 1930-32 councils), Indians have held the position of alcalde three times, in 1925, 1932, and 1944. The alcalde who took office in 1944 was soon replaced by a mestizo, however, so only two Indians have served out the term. Since the establishment of the council, then, the mestizos have predominated in its administration, although by 1912 it was accepted that Indians could be members.

The administrative posts of the Indian community which were described earlier were eliminated in 1891. When Muquiyauyo became a district and the district administration was established, the position of the Indian officers and their responsibilities became somewhat ambiguous. As long as Huaripampa was the district capital, the *alcalde de vara* and his assistant had some responsibility for control of the Indian population; when mestizos took over similar district duties in Muquiyauyo itself, they were in more immediate contact with the Indians of their own community and conflict over jurisdiction was soon felt.

The particular issue which brought the problem to a head was over the right to control the piece of land called Tasa. Tasa was part of the Indian lands; unlike the rest of them, however, it was not considered available for private use by any of the Indians but was assigned to the Indians who were designated by the district officials to act as *comisionados*. Late in 1889, a group of Indians, led by the Indian *alcalde auxiliar* and a mestizo, proceeded to divide up Tasa because it had not been used recently. The district council reacted violently to this. In a council meeting the act was denounced, and it was decided to take the case immediately to the provincial council in Jauja in order to castigate the ringleaders. In April, 1891, the results of the dispute were returned from the provincial council entirely in favor of the local district officers. The council claimed that the *alcalde auxiliar* had intentionally disobeyed the district authorities in favor of following the orders of the mestizo president of the Sociedad del Porvenir. Further, the act by the *alcalde auxiliar* had been intended to foment trouble "between the two parts of the town, the Indians and *Castas* [mestizos]." As a result, the council abolished the post of *alcalde auxiliar*, adding that "there do not exist rivalries between those called castas and *indígenas*."

This was the official end of what had for some centuries been the *comunidad indígena* officialdom of Muquiyauyo. Evidence points to the fact that it was not a change of major importance. The *comunidad* officers had ceased to be of much importance with the establishment of the district in Muquiyauyo; their old functions of necessity had to conflict with those of the newly installed district officers. Furthermore, the dropping of the *comunidad* officers did not mean that the Indian community ceased to have any voice in its own affairs. Dating from March 4, 1895, we have a session book entitled Book of Agreements of General Interest Between the Authorities and the Comunidad. This is not the district record book but is the record of a series of meetings held between the district officers and the members of the *comunidad*. The authorities in this case were the members of the municipal council, the *gobernador*, and the justices of the peace.

Probably in response to the liquidation of the *comunidad* officers the Indians formed a group made up of twelve of their leaders. These twelve men were known as the Indian *personeros*. It is not known exactly when the *personero* group was formally organized. It was of considerable importance for the Indians of the town to retain some order in their affairs, for the Indian community as such was the legal owner of 109 hectares of land. No complete account exists of the activities of these *personeros* before early in the twentieth century.

Meetings between the authorities and the *comunidad* continued until 1906. During this period, the chief business of these meetings was the renting of those *cofradía* lands not being used for fiestas or being used only in part for that purpose. In the 1742 repartition of lands, the *cofradía* lands were stated to belong to the "five *cofradías* which the town has." Thus the benefits from the *cofradía* lands were considered to belong to the town as a whole and not specifically to either the district or the church. However, since they belonged to the *cofradías*, they were still theoretically within the dominion of the parish priest. In a meeting held on March 4, 1895, it was arranged that the town should take over the right to exploit the *cofradía* land of San Juan under the following conditions: (1) the town would appoint a treasurer to handle the funds from the seeding of alfalfa on the land; (2) the *mayordomos* of the fiesta of San Juan would have the rights to one cutting of alfalfa in order to pay the parish for the fiesta; (3) the rest of the money from the land would be the exclusive property of the town, not to be confused with either ecclesiastical or district funds; (4) this money could be loaned out at an interest rate of 2 per cent monthly; (5) anyone who used the land without proper authorization would be refused all rights to irrigation water; (6) anyone who allowed his cattle to graze on the land would be fined.

By 1899 there had evidently been some irregularities in the handling of these funds, and a strict set of rules was drawn up which limited the activities of the treasurer. Among other items mentioned was that he was allowed to lend up to fifteen *soles* (S/. 15), [16] and that a commission made up of two men from each *cuartel* would review the books at the end of each year.

By 1902 the town felt that it was having such success with the rental of the *cofradía* land of San Juan that a similar arrangement was made with the parish priest over the *cofradía* lands of Amo Grande and Yauyos Señor. Separate treasurers were installed and part of the rents received were to be paid, as before, to the priest for the fiesta. It was specified, however, that the money from the lands was to be used only for the religious part of the fiesta, and not to defray the expenses for any of the "ancient customs" connected with the fiesta. In 1903, a further alteration was made whereby the responsibility for the funds was split between two treasurers, one from each barrio, or half, of the town. In addition, the treasurers

were made personally responsible for money loaned to members
of the community.

Toward the end of 1904, the *personero* group, under the direction of Melchor Soto, formed the Sociedad Pro-Indígena in order
to divide up the communal lands which belonged to the Indians. For
this division, a list of all the 239 adult Indian family heads in the
town was made; a plot of irrigated land and a plot of unirrigated
land were portioned out to each. This was the principal accomplishment of the *personero* group. The partitioning was started in October, 1904, and completed in February, 1905. This was the final
step in the dissolution of the *comunidad indígena* as a specifically
Indian concern. From this time on, although the term *"comunidad
indígena"* continued to be used, it tended to refer to the entire town,
mestizos and Indians alike.

It was felt at the time and has been thought since that this repartitioning was the most important act in the recent history of the
town, since it symbolized the official extinction of the differences
between Indians and mestizos. Of course, a single act could not and
did not succeed in bringing about a social revolution of this kind;
it did, however, serve to remove one of the strongest symbols of
Indianism, the possession of communal lands apart from the mestizos. While the Muquiyauyinos have often felt that they were highly
original in this move, there was in fact considerable precedent.
Ever since the establishment of the republic and Bolivar's decree
of 1824, [17] there had been occasional decrees ordering the repartitioning of communal lands among individuals. Castro Pozo tells
of the town of Huanec in the province of Yauyos, Department of
Lima, which first divided up its lands in 1888 and made a further
and final division in 1908. [18] It is certain that locally the repartitioning of the communal lands was felt to be a great social advancement. The plan to parcel out the Muquiyauyo lands was first set
up in 1901, and it was in that year that consistent Indian representation on the district councils began.

In 1906 the town, now referred to as the "community, " took
another step toward the consolidation of a new community organization as opposed to the district organization. A *junta directiva* was
established, to be composed of three men from each of the four
cuarteles. Within this group there were to be president, vice-
president, secretary, and *pro-secretario;* the remainder were to
be *vocales*. The junta was to deal with "communal matters, " and
to meet regularly every three months, with extraordinary sessions whenever necessary. The officers were to be re-elected each
year on the first of January. This group was composed of an equal

number of mestizos and Indians in 1906. To it were added the three
treasurers who formerly took care of the funds of the *cofradía*
lands. This organization gradually evolved during the next few
years in response to new necessities. By 1910, the funds had so
increased that it was decided that a treasurer from each *cuartel*
was necessary. In 1913, a separate secretary and an administrator
of income to supervise the treasurers were appointed. In the same
year, since the size of the group was growing, the number of representatives from each *cuartel* was reduced from three to two.

By 1916 the formal organization had so expanded that all the
following positions were named annually: administrator of income,
secretary, prosecretary, four *cuartel* treasurers, two representatives from each *cuartel*, two municipal agents to act as liaison
between the district council and the junta, four inspectors of accounts (one from each cuartel to keep track of the activities of the
treasurers at the end of each annual period), one *comisionado* from
each *cuartel* to carry out the orders of the council in the town, one
comisionado from each *cuartel* to carry out the orders of the governor, one *comisionado* from each *cuartel* to be responsible for
civic property, a sexton, a church warden, and finally an inspector
of the income from renting the waters of the canal of Unso. The
magnitude of this organization not only reflects the importance attached to it by the community members, but also indicates the
usurpation of various functions of the district council.

The district, at the beginning of the twentieth century, had charge
of appointing the various *comisionados*, the district agents, the
sexton, and the warden, and was responsible for the irrigation waters. The assumption of these functions of the district by the junta
evidently occurred with little friction. The principal reason for
this was that there was a constant and heavy overlapping of officers. While a man would not hold positions in both the council and
the junta at the same time, he might be in one one year and the
other the next. Furthermore. the alcalde, *gobernador*, and justices of the peace were also, because of their positions, members
of the junta.

The general structure of the junta outlined above remained in
force until 1922 when it was reorganized by the provincial alcalde.
Although the older list of officers had been appointed in January
of that year, the provincial alcalde had become incensed over an
issue connected with the newly completed power plant (the community had left some electric wire poles around Jauja), and as a result, he set up a new junta in March, with himself as director, and
required that it be composed of twelve persons from each *cuartel*,

making a total of forty-eight members of the new junta. There does
not seem to be any note made in the record books of this change
other than that it occurred. One reason for this is probably that
the community was so involved in what they considered a much
more important venture and a group of much more important positions that they did not much care what happened to the junta for
the time being. This new venture was the establishment of the
communally owned hydroelectric plant.

Through the *cofradía* lands that had been rented out annually
and the interest on loans made to community members, the *cuarteles* had built up a considerable bank account by 1918. Men who
had been working at the mines had for some years been thinking
of the desirability of having electric lights in their native town,
and the subject had received considerable discussion in Muquiyauyo. Early in 1918 the community decided to build such a plant,
and a commission was named from the *cuarteles* to look into it.
Each *cuartel* was to contribute S/. 2, 000, and the *comunidad* itself had another S/. 5, 000. Later, in order to get more funds, each
member of the community was assessed S/. 20, and all debts due
the community were called for payment. Word went out to the
Muquiyauyinos working at the mines to look for an engineer who
could be employed to do the work, and the men from the mine at
Morococha sent one. By May, 1918, a contract had been signed
to design the plant. Payments were made on the generators during
the next two years. A contract was made with the provincial capital, Jauja, to supply it with power, and a loan was made by a
man in a neighboring town to pay for the final installment on the
machinery; later, in order to pay him, a loan was taken out on a
bank in Huancayo.

The new venture was christened the Empresa FEBO, after the
god of light. In order to be legal owners of the plant, the various
cuarteles and the community had to assume legal standing. Consequently, each *cuartel* took a name and set up a junta. This permitted each *cuartel* and the community to act as one of the five
accionistas or co-owners of the enterprise. The *cuarteles* were
renamed as follows:

Cuartel 1: Sociedad Obreros (Worker Society)
Cuartel 2: Sociedad Industrial (Industrial Society)
Cuartel 3: Asociación Obrera (Worker Association)
Cuartel 4: Sociedad Unión Progresista (Union Progressive So-
           ciety)

An interesting example of the strength of traditional ways of doing things appeared in 1921 when one member of the community suggested that the running of the new light plant ought to be in the hands of a committee made up of one person from each *cuartel*. Fortunately for the effective functioning of the enterprise and the machinery, it was pointed out and accepted that a qualified electrician should be in charge of actually running the plant; that it was not a job which needed the representation of the various *cuarteles*.

In order to put up the building for the plant, each *cuartel* was assigned to supply two thousand adobes, two hundred worked stones, and twenty beams. In addition, each townsman was responsible for giving one roof tile.

By 1923 it became evident that even with the money and work which had been expended, the new enterprise was starting out deeply in debt. As a result, it was decided to let the running of the plant out on contract in order to be assured of a specific sum annually to pay off the debt. A Muquiyauyino took over the running of the plant.

The building of the light plant is looked back upon by the Muquiyauyinos as a time of tremendous communal activity; it is said that the men worked so hard on its construction that the women took over all the agricultural field work.

During this period another event took place which was to play an important role in the development of the local political history. In 1919, Leguia assumed the presidency of the republic and put an end to district elections. Instead, district councils and officers were to be appointed by the province in Jauja. It was on an interpretation of this change in policy that the subprefect in Jauja felt that he could, by order, reorganize the communal *junta directiva* in Muquiyauyo in 1922. This removal of the elective system for district officers later provided an issue which was to produce conflict between the junta and the district council.

One further issue which was settled about this time concerned membership in *cuarteles*. Being a member of a *cuartel* not only involved rights to the use of canal water for irrigation, but also subjected one to participating in regular projects for cleaning up the canals and roads, or paying fines if one did not so participate. By not joining a *cuartel*, a citizen avoided these issues and paid a little for the use of the water. The session books of both the junta and the district council from the first decade of the century on are dotted with comments and complaints concerning those people who would not join the *cuarteles* and participate in the work. It was ultimately decided that since there was no way to force membership, each person could make his own decision, but those who did not join would have to pay for any services made possible by the *cuarteles*. Later, of course, this included the right to use electric power.

By the middle of the third decade of the century, then, there was a *cuartel* and communal structure in the town, but the membership of these organizations did not include the entire population of the town. There were district offices filled by appointment from the province, but the district officers were in charge of the entire territorial district, not just the town of Muquiyauyo. There was no specific town government which included all townspeople and excluded others of the district. This was basically the same situation that had existed before the dissolution of the old *comunidad indígena,* except that at that time the mestizos were excluded from the community organization.

The last major step in the formation of the community government as it is today was the immediate result of a problem caused by the establishment of the light plant, the setting up of the district council by appointment, and the growing lack of sympathy between the council and the junta. In 1929 the community was involved in two legal disputes. One had to do with the electric plant, which had been turned over to a private individual on contract in 1923; he was supposed to run the plant for a period of six years, during which he was to pay off the outstanding debts incurred and pay the community a specified sum annually in rent. When the six years were up, in 1929, the community wanted the plant back. The contractor, in the meanwhile, had found the venture very profitable, and with the termination of his contract in sight he arranged to have himself appointed district alcalde in both 1927 and 1929. He hoped, by holding this position, to force the community to renew his contract; when the community objected, he took the case to court.

At the same time, another dispute arose over the lands of Tunancancha. There was a private claim to these lands which the municipality had purchased in the nineteenth century. When the community became established, these lands were assumed to belong to the community and not to the district as such.

In order to deal with the legal difficulties which were arising, one member of the communal junta suggested in January, 1930, that stronger communal government be established. Heretofore, the officers of the community existed only to handle the funds of the community; outside of the participation in the Empresa FEBO, they had no legal existence. Now the idea was put forward to elect a communal president who should be the leader for all the *cuarteles*. The district alcalde, present at the meeting of the junta, tried to put a stop to the action by claiming that the administrator of income was such a person. But other members replied that he had charge only of the funds. It was decided unanimously, except possibly for the alcalde's vote, that a communal president would be elected; each *cuartel* was to supply one name, and a general community election would be held to decide who should hold the post. The record concerning this meeting in the session book states that the alcalde sadly reflected that now it would be necessary to change the regulations!

The establishment of a formal community government, specifically officered by elected personnel, and to which each member *cuartel* was subordinate, was a departure from the general pattern of *cuartel* dominance on the one hand and district control on the other. It may be said to be the specific contribution which Muquiyauyo made to the development of local government in that region. Other towns soon imitated the change. The pattern now established of a junta composed of one man from each *cuartel* and the selection of posts for these four men by general election was new, although the idea of the communal junta itself was old.

One of the first moves of the new communal government was to forbid that the alcalde (the man who had held the light plant contract) could become a member of a *cuartel*. Shortly thereafter it was decided to name the new organization the Confederación Obrera de Muquiyauyo (Working Confederation of Muquiyauyo); there was reluctance on the part of some of the community members to use this name since, as they pointed out, not all Muquiyauyinos were workers; some were even doctors and lawyers!

In August, 1930, there was a successful revolution at the national level by Sanchez Cerro against the dictator Leguia. The reaction of Muquiyauyo to this incident reflects a great deal concerning the feeling of the new *comunidad* about elections and the district offices. Immediately upon receiving word of the revolution's success, the council and district officers who had been placed by appointment were denounced, many of the officers resigned, and the community elected new district officials. The spirit of the occasion so carried them away that they decided to remove the sign *"Municipalidad, "* the official name of the district government buildings. Since the *comunidad* was the organization of all community members and had built the buildings, they felt they should be turned over to the *comunidad*. This reaction was in part stimulated by the platform on which Sanchez Cerro had been fighting; he claimed that his revolt was a "pro-Indian" revolt. The excitement soon dissipated when it became apparent that once in, Sanchez Cerro had no intention of allowing district elections. It was decided not to change the name.

Another result of the enthusiasm of the new *comunidad* was the decision that the communal lands of Isla should be divided up. While time was allowed for individuals to present their private claims to parts of these lands, no one put in any claims until the decision to make the division was final. Then members of several families and of the village of Ataura across the river put in claims. The community, now feeling its strength, decreed that any townsman who brought suit against the community should be excluded from any further rights in the community. By the end of 1932, the local justice of the peace had decided in favor of the community in all except one of the claims; some of the other claimants then carried their cases to a higher court and were written out of community membership.

The feeling against the district organization that began when the alcalde tried to keep the electric plant evidently continued. In 1932 the communal vice-president, who had been recently named as a member of the district council, was asked to vacate his position in the community organization and was replaced.

During these years the new community was increasingly active in numerous projects. They started a library in order to encourage the young people of the community to read. They considered various possibilities to get drinking water; among ideas suggested and rejected or not followed up were piping it in from springs in Ataura and construction of wells by each of the *cuarteles*. They began the construction of the present bridge which spans the Mantaro near Jauja.

Unfortunately, I was unable to locate a copy of the regulations of the new community government before those dated 1940. In 1934 the name of the organization had been changed to the Comunidad de Industriales Regentes Muquiyauyo (Muquiyauyo Community of Regent Industrialists).

In the regulations for the community published in 1940, specific note is taken of the fact that some of the people who live in the town are not members of one of the four cuarteles but that the communal organization includes as well "all the small agricultural land owners who are not inscribed. " In this way the longstanding problem of the status of the town's dwellers who were not *cuartel* members was solved: they were to be included as community members anyway.

In the period of some five centuries since the Inca first conquered the Huanca, the sociopolitical structure in Muquiyauyo had undergone a number of pronounced changes. To review this briefly, we can conveniently distinguish six periods of development:

1. Pre-Inca or Huanca (?-*ca*. 1450). This is the period prior to the Inca conquest; we know practically nothing about the political structure in this period.

2. Inca (*ca*. 1450-*ca*. 1540). In this period, the Incas set up their own officials over the Huanca province and moved in some colonists from the neighboring province of Yauyos. The principal local officials were the *curacas*. This was the beginning of a dual strata system, in this case with the Incan society on the top and the provincial, conquered Indian on the bottom.

3. Conquest and early colonial (*ca*. 1540-*ca*. 1700). This is a complex period which can be subdivided. The first major change was the removal of the Inca superstructure, and its replacement with the *encomenderos*. The substructure remained, although its functioning was very much altered. This lasted until about 1600, at which time the *corregidores* were gradually being substituted for the *encomenderos* and the term *curaca* was generally replaced by cacique. Sometime in the seventeenth century the town of Muquiyauyo was formed of five *ayllus* of Huanca and Yauyos Indians. Also during this century, the first Spaniards established claims to land in the present area of Muquiyauyo. The dual stratification was continued and accentuated by the colonial system, with Spaniards on top and Indians on the bottom.

4. Late colonial (*ca*. 1700-*ca*. 1821). The date of 1700 is chosen as a marker because sometime between 1662 and 1735, the dates of the various land claim papers, the terms cacique and *ayllu* began to be of less importance in the Indian organization and the new colonially established Indian officers (alcalde, *principales*, *regidores, mandones,* and so forth) began to assume greater importance. This signified gradual loss of importance of the intra-Indian divisions of the *ayllus*, and the establishment of a total Indian organization under a single set of officers. The *ayllus* continued to exist until the republican period, but with decreasing importance. The dual stratification became stronger with an influx of more Spaniards, creoles, and mestizos into the upper strata and with gradual unification of the Indians in the lower strata. In the general political structure, the *corregimiento* system ended in 1784 and was replaced by the new *intendencia-partido* system. This did not have an immediate effect on the local social structure, however.

5. Early republican (*ca*. 1821-*ca*. 1890). The effect of the *intendencia-partido* divisions was felt in that they were the basis of

the new republican demarcation; within the new provinces, districts were established on the basis of former Catholic Church parishes. This brought Muquiyauyo under the control of Huaripampa, and while the district organization was run by Spaniards and mestizos, they were not Spaniards and mestizos of Muquiyauyo. The Indian organization was by this time nearly crystallized into a single unit; the caciques and *ayllus* were very much reduced in importance and the *comunidad indígena* began to be the principal Indian social unit. Sometime in this period the *cuarteles* may have started, but they were not specifically organized until the very end of the period. The fact that the Muquiyauyo mestizos were politically important in this period may have tended to throw them closer to the Indians; both held rancor against the mestizos of Huaripampa. Late in the period, Muquiyauyo achieved political independence from Huaripampa, and this was followed shortly by the formal dissolution of the Indian community. At the end of the nineteenth century, then, there existed a sociopolitical structure in which the mestizos and Indians now formed the dual strata, but the strata were increasingly poorly defined; the end of the *comunidad indígena* organization took away the political differences, and this was to be followed shortly by the repartitioning of the communal lands, the end of the last formal economic difference.

6. Contemporary *(ca.* 1890-present). This period may be said to start with the formation of the *junta directiva* to handle the renting of *cofradía* lands by the Indians and mestizos together, and the formalization of the *cuarteles* as organizations including members of both social strata. From the beginning of the century until 1930, the political structure led to mestizo superiority in district matters and Indian-mestizo equality in communal matters. With the establishment of the new communal organization in 1930, the community became of greater local significance than the district. For the first time the old horizontal division of mestizo and Indian was completely cut by a vertical political division into district and community groups with mestizos and Indians participating in both.

There is another significant aspect of the establishment of the community organization in 1930, to be considered against the background of all of Latin America. With the community organization, Muquiyauyo took an important step away from the centralization which characterizes the political systems of most of the Latin American countries. The political district is and has been distinctly a subunit in the national administrative hierarchy. The district officers exist principally to keep order, collect taxes, and carry out instructions for the provincial, departmental, and national governments; they are, therefore, concerned with specific territorial subdivisions of the country, and not with specific human populations. That is to say, in terms of the Anglo-American structure used earlier, the "county" territorial unit has been more important than the separate urban and rural populations within it.

The important feature of the development of the communal organization in Muquiyauyo is not that it is a continuation of the old Indian community, a doubtful theory in view of the social changes involved, but that for perhaps the first time in Peruvian history (and in much of Latin America) a small, agriculturally oriented community developed a political administration which was designed for and adjusted to the needs of a specific town population. To persons of Anglo-American traditions, this may not seem extraordinary; in their social heredity the importance of the autonomous town government has rarely been questioned. However, if the suggestion were made that the Anglo-American town government be destroyed and replaced by appointed officials of the states, and in turn that the state governors be appointed by the president, then the degree of difference involved would become apparent. For this latter system is what exists, in effect, as a part of the colonial heritage of the Latin American republics. The real, and almost astounding, accomplishment of Muquiyauyo is that in the process of trying to solve its own immediate problems, and without any evident borrowing from Anglo-American areas, the town developed a governmental form in direct opposition to the centralized traditions of its own country and heritage and established the type of local autonomy and government which is the absolute *sine qua non* of democratic government as it is known in the Anglo-American countries.

Outside of the Jauja valley, Muquiyauyo has been better known for its progressive steps in establishing an electric light plant and other public works; none of these material gains, however, can compare with the creation of the communal government as an organization independent of the district. Other towns in the valley have tended to realize this more than have outsiders. In a number of neighboring communities similar communal governments have been established.

Two more aspects of the creation of this community organization should not be overlooked. One is that it was not the product of a single visionary or of extensive planning; the other is that it was in part a product of the relentless pressure of the growing population. No one, in 1850, or 1900, or even in 1925, sat down and described to someone else the creation of such a governmental form.

There was no utopian foresight involved, no long-range preparation and planning. It could not have occurred without the many
steps which led up to it: the breakdown of the caste system, the
dissolution of the Indian community organization, the formation
of the community *junta directiva,* the funds and sense of unity derived from ownership of the light plant, the preceding organization
of the *cuarteles,* and so forth. But none of these things was done
with the final establishment of such a communal organization as
the goal; each was done in answer to some immediate and pressing
problem. This illustrates as well as any case with which I am familiar the degree to which cultural change depends upon gradual
steps and can be viewed in terms of problems and their solutions.
In a very real sense, this evolution is without direction. The direction depends entirely on the degree to which the culture at a
given moment directs the solution in a certain path, and the degree
to which this solution actually solves the problem at hand.

The last point is important, because often the attempts to solve
a problem do not, in fact, permanently solve it. Such has been the
case with many of the problems resulting from population growth.
Population growth was an important factor in the creation of Muquiyauyo as a separate district; in the repartitioning of the Indian
communal lands; and in the renting out of the *cofradía* lands, which
in turn was the immediate reason for the creation of the *junta directiva.* The pressure of population cannot tell a people what to
do, but it keeps telling them that something must be done.

DEVELOPMENTS IN THE RELIGIOUS ORGANIZATION

RELIGIÓN has always played an important role in the lives of the Muquiyauyinos. It seems likely that the very founding of the town was due in part to the desire of the Spanish to bring the Indians together so that they might be more easily evangelized. The organization necessary to support the church and to sponsor the Catholic rituals has molded many of the activities of the town and has in turn been molded by the basic distinctions which exist in the social organization of the community.

Our information on the early history of the religious organization of the town is as sketchy as our knowledge of early political events. It was Catholic practice then, as it is now, to divide territories and their populations into parishes. At the time of the visit of Vázquez de Espinosa in the early part of the seventeenth century, both Huaripampa and the "Yauyus" were in the priory of Jaua. It is not known what took place between that time and the dispute of 1819, but by the latter date the parish was established in Huaripampa and evidently had been there for some time.

The first fairly sound information on the nature of the organization established to promote religious activities comes from the land repartitioning document of 1742, wherein it is specified that fifty-six *topos* of land were to be set aside for the five *cofradías*[1] of the town. These five *cofradías* are by tradition San Juan Bautista, Amo Grande, Asunción, Yauyos Señor, and Purísima. One cannot be certain today how these *cofradías* were organized. It has been suggested that they were identical to the *ayllus*, which still existed at that time. While this seems logical, it does not seem possible in view of the fact that according to the 1742 document, Huaripampa is given land for five *cofradías* but has only three caciques, or chiefs of the *ayllus*.

In the same document, it is indicated that at this time the Muquiyauyinos were fairly satisfactory participants in religious activities. In the section which deals with the repartitioning of the Huaripampa lands, it is noted that almost half the Indian *tributarios* of that town had not been participating in church activities, and that they had refused to leave the *puna*, thus avoiding the church exercises. Because of this, certain of the Huaripampa *tributarios* lands are being assigned to the Muquiyauyinos, who have attended the religious events regularly.

Papers of the religious association of Santo Cristo dating back to 1811 provide general information about many phases of religious organization in Muquiyauyo. But the 1819-20 dispute between Huaripampa and Muquiyauyo throws more light on the social relations of the period and provides the first clear picture of the religious organization. The Muquiyauyinos had evidently become very irritated by the manner in which the church was treating them. The parish priest, who lived in Huaripampa, expected them not only to attend religious affairs of Muquiyauyo, but also to attend and contribute to the affairs of Huaripampa, the parish seat. The dispute was settled in favor of the Muquiyauyinos by the subprefect of the *partido* of Jauja. During this phase, the principal persons involved had been the lay leaders of the two towns. When the decision went against Huaripampa, however, the priest himself entered the fray and carried the appeal to Lima. He objected to the decision and maintained that it was not fair to expect him to handle efficiently the affairs of two distinct churches, those of Muquiyauyo and Huaripampa, and that the people of Muquiyauyo should continue to support the Huaripampa church. He considered the parish to be a single unit and felt that the political authorities had no right to direct parish affairs. The final decision handed down in Lima was the same as the first, in favor of Muquiyauyo. It pointed out that according to a law of 1684 it was illegal to force Indians to support more than one church. The fact that this had been going on in the Huaripampa parish was no reason to perpetuate the injustice.

The long dispute brings out a number of features of the interrelations of the period. First, there was clearly bad feeling between the Huaripampiños and the Muquiyauyinos; the documents occasionally verge on namecalling. Second, there is obviously ill feeling between the priest and the Muquiyauyinos; this relationship continues to the present day. And finally, there is considerable indication in the phraseology of the document of cooperative effort on the part of the "Spaniards, mestizos, and creoles of Muquiyauyo," and the "community of natives." This is evidence that even at this early date the people of the two social classes were acting in some unity.

While not mentioned specifically, the *cofradía* lands apparently grew between 1742 and 1820, and the *cofradías* themselves increased in number. *Cofradías*, however, were only one of the organizations which sponsored fiestas in Muquiyauyo at this time. At some time before 1811 the associational type of sponsorship, variously called *sociedades* and *hermandades*, started. The difference between these associations and the *cofradías* was principally that the former had no lands from which they could earn money to pay for the celebration of the saints' or holy days to which they were devoted. As long as there were *cofradía* lands, it was not necessary for the *cofradías* to maintain any permanent organization from one year to the next; a few *mayordomos* in charge of the lands could handle the sponsoring of the fiestas. The associations, however, depended upon a constant membership for contributions. Furthermore, the *cofradías* were theoretically supported by everyone of a particular social caste; there was nothing clublike about them. Thus the *cofradías* of San Juan Bautista and Yauyos Señor were in the charge of the Indians of the town, while the Amo Grande and Asunción were the responsibility of the mestizos.

The establishment of the *cofradías*, as they were found in Muquiyauyo, was evidently a part of colonial policy. As a result, we have the official assignation of lands to the *cofradías* in 1742. The development of the associations was probably a more casual diffusion to the New World. The clublike association of people devoted to a specific saint is an old Spanish pattern, while the development of the *cofradía* seems to be a result of the imposition of a Spanish colonial idea on the local Indian and mestizo society.[2] As will be seen shortly, the *cofradías* which were formed in Muquiyauyo were usually based on ethnic, barrio, and sex lines.

In the dispute of 1819-20, one of the points mentioned by the Muquiyauyinos is that there was no longer enough land to go around to handle all the expenses. The reply from Jauja on this matter was, as might be expected, that all land belonged to the crown anyway, and when it became necessary the land would be repartitioned to take care of the new needs. The final decision on this case, with the suggested repartitioning, arrived in April, 1820. In the following year, San Martín entered Peru and Spanish colonial rule virtually came to an end. The establishment of the republic turned all lands into private property and ended the practice of assignment by a higher authority of lands for the use of *cofradías*. The information provided by the 1819-20 dispute documents, therefore,

gives essentially the status of the *cofradías*, associations, *cofradía*
lands, and fiestas celebrated at the end of the colonial period. It is
unlikely that these things changed markedly between 1821 and 1950
since there was no authority to institute or enforce such changes.
As a result, by comparing data on the *cofradia* lands available in
1938, at the time they were finally purchased by the community,
with the data from 1819-20, it is possible to outline the status of
the religious organization for the earlier period.

Among the documents surviving from the litigation between the
two towns is one in which the priest lists his various duties in Muquiyauyo. It states that the duties which he had in the "vice-parish"
of Muquiyauyo were "All the Sundays of the year the Mass of the
Holy Sacrament, the cost of which is 117. "[3] In addition were the
special Masses with the indicated costs in pesos and *reales:*

January:	Misa de los Alcaldes	004.4
February:	Misa de Candelaria	004.4
	Lunes de Carnestolendas	
	y Misa de los Hueros	004.4
March:	Fiesta de la Encarnación	013.4
June:	Fiesta de Santísima Trinidad	006.0
	Fiesta de Corpus	008.2
	Octava de Corpus	006.0
	Fiesta de Nuestro Amo	012.0
	Aniversario de Nuestro Amo	005.74
	Fiesta de San Juan	012.0
	La Misa de Fundación	002.2
	Aniversario de San Juan	005.7 1/2
July:	Fiesta de Santiago	002.2
August:	Fiesta de la Asunción	006.0
	Novena de la Asunción	020.0
	Octava de Santa Rosa	012.0
	Misa del Niño de la Asunción	004.4
	Aniversario de Santa Rosa	005.7 1/4
September:	Octava de la Exaltación de la Cruz	006.2
October:	Fiesta del Ángel de la Guardia	006.2
November:	Misa de Finados	013.4
	La Cofradía de San Juan	002.2
	La Cofradía de Nuestro Ámo	002.2
	La Cofradía de Purísima	002.2
	El Santo Cristo	002.2
December:	Fiesta de Purísima	012.0
	Novena de Purísima	020.2

December:	Aniversario de Purísima	005.7 1/4
	Misa de Navidad	002.2
	Misa de Nuestra Señora de Belén	002.2
		331.0
Thirty-six Masses annually with the		
Doctrina at two pesos, two *reales*		081.0
Twenty-five pesos, 4 *reales* for Holy Week		025.4
		437.4

Of these thirty-two fiestas, at least twenty-three were paid for with money taken from *cofradía* lands. In addition, although not mentioned, the fiesta of Yauyos Señor surely must have been held at that time, and was paid for from *cofradía* produce. The breakdown of fiestas by *cofradía* responsibility was as follows:

Cofradía	Fiesta	Month
Amo Grande	Fiesta de Nuestro Amo	June
Amo Grande	Aniversario de Nuestro Amo	June
Amo Grande	La Cofradía de Nuestro Amo	November
San Juan	Fiesta de San Juan	June
San Juan	Aniversario de San Juan	June
San Juan	La Cofradía de San Juan	November
Asunción (Asunta)	Fiesta de Asunción	August
Asunción (Asunta)	Novena de Asunción	August
Asunción (Asunta)	Misa del Niño de la Asunción	August
Purísima	La Cofradía de Purísima	November
(Purísima Pata)	Fiesta de Purísima	December
(Purísima Pata)	Novena de Purísima	December
(Purísima Pata)	Aniversario de Purísima	December
Trinidad Pata	Santísima Trinidad	June
Octava	Fiesta de Corpus	June
Octava	Novena de Corpus	June
Santa Rosa	Octava de Santa Rosa	August
Santa Rosa	Aniversario de Santa Rosa	August
Candelaria	Candelaria	February
Ánimas	Misa de Finados	November
Santa Iglesia	Holy Week	variable
Dolores	Holy Week	variable
Ángel de la Guarda	Ángel de la Guarda	October
Various lands	Fiesta de Encarnación	March

Of the remaining nine fiestas, Santo Cristo had an association which we know existed before 1819. Santiago continues today but under a different form of sponsorship. The Misa de los Alcaldes is now part of the New Year fiesta; the Misa de Navidad and the Misa de Nuestra Señora de Belén are parts of the Christmas fiesta. I heard no mention of the fiestas called Misa de Fundación and Octava de la Exaltación de la Cruz. They were probably discontinued sometime during the nineteenth century. Lunes de Carnestolendas is one of the days celebrated today as Carnaval; I have not been able to identify the Misa de los Hueros, but, since it is mentioned together with Carnestolendas, it seems likely that it is also part of the Carnaval celebration. The modern celebration of Carnaval was described in later sources.

In this résumé are a number of points of interest. By 1819, at least eight more *cofradías* had been established beyond the original five of 1742, and, according to the bill of sale of 1938,[4] two of these had two pieces of land:

Cofradía	Number of Pieces of Land in 1938
Santísima Trinidad	1
Corpus	1
Santa Rosa	1
Candelaria	1
Ánimas	2
Santa Iglesia	2
Dolores ("Semana Santa")	1
Ángel de la Guarda	1

This means that between eight and ten new pieces of land had been incorporated into the *cofradía* system between 1742 and 1819, or in a period of seventy-seven years. That these were probably not cut out of the five *cofradías* established in 1742 is suggested by the fact that four of the original five accounted for thirteen different religious events in 1819; had they been cut up, they could hardly have produced enough money to pay the expenses of three or four events each.

With the beginning of the republic, the status of *cofradía* lands became confused. This did not become apparent to the Muquiyauyinos or other valley dwellers for almost three-quarters of a century, but there is nothing in the colonial documents to state precisely to whom the lands belonged. The 1742 repartitioning document directed that the five pieces of land assigned to *cofradías* belonged to the "five *cofradías* which the town has. " In view of the facts that the *cofradías* were not clubs but rather were made up of segments of the population and that the town was considered as "having" the *cofradías*, the ambiguity of the situation could not fail to cause some trouble. We shall see later just how this trouble developed, how it was resolved, and the important effects it had on the development of the community.

Something of the development of the associations in Muquiyauyo can be seen in the papers relating to the Sociedad de Santo Cristo. [5] These papers unfortunately consist principally of lists of members' names, but enough other items are mentioned that it is possible to piece together something of the history of the organization. We do not know when the association was founded, but the records begin in 1811. At that time the association met each February to elect the officers for the following year. For the first day of the fiesta there were two *mayordomos*, two *priostas*, two *mayorales*, and two *alféreces;* for the second day there were a different pair of *mayordomos, mayorales*, and *priostas*. In addition, individuals referred to as *mayordomos* were appointed separately to take care of the rodeo and the *tumbamonte* (a tree-cutting game), and to pay for the music. The structure of this group of officers underwent certain changes. By the middle of the century, the number of *alféreces* increased, varying between thirty and eighty. The *alféreces* by this time evidently became simple contributors to the fiesta. In general, the *mayordomos* were men and the *priostas*, women; there are variations in this, however, and sometimes the positions are reversed. The pattern by the end of the century was for each *mayordomo* to have an accompanying *priosta*. There were three such pairs for each of the two days of the fiesta. In 1893 it was recorded for the first time that the funds collected by the society were lent out for interest; in that year, twenty-seven people took out between three and seventy centavos each for which they were expected to return to the society from five centavos to S/. 1.50. In most cases, this interest amounted to between 50 and 100 per cent per year, but the object was not so much to lend money to those who needed it as it was for the members of the society to contribute. This also avoided the necessity of having a treasurer to guard the money during the year; each person was responsible for a small portion of the funds and was expected to put back a specified amount over what he had received.

At least by 1873, the term *sociedad* in connection with the Santo Cristo association had been changed to *cofradía*. In 1902, for the

first time, it was mentioned that the association had a piece of
land, and a discussion was held that year about building a wall
around it. Since the term *cofradía* in Muquiyauyo is usually used
specifically for those groups of people who are active in sponsoring a fiesta for which there is *cofradía* land, this change in terminology reflects the fact that sometime during the middle of the
nineteenth century the association purchased a piece of land in
order to use it as the *cofradías* did. Since this was after the Muquiyauyinos stopped participation in the parish affairs of Huaripampa, this land was not classed as one of the old *cofradía* lands;
it belonged to neither the town nor the church but to the association. Some of the other associations bought lands for this purpose,
and these lands have always been considered as their private property.

Once the association was using the land, the task of the *mayordomos* became one of looking after the property and calling work
sessions of the members to plant and harvest. Among the items
for which the money from this land was used were the annual fiesta
of the association and the purchase of the candles to be burned every
Sunday and on the occasion of the death of a member of the association.

The histories of the various associations and *cofradías* have come
down to us in fragmentary form. It is possible to put some of the
fragments together, however, and see something of the major
changes which these organizations have undergone in the past seventy-five years. By 1819 four of the first five *cofradías* named
on the priest's list supported thirteen different religious observances out of the more than thirty annual fiestas. By the time that
our district records (1887) and community records (1895) begin,
there is no indication that this multitude of religious events was
observed. According to informants, the five *cofradías* followed
a fairly symmetrical pattern of sponsorship. Two were sponsored
by Indians, two by mestizos, and one by the town as a whole. The
cofradía of San Juan Bautista was that of the patron saint of the
town and was sponsored by Indians; it included a Mass and procession on the first day and a bullfight on the second. On the second
day, also, the mestizos sponsored a Mass and procession from
the *cofradía* of Amo Grande. This was the fiesta known as Señor
del Amo. The *cofradías* of Asunción and Yauyos Señor worked in
just the reverse order. The first was sponsored by the mestizos
and involved the Mass and procession on the first day, with a bullfight on the second, while the Indians paid for a mass and procession from the *cofradía* of Yauyos Señor on the second day.

The *cofradías* had other traits in common. The fiestas of each were in the hands of *mayordomos*. No special costumes were used, and everyone danced. Each group which had to sponsor a bullfight also appointed an extra series of officers, a *capitán*, who killed the bull with a lance on horseback, and assistants to help him should he have difficulty.

The records indicate, and informants agree, that by 1894 the celebration of these fiestas had become very simple and in general had lost the interest of many of the people of the community. Also by that date the *cofradía* lands supporting these fiestas were recorded as having been out in *remate* to various people of the town. To place a piece of land or other capital goods in *remate* meant that they were rented out for a stated period, usually a year, to the highest bidder. In this way it was possible to get an acceptable amount of money out of the lands without being concerned over who did the work. The district council in 1894 decided to take over the responsibility of sowing the *cofradía* land of San Juan Bautista in alfalfa, and to name a treasurer for the project at a community meeting. It was at this meeting, and over this issue, that the first community junta, described in the last chapter, was formed.

With this decision, the regulation of *cofradías* gradually became the responsibility of the general community and the community authorities. In 1895 a formal system for use of the lands was drawn up. It was established that a resident of the town would take the *cofradía* land out in *remate* from the priest by contract and agree to sponsor the fiesta; the town was to pay this man for his part in the agreement, however, and it was the town that actually gained control of the land. The four *cuarteles* were to take turns in cutting the alfalfa, and the treasurer elected was to be responsible for the funds. The money was to be the exclusive property of the town, distinct from either church or communal funds. The subsequent development of the power of the junta has already been traced.

In February, 1902, the junta decided to place the old *cofradías* of Amo Grande and Yauyos Señor in *remate* in this way. With respect to paying for the fiestas, however, it was specified that only the religious part of the fiestas would be subsidized, and that none of the "ancient customs" of the community could be underwritten by funds stemming from the lands. In 1909 the junta took over the remaining *cofradía* lands in the same manner.

The subsequent history of the fiestas is confused. Informants with whom I discussed these events agreed that community celebration of these five fiestas had stopped by 1920. The earliest indication of the decline in interest is in an 1887 entry in the district record

books which notes that there are no longer any *mayordomos* to celebrate the fiestas of Purísima and Encarnación de Nuestro Señor.
The district council felt at that time that it was responsible for see-
ing that these fiestas were sponsored. It was specified, however,
that the fiesta would consist only of a Mass. Payment of the priest
was put in the hands of the district *síndicos*, who were to take the
money from the *cofradía* lands.

I found no evidence that the fiestas of Amo Grande and Asunción
are celebrated in Muquiyauyo today. The last mention in the district session books of the former celebration is in 1912, while the
last observance of the latter was about 1920. Although informants
claimed that the other three fiestas had all stopped by 1915, the
1950 census which I took in the town revealed that there were still
at least twenty-nine families celebrating the fiesta of San Juan Bautista, eighteen celebrating the fiesta of Purísima, and one claiming to celebrate that of Yauyos Señor.[6] There was evidently little
or no organization connected with the San Juan Bautista celebration;
the district session books of 1943 record a suggestion by one
of the townsmen that some recognition be taken of the day of San
Juan since he was the patron saint of the town. Of the twenty-
nine families still observing San Juan in 1950, nineteen were included in a social class delineation sample; of these, ten were considered to be Indian, one mestizo, and eight undecided. (This social
categorization is described in chapter 5.) Of the families still observing the fiesta of Purísima, five were considered to be Indian,
five mestizo, and one undecided. The general distribution of the
social groups participating in these two fiestas agrees fairly well
with the opinions expressed by informants concerning such participation in the last century. The fiesta of Yauyos Señor was observed
only by a widow seventy years of age. In the social class sample,
she was classified as "undecided."

The continued celebration of these three fiestas is principally a
family concern. The dates set by the informants as the termination of the fiestas refer to the time at which they ceased to be observed by the community as a whole and the town ceased to support
them with funds from the *cofradía* lands.

Among the religious celebrations included in the priest's list of
1819 were an additional eight that were evidently supported by
cofradía lands. Of these, five have disappeared and we have practically no data on the nature of the disappearance. The fiesta of
Encarnación, which evidently depended upon the *cofradía* lands of
other fiestas, was mentioned in 1887 as having no *mayordomo*. The
celebration of Corpus Cristi stopped at the time of the sale of the

cofradía lands in 1938. The fiesta consisted only of the Mass and procession and had no other activities connected with it, nor any special group to sponsor it. No information was collected on the fiestas of Santísima Trinidad, Santa Rosa, and Ángel de la Guarda. All had *cofradía* lands which were included in the 1938 sale, but evidently they ceased to be observed long before this time.

The other three fiestas which depended upon *cofradía* lands, Holy Week (the lands of Dolores and Santa Iglesia), Misa de Finados (the "Day of the Dead," with the *cofradía* of Ánimas), and Candelaria, are all held today. The Holy Week celebration in 1819 was evidently one of the most expensive of the year. By 1949 it was still fairly complex but was paid for entirely by volunteers who agreed the previous year to take over specific responsibilities. There are today three sets of two *centuriones* each, accompanied by an indefinite number of *alféreces* who help them bear the expenses for which they volunteer. One set of *centuriones* takes care of the fiesta and the procession on the Friday before Holy Week (Viernes de Dolores), another is responsible for the Wednesday of Holy Week (Miércoles Santo), and the last set does the honors on Maundy Thursday (Jueves Santo), the Mass and procession of Good Friday (Viernes Santo), the Mass on Holy Saturday (Sábado de Gloria), and the Mass and procession on Easter Sunday (Domingo de Pascua). In addition, the Sociedad de San Juan Chico begins its celebration on Lunes de Pascua, the day after Easter Sunday, and continues for three days. Until sometime between 1920 and 1930, San Juan Chico was one of the group of associations which celebrated during Carnaval. The general pattern of sponsorship of San Juan Chico remains similar to the other associations in the Carnaval group and is better described there.

All Saints' Day and the Day of the Dead originally had the *cofradía* land of Ánimas to pay for the Mass and procession, but today this Mass is paid for out of the funds which the town holds in the bank for the payment of the *cofradía* lands. It is a fiesta in which almost the entire town participates; each family visits the tombs of its dead in the cemetery and places flowers.

The celebration of the fiesta of Candelaria has evidently been elaborated upon since 1819. At that time, there was a single Mass held. Today, this fiesta has been combined with the New Year fiesta, and each is sponsored by groups within one of the two principal barrios. Candelaria will be discussed below in connection with the New Year fiesta.

Of the remaining fiestas mentioned in the list of 1819, four others have disappeared and left no trace. Lunes de Carnestolendas, the

Misa de Hueros, the Misa de Fundación, and Octava de la Cruz
are neither observed nor remembered by any of the Muquiyauyinos
with whom I discussed the subject. A fiesta which is not mentioned
on the 1819 list, but which was observed during the nineteenth century and which disappeared during the first decade of the present
century, is the Cruz de Mayo. It was sponsored·by two barrio
groups of unmarried Indian men. Informants say that all members
wore a regular suit of clothing with ornate leggings, called *botas
postizas*, and a woman's carrying blanket, the *uishkata,* tied across
one shoulder.

Besides Holy Week and the Day of the Dead, seven major fiestas
and five less important ones are celebrated today in Muquiyauyo.
The principal fiestas are the New Year celebration, Candelaria,
Carnaval, Holy Week, Jueves de Comadre, Santiago, and Christmas. The New Year celebration is evidently an elaboration of the
old fiesta of the Pascua de los Reyes held on January 6. In the 1819
list, the forerunner of this is mentioned as the Misa de los Alcaldes. Until the abolition of the post of *alcalde ordinario* and the
other Indian community offices at the end of the nineteenth century,
these positions were filled anew each year on this day, and the
alcaldes were responsible for sponsoring the Mass. Today, however, this fiesta and Candelaria have developed parallel celebrations. Each formerly had *cofradía* land (although the land of the
New Year fiesta group is not mentioned in the sale list of 1937)
but neither depends upon this land today. Now each is sponsored
by groups within one of the two barrios.

The lower barrio is that half of the town to the south of the plaza,
and the upper barrio is the section to the north of the plaza. In
general, the lower barrio is composed of people of the first and
second *cuarteles,* while the upper barrio is composed of the people
of the third and fourth *cuarteles.* The barrios are, however, territorial designations, and they have no formal organization such as
do the *cuarteles.*

In 1911 and 1918 the·*cofradía* lands of the upper barrio group
which sponsored the New Year fiesta, and those of the lower barrio
group which sponsored Candelaria, were taken over by the town.
With the removal of the lands, associations were formed in each
of the barrios to continue the fiestas. In the lower barrio, the
Sociedad de la Vírgen de Candelaria was established, and in the
upper barrio, the Sociedad del Niño Jesus. These two associations are the only ones today continuing to hold fiestas which
were formerly financed by *cofradía* lands and which turned to the
association method to perpetuate themselves.

One of the liveliest fiestas held during the entire year is Carnaval. The only mention of it in the 1819-20 documents is the Monday of Carnestolendas and the Misa de los Hueros. Santo Cristo was evidently not celebrated as a part of Carnaval at that time, for it is listed as a November fiesta. Since that time, the associations of Santo Cristo, San Pedro y San Pablo, San Miguel, San Juan Grande, and San Juan Chico have all begun celebrating Carnaval. As was noted earlier, the last of these was shifted to the end of Holy Week a few decades ago.

The associations are so similar that certain characteristics can be cited for all of them. Their time of origin is unknown, although their attachment to Carnaval seems to have taken place during the last century. Each association holds a Mass, a procession, and an evening of prayer on the night before their Mass. All five groups are now in the charge of directive groups. Sociologically all are similar, being composed of sets of families who have through the years formed the main body of membership. All the groups together include a large proportion of the town's families. Individuals are not required to follow their families in membership, but they usually do.

There are also some variations among these associations. Three of them, Santo Cristo, San Pedro y San Pablo, and San Miguel, have bought lands within the last century, ranging in size from one-half to two and one-half *yugadas* (1, 500 square meters to 7, 500 square meters) to help defray their expenses. These have been called *cofradías* but, as we noted earlier, this is not a standard use of the term. These lands are the private property of the society concerned and neither the church nor the town has any claim on them.

Although I inquired whether these associations were particularly related to one or another of the social classes, the only reply I received was that the Santo Cristo and San Pedro y San Pablo associations were generally made up of the "better" people, the San Juan Grande and San Miguel of "middle" people, and the San Juan Chico association was composed of "lower" people. On the basis of the data collected during the census of families, however, there seemed to be substantial correlation in the associations between barrio and *cuartel* membership on the one hand and class assignment on the other.

As can be seen in the tables below, the associations of Santo Cristo and San Miguel are composed predominantly of people of the third and fourth *cuarteles,* or upper barrio. The members of the other three societies come predominantly from the first and second *cuarteles,* or the lower barrio. Also, three of the groups are composed of both mestizos and Indians, while San Miguel and San Juan Chico are composed predominantly of Indians, and no mestizos were

NUMBER OF FAMILIES BY *CUARTEL* AND CLASS
IN THE CARNAVAL RELIGIOUS ASSOCIATIONS

	Cuarteles				Not Member of *Cuartel*
	1	2	3	4	
Santo Cristo	14	20	30	73	8
San Pedro y San Pablo	17	38	11	8	2
San Juan Grande	32	22	8	3	0
San Miguel	2	0	16	9	0
San Juan Chico	9	7	0	1	4

	Social Class Assignment			
	Indian	Undecided	Mestizo	Not in Sample
Santo Cristo	46	33	27	39
San Pedro y San Pablo	20	16	13	27
San Juan Grande	19	21	8	17
San Miguel	13	8	0	6
San Juan Chico	7	5	0	9

recorded as members. Also significant is the size of the membership of these groups. The groups are classified below according to their predominant *cuartel* and class affiliation, and the number of families with members in each category is given.

	Cuarteles 1 and 2		*Cuarteles* 3 and 4	
		Families		Families
Indian and mestizo	San Pedro y San Pablo	76	Santo Cristo	145
	San Juan Grande	65		
		Total 141		
Indian only	San Juan Chico	21	San Miguel	27

It can be seen from this grouping that the San Pedro y San Pablo and the San Juan Grande groups taken together have a total membership just slightly below that of Santo Cristo; similarly, San Juan Chico has a membership just slightly smaller than San Miguel. The two predominantly Indian societies are very small and seem to be associations of poor people. Of the three mixed (Indian and mestizo) associations, two are made up of members primarily from the first and second *cuarteles,* while only one has a membership primarily from the third and fourth *cuarteles.* This fact suggests that at one time there may have been a single group in the first and second *cuarteles* which later split in two, but I heard no mention of this.

The fiesta of Jueves de Comadre or El Señor de Paca is unique in being the only fiesta promoted by another town in which a regular group of Muquiyauyinos participates. According to one informant, the fiesta was started in the town of Paca (just to the north of Jauja) in 1813. In recent years the active number of Muquiyauyinos has evidently declined, and now only specific families observe the fiesta. Just when the Muquiyauyinos started to participate in the fiesta is not certain. One informant thought they had joined in it at the start; another said that they did not participate until 1905. Through the years almost all the towns in the Jauja region have joined in the celebration. The group leaves Muquiyauyo about four in the morning on the day of the Mass and travels to Paca by bus (formerly on foot) in time to hold their Mass at nine. The whole group then dances around Paca for some hours, and finally dances all the way back to Muquiyauyo, a distance of about thirteen kilometers. The next day another Mass and another procession are held in Muquiyauyo, together with a *tumbamonte.* The Mass and orchestra are paid for by volunteers. Many people who are not regularly members join in the trek to Paca for the entertainment offered by the dance back! According to one informant, the observance used to include a fiesta on the day of Jueves de Compadre, two weeks before Jueves de Comadre, but this is no longer observed.

The fiesta of Santiago was apparently not very elaborate during the nineteenth century. Until 1925 it was sponsored by only one group, but since that date new groups have been formed so that today there are eight separate groups, each of which has an image of the saint. This fiesta is specifically concerned with the branding of animals. Local tradition has it that the fiesta stems from a pre-Spanish observance in which the llama was the focus of the fiesta. According to the folklorist Quijada Jara, Santiago is celebrated by Indians throughout the sierra as the "day of the animals and shepherds, based on the superstition of considering *Taita-Huamani* as the owner and señor of the mountains."[7] The various groups which celebrate the fiesta in Muquiyauyo are composed of members of specific families. There is Santiago de Cáceres, Santiago de Lamberto, Santiago de Losano, and so on. Santiago is evidently observed by families of both the Indian and mestizo classes. Of the sixty-two families recorded as observing it in my 1950 census, forty-five were included in the class membership analysis; of these, twenty-two were classed as Indian, twenty as undecided, and three as mestizo. The various families by whom it is sponsored each year evidently keep no records, and the stimulus for sponsoring comes from one or a few individuals in each group. Since the days on which Santiago is celebrated, July 25 and 26, come between the older paired fiestas of San Juan and Amo Grande in June and Asunción and Yauyos Señor in August, it seems not unlikely that the decline in the celebration of these fiestas may have spurred certain of the townspeople to promote the celebration of Santiago.

The Christmas fiesta has long been observed in Muquiyauyo. The 1819 list of Masses held by the priest includes two, the Misa de Navidad and the Misa de Nuestra Señora de Belén, which were part of the Christmas observance at that time. As is the case with most of the other religious observances, however, this situation changed in the intervening years. By 1880 there were six different groups of dancers celebrating this fiesta. The upper barrio and the lower barrio each sponsored a group called the Chacra Negros and one called the Pachawara or Negrito. The Pachawara is reputed to be older than the Chacra Negros.

The barrios competed with each other for the privilege of paying for the midnight Mass, the Misa de Gallo, on Christmas Eve. Whichever of the two lost automatically paid for the Misa de Aurora, which followed at five o'clock on Christmas morning. Paying for these was a barrio affair: every year from each barrio a *caporal* would be chosen who was responsible for paying for the Mass, contracting for the orchestra, and so on. He was liberally helped by other members of the barrio. The dance groups themselves did not hold any Mass or religious observance apart from those sponsored by the barrio. The dancers devoted their time to dancing, eating, drinking, and not infrequent fights with members of the other barrio.

In addition to the four barrio-sponsored dance groups, there were two other dance groups, the Huaylijía and the Pastores. The Huaylijía, it is said, was composed of persons of the town who lived in the area one block wide which existed between the upper and lower barrios. This area was known as the Chaupibarrio or Barrio del Centro. The Huaylijía seems to be based on membership in certain families, and the traditional middle barrio origin has lost all meaning. So long as the Huaylijía was based upon the Barrio del Centro, it was run in much the same way as were the Negro groups of the two major wards. In 1895, however, the *caporal* had a dream in which he was told that the group should devote itself to San Juan Evangelista; shortly thereafter he mysteriously discovered an image of this saint in his back field. This was a sufficient omen to the group and they reconstituted themselves as a formal association devoted to this saint. They started to hold their Mass and procession on December 27, and have continued until the present with little formal change. At present the Huaylijía is composed of both Indians and mestizos.

The Pastores (shepherds) is a group which consists of young people, principally girls. It is said that formerly the women stayed in the group throughout their lives but in recent years it has become an age-based association. When a girl becomes old enough to marry or goes away to high school, she drops out of the group. The fathers sponsor the group, but it is a small and poor one. Young men may join of their own accord if they are attracted to one of the girls, but few do. The Pastores bought their image only a few years ago; earlier they used one which belonged to another association and which was available in the church.

Around 1880 a new dance group was started by a number of young mestizo men. They introduced a series of dancers called the Tunantes, together with a new set of costumes. As the years passed, this group became extremely popular, and as the class barrier was being weakened many people joined it. This process evidently served to drain the younger generation from membership in the Negro dance societies. The Negro groups declined in popularity, and one of them, the Pachawara of the upper barrio, disappeared altogether about 1915. The Tunantes, on the other hand, continued to grow until 1946, when a large group, mainly men from the lower barrio, split off and formed a new Tunantes group. The older group remained predominantly in the upper barrio. In this way barrio balance was again achieved.

Through their early years the Tunantes never bought an image nor sponsored a Mass. They maintained the group purely for the entertainment of the members and the townspeople. By the time the division occurred, criticism was beginning to grow to the effect that they were an unchristian group and that they should sponsor a Mass. Consequently, within the last five years, the Tunantes of the lower barrio began sponsoring a Mass on Christmas morning, the Misa de Ocho, while the upper barrio Tunantes sponsored one on

December 28. By this time, also, both groups had formed along associational lines, following the old pattern. Each had a *junta directiva*, consisting of an elected president, vice-president, secretary, fiscal, treasurer, and *vocal*. The financing of the Mass and other expenses was done voluntarily by the members of the group.

According to the information I gathered in my 1950 census of the town, there seems to be no class significance attached to membership in any of these Christmas groups. Both mestizos and Indians are to be found in all of them. The two Tunantes associations, the Sociedad de Auxilios Mutuos del Niño Jesus of the upper barrio and the Sociedad Cooperativa del Niño Jesus of the lower, are by far the most active of all the Christmas groups at present.

Five smaller fiestas are celebrated by groups which have originated in the town within the last eighty years. The associations sponsoring these celebrations are the Franciscanos, the Hijas de María, the Sociedad de Artesanos, the Sociedad del Señor de los Milagros, and the Sociedad de la Vírgen del Perpetuo Socorro. All of these groups emphasize the religious aspect of their fiestas; they have no particular dance groups nor do they sponsor any other large-scale diversion.

The fiesta of San Francisco de Asís was started toward the end of the last century under the stimulus of the Franciscans from the monastery of Ocopa near Concepción, some miles down the Jauja Valley from Muquiyauyo. The activities of the group consist principally of an annual trip on the second of August to the monastery for Mass, Communion, and confession, and an annual meeting in October for the business of the association. In former years, it is said, the membership included both men and women and Indians and mestizos. Today, however, the group is composed principally of mestizo women of the upper barrio.

The association of the Hijas de María evidently started about the same time as the Franciscans. I could find nothing of its early history, but its membership evidently includes any woman who wishes to join. It is run along the same general lines as its sister organizations in other parts of the Catholic world, with evening prayers at the church during the month of May and a final Mass and procession on the thirtieth of that month.

The Sociedad de Artesanos, dedicated to San José, and that of the Señor de los Milagros can be considered together since they were both recent innovations and were started by a father and son respectively. The first was initiated about 1900 primarily for artisans, but has since diminished so that it has a very small membership of mestizos. The Señor de los Milagros association was started in 1946 specifically for mestizos. Both associations hold a Mass and employ a band for a social dance following the Mass. The Sociedad de la Vírgen del Perpetuo Socorro is very similar to these two in its activities but it is evidently an older organization. Formerly it was predominantly mestizo, but early in the century it began to be mixed in composition. At the annual luncheon following the Mass, however, members of the two classes sit in separate rooms.

This review of some of the changes which have occurred in religious organizations and fiestas in Muquiyauyo during the past century brings out a number of trends. First, we can distinguish two rather different kinds of fiestas which, for the sake of convenience, we may call the public and the private. Christmas, the New Year, Candelaria, Carnaval, Holy Week, the Day of the Dead, and Jueves de Comadre are public fiestas in which anyone may participate, although their sponsorship is generally limited to a specific group. In the past, the fiestas of San Juan Bautista, Señor del Amo, Asunción, Yauyos Señor, Purísima, Encarnación, Corpus Cristi, and various others were of this nature. One trend, then, has been the gradual disappearance of some of the public fiestas; we know that many have disappeared and no new ones have been started.

Second, where public fiestas have not disappeared, their sponsorship has tended to change. Whereas the New Year fiesta and Candelaria were formerly sponsored on the basis of *cofradías,* they are now run by associations of individuals. The Christmas fiesta used to be sponsored by the entire membership of the barrios; the various dance groups and fiestas are now run by associations of individuals. While in many cases these new associations are still predominantly composed of people from the same barrios as before, only members of the association, rather than an entire barrio, are responsible for the fiesta. The only fiesta which continues in the general pattern of the past is Holy Week; it has as yet no associations, and volunteers are drawn from among the townspeople to sponsor it. A second trend, then, has been the change of sponsorship in the public fiestas from entire territorial groupings to specialized associations.

Third, since the latter part of the nineteenth century there have appeared at least four and possibly five new fiestas: San Francisco, Hijas de María, San José, and Señor de los Milagros; the Sociedad de la Vírgen del Perpetuo Socorro should probably be included in

this group, but we do not know the date of its founding. Characteristic of the four new fiestas is that they are private fiestas: each
is run by a small and somewhat closed group of people. Membership is always theoretically open, but it is actually restricted,
usually to mestizos. Thus, another trend is the formation of new
fiestas on a private basis. The creation of the Sociedad de San Juan
Evangelista, or the Huaylijía, and the Tunantes groups can be interpreted in somewhat the same manner although they are parts of
public fiestas.

A final trend may be seen in the fact that of the older fiestas, all
those which were sponsored on the basis of an entire class, such as
all the Indians or all the mestizos, and known to be sponsored specifically on that basis, have disappeared. Thus San Juan Bautista,
Señor del Amo, Asunción, Yauyos Señor, and Cruz de Mayo have
all disappeared completely, while the Fiesta de la Vírgen del Perpetuo Socorro, which used to be strictly a mestizo group, has
changed so as to include both mestizos and Indians. All public
fiestas which emphasized the differences between the classes, or
at that time castes, have either disappeared or changed in such
a way that they no longer place emphasis on the class distinctions.

There is no evidence that there has been any decrease in interest
in fiestas as such. The attendance at public fiestas is usually very
large and the townspeople look forward to the three- and four-day
celebrations. The dance groups show numerous features of recent
elaboration in costuming, and there is no evidence that the main
dance groups are declining in importance. Some of the very old
groups, such as the Principales (New Year) and the Negritos
(Christmas), now have very few members and may possibly die
out in a decade or so, but the larger groups seem to be on the
increase.

Similarly, the private fiesta groups show no decline in interest.
Rather, new groups are being formed from time to time, and as
will be noted later, the present status of the social class system
seems to be encouraging the formation of such private groups.

These trends in increase and decrease in certain phases of the
fiestas may be traced in great part to three factors: the desire for
greater local autonomy, the increase in population, and a tendency
to put aside traits which reinforced public recognition of mestizo-
Indian differences. The desire for local autonomy was first manifest in our records in the long litigation of 1819-20 in which the
Muquiyauyinos disagreed with the parish priest in Huaripampa.
The townspeople were upheld in this effort and the authority of the
parish priest was to that degree weakened. Thus local autonomy

.n religious celebrations was achieved two-thirds of a century before political individuality was won through the creation of the separate district of Muquiyauyo.

It has also been shown that during the nineteenth century the population of Muquiyauyo practically doubled. This population growth
resulted in the fact that fiestas which were supposed to be sponsored
by entire caste (Indians or mestizos) and territorial (the entire
town or entire barrios) groups became unwieldy. The abolition of
the Indian community officers in 1891 put an end to the existence
of an Indian authority which could promote and regulate the activities of the Indians. The pressure for effective organization of the
growing number of townspeople for sponsoring fiestas was felt before this time, however, as is indicated by the appearance before
1890 of the Tunantes group in the Christmas fiesta and the private
societies of the Franciscanos and the Hijas de María. The effect
of population increase may be seen in the fragmentation of sponsorship and the rise of associations and private fiestas.

The final factor in the trends observed is the breakdown of the
caste system. This too, as will become evident in the next chapter, was in part due to an increase in population. Its specific effect on the fiestas was an increasing lack of interest in those fiestas which were supposed to be sponsored by an entire caste group.
Important elements in this process were the breakdown of the Indian communal authority, the increasing Indian-mestizo solidarity
that developed during the nineteenth century, and the weakening of
the priest's authority. Presumably, had a priest been active in Muquiyauyo through these years, he could have exerted some influence
against the gradual disintegration of the caste and territorial spon-
sorships; but no one in power was any longer specifically interested
in maintaining the sponsorship of the old fiestas on the caste and
territorial bases.

Thus three factors, population increase, increased local autonomy, and the breakdown of the caste system, brought about the
trends mentioned earlier: the gradual disappearance of some public
fiestas and a shift of sponsorship to specialized associations in
others; the formation of private fiestas and specialized sponsoring
associations; and the disappearance or change in form of sponsorship of fiestas which were based on caste or territorial groupings.

An important group of associations, those of Carnaval, might,
on the surface, seem to contradict these trends. It will be remembered that these groups are still operating on what appear to be
both barrio and class bases. Closer examination, however, reveals that these fiesta groups do not contradict the trends but

rather fall in line with them. Of the five groups, Santo Cristo, San Pedro y San Pablo, and San Juan Grande are composed of both Indians and mestizos. What evidence we have points to the fact that they have been so sponsored since early in the last century. Thus, the continued existence of these groups fails to contradict the trends toward associational sponsorship and a mixing of the classes, but rather indicates that an early form, or possibly the original form, of the Carnaval groups was a forerunner of the form which other groups have taken in more recent years. The two smaller associations, San Miguel and San Juan Chico, seem to be class-based in that they are composed principally of Indians. We cannot interpret this membership as being exclusively Indian, however, since the other societies are mixed. Rather, it must be interpreted as a matter of wealth and standing in the general social scale; some Indians are wealthier and associate more with mestizos than others.

The apparent territorial basis of these five groups, three composed predominantly of people from the first and second *cuarteles* and two composed predominantly of people from the third and fourth *cuarteles*, does not mean that they are sponsored by the barrios or the *cuarteles* as such. In no case is the membership exclusively from one *cuartel*, and in all cases the sponsorship is based on an association of individuals rather than on a territorial association. The barrio characteristics of these associations doubtless reflect a situation in the past when barrio membership was of greater significance than it is today. As is the case in the contemporary Tunante groups, members tend to be drawn from one or another of the barrios. The fact of general territorial proximity should not obscure the fact that it is not the members of a given territory as such who sponsor the fiesta.

There is yet another trend which should be noted. While at the end of the last century the caste breakdown was an important factor in the disappearance of certain fiestas and in the change in membership of others, recent years have seen a trend among mestizos to re-establish the class basis for some of the private fiestas and sponsoring groups. Recently, perhaps beginning as early as the 1920's, but more strongly in the 1930's, the membership of the Sociedad of Artesanos (San José) and the Franciscanos have tended to become mestizo. In addition, the Sociedad del Señor de los Milagros was formed in 1946 as a purely mestizo group. In the next chapter we shall see how this reflects an attempt to re-establish certain of the class distinctions which were temporarily put aside when the caste-based fiestas disappeared early in this century.

This re-establishment of mestizo-Indian distinctions in the sphere of religious organizations, however, is occurring in the realm of private, not public, fiestas.

It is important at this point to continue the story of events which led ultimately to the purchase of the *cofradía* lands by the town. In 1909 all the remaining *cofradía* lands except Dolores and Candelaria were rented out in *remate* and thus put in the same status as the lands of San Juan Bautista, Amo Grande, and Yauyos Señor; in 1915 it was arranged that a single *rematista* should make a contract with the priest for all the lands then in *remate*. The lands of Dolores and Candelaria were handled this way in 1916 and 1917. In 1920 it was decided to make a contract directly between the town and the priest, but by 1923 this still had not been done. In 1926 funds gained from the lands were still being used by the town when an individual from the town made a contract with the priest to rent the lands for his private benefit. This was strongly denounced; it was publicly claimed that the lands actually belonged to the community, even if they had been rented from the church, and that this individual, therefore, had no right to make a contract with the priest. Evidently the question of who actually owned the lands went undecided, but the man dropped his contract with the priest.

This uncertain state of affairs had apparently gone far enough by 1931 to cause concern to the church. Sensing that the lands might be lost outright, as had happened after the revolution in Mexico, the archbishop authorized the various priests to sell the *cofradía* lands. This upset the community, since some members felt strongly that the church had no right to rent, much less to sell, lands which already belonged to the town.

In 1924, one of the leading citizens, Gabriel Bustamante, had pointed out that there was in the council archives a document which made the lands the property of the community; but he never pressed the point and later came out in favor of purchasing the lands from the church. In 1926 the next major town to the south, Sincos, had called a congress of districts to try to convince the various alcaldes that they should expropriate their respective *cofradía* lands with no further concern for the church; the community of Muquiyauyo decided not to attend this meeting. When the priest announced the decision of the archbishop in 1931, the community immediately named a commission to prevent the church from selling the land until the town could decide what it wished to do. The records of the meetings of that year are full of this subject, and diverse opinions were expressed on the matter. One member felt that since Muquiyauyo was

no longer a purely Catholic community (some members had been
converted to Protestantism in 1920), the lands were communal and
that no contract was necessary; another said that the church had
caused humanity little but trouble, but that in order to avoid more
trouble, it would be simpler to buy the lands and have nothing more
said about it.

In 1932 the priest offered the community two choices, either to
buy the lands outright for S/. 10, 000 or to continue renting them
for another year at S/. 350. The community chose to do the latter
Later, in 1935, the community had apparently been lax in its
payments to the church, and the priest threatened to sell the lands
to an outsider if payment was not made immediately. The same
year the community sent a committee to the national congress to
try to determine whether the lands really belonged to the church or
the town. The next year they sent another commission to the bishop
and again the meetings were full of the subject. More persons tried
to buy the lands outright, and finally in 1938 the community purchased the lands for S/. 15, 000.

This history of vacillation over what should be done with respect
to the *cofradía* lands is in considerable contrast to the attitude manifested toward the transaction when I was in the town. Had it not
been for the unmistakable story told in the session books, I would
have believed the claims of many informants that the lands had been
purchased with a long-range and careful plan in mind. The transaction finally made was rather to the credit of the town, but only
reasonable in the light of the fact that a number of towns, Sincos
among them, had refused even to deal with the church and had simply assumed ownership of the lands. In the contract signed with
the bishop, it was agreed that S/. 6, 000 of the total sum paid was
to be used by the church, in repairs on the Muquiyauyo church
building, while the remaining S/. 9, 000 was to be deposited in the
bank and the interest thereon was to be used to pay the priest for
Sunday Masses or, as it was expressed, "to cover the expenses of
the cult." Apparently the church was not alone in its earlier fear
that the lands might be seized by the government; when the contract was made, one community member remarked that it was important to get the transaction in writing since the community might
otherwise eventually lose the lands to the national government.

A view expressed by some informants suggested that the final
purchase of the lands was due to the fact that the president of the
communal organization in 1938 was a Protestant. It is entirely possible that this influenced the final effort to bring the transaction
to a close. In any case, the removal of the lands from any claim

of the church was another step in the long pull away from the system which had been established during the early colonial period. The decline in the use of *cofradía* lands to sponsor fiestas at the end of the last century reflected not only a breakdown of distinctions between the castes and a need for the lands because of the expansion of the population, but also a further degeneration in the relationship between the townspeople and the clergy. One of the most respected priests in recent Muquiyauyo history, according to informants, was Padre Guzmán, who lived in Muquiyauyo even though the parish seat was in Huaripampa. However, an early entry in the district session books in 1887 reveals that this man had just used his influence in Jauja to get the Muquiyauyo governor removed from office in order to replace him with another man who would agree to an increase in the church income. The council objected, both to the raising of the taxes and the high-handed method employed to do it. In the following year, the priest complained to the vicar general that Muquiyauyo was not showing sufficient respect for its priest; the town council heard of this and replied that they would show more respect if and when the priest began to hold his Masses regularly. In the same year the council decided that the old custom of *pri-nacias*, the donation by each member of the parish of a yearly gift of an arroba (twenty-five pounds) of grain, should be changed; the donations were to be taxed, and hereafter the priest would pay /. 2 for each arroba he received.

For many years a point of friction between the town and the priest was the mill. The town, through an error, built a water mill on and owned by the church. Thereafter the priest demanded that all profits from the venture be sent to him, and the town resentfully but dutifully complied. Early in the twentieth century the mill broke down and the priest asked that it be repaired. The town council replied that they had no intention of repairing it merely to provide him with more profits; and it never was repaired.

The recent history of the town is full of unpleasant incidents between the town and the priest; in 1911 the town threatened to publish in a Lima newspaper a letter from the priest excusing himself from having been absent a number of times from Mass; in 1912 the town wrote the bishop complaining that no two priests charged the same price for Mass; in 1916 it was reported that the priest had acted very badly after a local fiesta, and the town wished to be made into a separate parish. During my own visit, the town was trying again, under a new *gobernador*, to have the town recognized as a separate parish. If this is accomplished, it will mean the breaking of still another tie with the colonial period.

Irrespective of the relationship with a particular priest, the cler
gy and the Catholic Church hold a very important place in the live
of the Muquiyauyinos. It is still remembered with great pride tha
in 1894, when the guardian father of the Franciscan monastery o
Ocopa some miles to the south wrote the district council asking fo
help in the rebuilding of his monastery, almost the whole town wen
down and worked for two and a half days.

Two factors underlie the troubled relationship. The first is tha
the priest almost always lives in Huaripampa, and this is a con
stant reminder that in this respect Muquiyauyo is still subordinat
to the neighboring town. The best-remembered priest is Guzmán
who chose to live in Muquiyauyo. The other factor is that there i
little doubt but that the quality of the Peruvian clergy assigned t
the parish has not always been very high. Thus some people wil
refuse their house to the priest as a person but will carefully in
vite him for the formal meal after Mass during one of the fiestas
they may say vicious things about the priest but highly resent hi
absences. The troubles over the *cofradía* lands might have bee
solved much more easily had the townspeople liked the priests per
sonally and had the priests lived in Muquiyauyo. The situation i
Muquiyauyo reflects a problem which is also to be found elsewher
in Peru.

A gauge of religious activity in Muquiyauyo can be made by a
examination of attendance at Mass. Attendance at every daytim
Mass which took place during the time of this study was observe
At Sunday Masses an average of about fifty to sixty persons, prin
cipally women and children but some men, regularly attended. .
typical attendance was as follows: seventeen families were repre
sented, of which five were considered to be Indian and ten mestiz
One family was of mixed ancestry, but generally thought of as mes
tizo. One elderly man whose class membership was undecided als
attended. The representatives of the Indian families were widowe
old people, two men and three women. Of the ten mestizo familie
three were represented by one person each, two married wome
whose husbands did not attend, and one young man. The other seve
families were represented by women and children, and in two case
the husband also attended.

In general, then, mestizos regularly attend Mass more than d
Indians, but among the mestizos it is principally the women an
children who go. Among the Indians it is principally the very ol
who attend. In terms of the town as a whole, however, very fe
people go to Sunday Mass; sixty may be considered as a good show
ing. Informants say that in the past Sunday Mass was much bette

ttended than now. Up through the last century the Indians were
under some pressure by the mestizos to attend, but this stopped
some time ago. One of the functions of the Indian *alcalde auxiliar*
was to make sure that the Indians went to church. In the district
session book for 1887 a petition was submitted by residents of the
own complaining that the *alcalde auxiliar* had abused them by oblig-
ng them to go to the fiesta of the Purísima. The council's only
omment was that the office of *alcalde auxiliar* was superfluous
anyway. By the end of the century this pressure had virtually
topped, and doubtless ceased completely with the abolition of the
ndian official posts. In 1891, however, the *gobernador* complained
hat the agents and inspectors of the district council had not been
ssisting in the "doctrinal exercises" which were supposed to be
nder the cognizance of the provincial alcalde. The council relied that the district agents were not obliged to implement any
ype of fiesta or diversion of this nature.

That there has been a decline in church attendance seems cer-
ain; the question is when it may have become noticeable. The de-
line of certain fiestas was well under way by 1890; the few notes
which appear in the district session books indicate that lack of in-
erest on the part of at least some of the population was evident at
his date also. In 1916 a very suggestive entry appears in the coun-
il book. A request was made asking whether it was permissible to
work on Sundays and fiesta days; the council decided that it was up
to the individual person to decide for himself, although the ruling
eretofore had been that work was prohibited. This indicates that
he problem of work on Sunday had probably been an issue for some
me; and since the council reversed the older ruling, it would ap-
ear that the old custom had not been strictly observed.

Since Mass today is attended primarily by mestizos and evi-
ence indicates that the Indians used to attend more frequently,
is reasonable to conclude that the main decrease in church at-
endance has been among the Indian population. It is likely that
he decline in the Indians' interest in church accompanied the de-
line of the importance of the Indian community officers and the
radual dissolution of the Indian community. The church had long
een not only a religious institution, but a means of subordina-
on of the Indians first to the Spanish and then to the mestizo upper
lass. The disintegration of the Indian group as a distinct socio-
ogical entity brought about the permissive abstention from weekly
hurch activities. With this turn of events, the intensive partici-
ation in religious affairs became a function of the upper class,
nd the private religious associations provided a most conveni-

ent means by which separate social participation could be main
tained.

Other factors led to less frequent attendance at Mass by the In
dians. Early in the century more and more Muquiyauyinos wer
going to work at the mining centers to earn their livelihood o
merely to earn extra cash. In those years very few of the mines ha
Catholic churches. This led to a decrease in active participation i
weekly church activities and also provided an open field for Prot
estant missionaries.

Another aspect of lack of interest in church affairs, and one whic
also reflects the conflict between the townspeople and the clergy, i
the long and unsuccessful attempt to build a new church building
The present church in Muquiyauyo is a small, probably eighteenth
century structure which has undergone considerable repair. Whil
it is ample for the small Sunday congregations attending it now
it is much too small for the large crowds of five hundred or mor
which gather at Christmas and during Holy Week. It was decide
some time in the 1880's that this structure was inadequate for
district capital. In the 1889 session book a decision is recorde
to continue the construction of a new church which had been hel
up by legal problems. There followed during the next ten year
an endless series of discussions and decisions with respect to th
work; orders were sent out to bring materials, provide workers
and so forth. By 1898 it was recognized that the district did no
have the funds to keep up the project. When both the priest and th
bishop refused to help in the financing, the work stopped; at tha
time, an entire stone foundation had been laid to a height of si
feet above the ground, across the plaza from the old church. Ther
was no further mention of the project for years. One of the mes
tizos explained to me that in the late 1880's the priest had disap
peared with the money to complete the building. As there was neve
a mention of such an event in any of the session books (and th
books are quite frank about calling people thieves), it is likel
that this was another instance of using the priest as a scapegoat
In 1944, on a list of possible communal projects, the constructio
of the new church was again mentioned, but by 1950 nothing ha
been done about it. It was the opinion of one informant that the ston
foundations would not be strong enough to support the building no
even if it were built. At present one side of the foundation serve
to support a wall of the girls' school and the other is occupied b
a new grain mill. The front area is used as the basketball an
volleyball court for the Avalanche Basket Club, with large letter
"A B C," painted on the stone wall.

An important religious change occurred when Protestantism was introduced into Muquiyauyo. The Protestant population at present numbers about twenty-two families. The organization to which they belong is the Evangelical Church of Peru, sponsored by cooperative efforts of British and North American missionary associations. The governing of the church, however, is in the hands of the Peruvian converts, and in the Jauja Valley there are no permanent mission stations.

Protestantism was brought to Muquiyauyo by four Muquiyauyo men who were converted while working at the mines in 1919. When they returned to the town from the mines, they were sent immediately off to the army. Upon their second homecoming they caused the community no overt trouble and were allowed to carry on their conversion activities as best they could. It was not until 1930 that one of the members of the Protestant Church, one of the original four and now minister of the group, achieved a place in the district government through being appointed to the post of *gobernador*. The only other major posts of authority held by members of this group were communal president in 1938, manager of the electric light plant in 1942, and *gobernador* again in 1949.

The general reaction of the town to the Protestants indicates that while the townspeople may have been a little apprehensive at first, they were fundamentally not very much disturbed by the introduction of another faith. After the Protestants had been in the town for twelve years, they began making requests to the district and the community for assistance in certain matters. In 1932 they asked the community organization and the district council for permission to use or rent one of the district buildings for their meetings. Records do not state what the community's reply was, but the district council refused. In the same year, however, it was agreed that since both Evangelicals (as the Protestants are called) and Catholics contributed work for the community, the former as well as the latter should be given electric light free. In 1938, when the Protestants again asked for the use of one of the community rooms for their "spiritual activities" for a period of three days, the request was granted.

The first indication in the records that another church had been recognized in the town was in 1927, when the expression "Church of the Catholics" was used instead of merely "Church," which before had been sufficient. In general, the Protestants have a limited group in the community, and in 1950 it did not appear that with their present organization they were likely to expand very rapidly. No mestizo ever joined the Protestant Church in Muquiyauyo; in the sample of social classes, sixteen of the twenty-two Protestant families were included, and of these, ten were judged as Indian and six as undecided. Informants agreed that "only North Americans and Indians were Protestants." In other respects, the Protestant population is similar to the rest of the Muquiyauyo townspeople. During the period of this study a large camp meeting was held in Muquiyauyo and attended by Protestants from all over the region, as well as by missionaries from other parts of Peru. One of the missionaries at this time commented that Muquiyauyo was a very fine place, that it was safe to have a camp meeting there; some time before, they had held one in Argentina and the Catholics had burned them out!

These aspects of religious activity in Muquiyauyo bring out changes in attitudes toward religion over the past years. Religion has, as the district council expressed it many years ago, become a matter for the individual to decide on. If a person does not wish to participate in a fiesta or in a Sunday Mass, he does not have to; if he does not wish to remain a Catholic, he may become a Protestant, or indeed may simply be nothing. But this does not mean that religion is unimportant or even becoming unimportant in Muquiyauyo. Rather, it has found new support. The mestizo class as a group is reinforcing its class position through emphasis upon constant religious activities and through the founding from time to time of new associations for celebrating particular saints. The town continues to hold its greatest celebrations on days of religious festivity; these celebrations are probably growing larger and more complex with the years, and the growth is in both religious and recreational spheres. The fiestas, instead of being supported by an entire segment of the population, are now being sustained by special associations which, in fact, frequently follow the old pattern in their formation; those formerly sponsored by a barrio are now sponsored by an association of people from the same barrio.

While it may be said that religion has been achieving new support, the church as an institution has not been growing stronger over the years. The long history of town-church relations is suggestive of the separation of the clergy from the life of the people. When the church originally came to Peru, it was in the role of a conqueror; it retained this role even into the beginning of the republic. During the nineteenth century, however, the Indians of Muquiyauyo evidently became disillusioned with the church; as the requirements for them to attend and support Sunday Masses and to sponsor fiestas weakened, they ceased to do these things. If asked today, all the Indians of Muquiyauyo except the Protestants would claim to be ardent Catholics. But by this they mean they are of the faith but hold little interest in the church. The church instead of being the leader of the religion has come to be merely the mechanism by means of which it functions. The mestizos, as has been noted, have a somewhat different point of view.

5

THE CHANGE IN SOCIAL CLASS STRUCTURE

IN THE previous chapters it has been necessary to refer to two major segments of Muquiyauyo as "Indian" and "mestizo."[1] We must now explore in more detail just what is meant by these terms. During my stay in Muquiyauyo, I only gradually became aware that these terms had a strong social significance to the townspeople. To an outsider, the townspeople appear to be dressed generally alike, to live in similar houses, to speak the same language, and to resemble any group of people among whom are both rich and poor. Little by little, however, differences became clear. At certain fiestas, for example, some people ate the fiesta dinner in one part of the building, others in another, and certain people always took the lead in certain kinds of activities. When it became clear to me that the terms "Indian" and "mestizo" had a social meaning beyond their racial connotation, I began to question informants concerning them and found that at least up to the beginning of the present century there existed a series of social distinctions which constituted a caste system. It will be remembered that in the documents relating to the feud between Muquiyauyo and Huaripampa in 1819-20 there were numerous references to a *comunidad* of *naturales* or *indios* on the one hand and the Spanish, mestizos, and creoles on the other; the entire sociopolitical history of the town is based on the existence of these two groups.

Since our descriptive data really begins only in the latter part of the last century, we will have to begin there. Informants agreed that about 1880 there existed a series of distinctive traits which served to distinguish one group in the community from the other. Characteristic Indian clothing was worn by Indian men and women, and European clothing was worn by the mestizos. Only Indians had usufruct of communal lands, and these lands were owned by the Indian community; this land was under neither the authority

82

nor the control of the mestizos. All Indians spoke the Quechua language, and some spoke Spanish; all mestizos spoke Spanish, although many also knew Quechua. Certain family names were known to be carried only by Indian families, others only by mestizos; an individual's ancestry was the primary determinant as to whether he belonged to one caste or the other. Indians were said to have physical features by which they could easily be distinguished from mestizos. Only Indians could hold office in the Indian community organization; only mestizos could hold office in the district government. While everyone was a Catholic, some of the fiestas were sponsored by the Indian caste and others were sponsored by the mestizo caste; some fiestas were based upon other social factors. Intermarriage between the castes was theoretically prohibited. In addition to these traits, others frequently mentioned by informants were these: Indians owned very little private land; Indians seldom traveled; Indians were poorly educated or had no formal education at all; Indians were never invited to the homes of mestizos for fiestas except in a subordinate capacity; Indians lived "much lower" than did the mestizos, and so forth. In the district session books of the period there are frequent references which distinguish one group from the other. It is evident that the mestizos preferred not to equate their own partial Indian ancestry with the contemporary Indians who lived in the same town as a lower caste.

It is impossible to estimate how strong this caste system was in the late nineteenth century. We have evidence that there existed a greater solidarity between the castes in Muquiyauyo than perhaps existed in most Peruvian mountain towns and that the Indian community as a political organization was on the verge of disintegration; it was only some twenty years until the Indian group divided up its communal lands and consequently disappeared as an economic entity. It is not possible to delineate either the absolute or relative sizes of the two castes in 1880 since there are available no lists of the population of the town. Fortunately, however, it is possible to determine the social composition of the Indian group at a date early in the present century. When the communal lands were repartitioned in 1904, a list was made of every person claiming to be Indian and therefore having right to a share of the land. This provided a basic list of family names and individuals as of that date for the Indian caste; for the mestizo caste, there was no comparable list.

In order to determine the general social composition in 1949, I obtained from each of the *cuarteles* a list of its current membership; these were mimeographed, and a copy of each list, with a total of 457 names, was given to each of four informants. The informants were asked to judge and to mark beside every name whether the person involved was looked upon socially as Indian or mestizo. In each case, we explained carefully that we were not interested in judgments upon race, and the informants understood this. Each individual was thereby judged four times, and the judges agreed that 64 persons, or 14 per cent, were mestizo; 224 persons, or 49.1 per cent, were Indian; and concerning the remaining 169 persons, or 36.9 per cent, the judges disagreed as to whether they should be called Indian or mestizo.

In a review of the list of 169 persons over whom the judges disagreed, it developed that there were two relatively objective reasons for confusion which accounted for about 50 per cent of the group. For the rest a variety of reasons emerged. The two objective reasons were (1) that the person in question, or more usually his parents, came from outside of Muquiyauyo; the judges did not know definitely how to classify the person and so followed one or more of a number of secondary criteria; and (2) that the person was of recently mixed ancestry, that he had one parent from each class (or caste), or his grandparents were of different castes. Under both these circumstances, since there was ambiguity concerning the person being judged, it was possible for various secondary criteria to influence the judge's opinion. It developed that there were five such secondary criteria: (1) whether the name of the person was the same as an old Indian or old mestizo name in Muquiyauyo; if it was neither and new to the town, there would be some reflection as to whether it was of Spanish or Indian origin, but this usually did not carry very far; (2) whether the newcomer lived "low" like an Indian or in better circumstances, like a mestizo; (3) whether the Muquiyauyino, the husband or wife, was considered to be Indian or mestizo; there was a tendency to equate a husband and wife; (4) whether, if a stranger, the person had distinctive Indian racial characteristics; (5) whether the person was perfectly certain of his own class antecedents; if a person claimed convincingly to be mestizo, and his name and physical appearance did not contradict him, he might be accepted as one. The above five points are listed roughly in order of their importance.

Legal recognition was given to the fact of being listed as either Indian or mestizo in the birth records until 1943. In 1905, 70 per cent of the births were recorded as Indian, but by 1940 this had dropped to 45 per cent; and from 1943 on, all births were recorded as mestizo. The use of these terms as a racial designation of the members of the present population and as a classification of social classes is clearly understood by the townspeople. When I first asked the informants to give their judgments concerning the various adults on the list, they claimed that it was impossible since racially everyone was mestizo.

In the past seventy-five or one hundred years, a great change has taken place in this social structure in Muquiyauyo. Some of the elements of this change have been described in preceding chapters. In general, people from both castes began to participate jointly in more affairs; together with this, there was a simultaneous borrowing of some culture traits and a merging of others. The result has been, in effect, to blend the two previously distinct sub-cultures of mestizos and Indians.

Economically, the most distinct difference between the castes was the existence of the Indian communal lands; when these lands were repartitioned among the Indians in 1904, an important symbol of differentiation was removed. There is no evidence that the majority of mestizos was pleased about the loss of this symbol, but there was recompense in the fact that the lands were now available for purchase. It will be remembered that these lands composed about 15 per cent of the total valley lands of the town. In terms of wealth, there is little doubt that the mestizos of the last century were better off than the Indians, but we have no specific data on this issue. By the time of the study in 1949, a number of Indians were quite wealthy. This wealth consisted principally of land and annual crops; several Indians engaged in minor commercial activities, but in general this was not a very important source of profit. Many Indians and some mestizos, however, were rather poor and had to depend in great part on annual work in the mining centers.

During the nineteenth century, the Indians' clothing was quite distinct from that of the mestizos. This is described in some detail later in chapter 11, and it is sufficient to point out here that the men wore short black wool trousers and jacket, while the women wore a single-piece long dress. By 1910, the last of the men had given up their Indian dress for mestizo clothing, and the women's dress was changing to a form which was being used by both Indians and many mestizos. The new dress, known as the *centro*, was composed of a cotton blouse and a skirt with a number of woolen underskirts. The mestizos have usually kept up with the changing urban styles for occasions, but many still use the *centro* for daily wear.

The language difference between the castes changes slowly, but the use of Spanish by Indians was well under way by the end of the

1920's. The entire generation of townspeople who reached adulthood in the 1930's and 1940's spoke Spanish with more ease than they did Quechua. Mestizos generally knew Quechua as well as Spanish, and many still speak the language with some proficiency. Only a very few people today speak Quechua in preference to Spanish in all situations and these people are, without exception, referred to as Indian. There is still a tendency among the poorer Indian women to speak Quechua among themselves in their homes.

The linked characteristics of name and ancestry, of course, did not disappear. By the end of the nineteenth century, marriages of people of recognized Indian ancestry with mestizos were not uncommon. Marriage records begin only in 1905, but in that year there were recorded six such marriages out of a total of thirty-two, and some were recorded during all succeeding years until 1943, after which all persons were listed as mestizo. There is little indication that many such marriages took place before 1890, but we have no real data to confirm this. Today, the feeling in the particular family determines to what extent pressure against such mixed unions may be applied. There is a definite tendency for members of mestizo families to marry within their own class; Indians who marry into the mestizo class usually do so with persons from outside the town. In all, however, ancestry and name are still the strongest social and symbolic elements determining a person's class position.

Physical appearance, while at one time doubtless practical for the differentiation of caste members, has long since become a confusing factor. Certainly by 1910 a great number of people could not be distinguished as belonging to one or the other class on the basis of physical features alone. Muquiyauyinos today recognize that little can be deduced concerning ancestry or social position from physical appearance. Racial characteristics are still occasionally referred to, however, if one wishes to indicate that a given person is really Indian despite the fact that he is socially recognized as mestizo.

Another major change which occurred as a part of the shift from the caste system to the class system was the alteration of the political system described earlier. This political change, combined with the fact that the usufruct of land was implicated in it, is from one viewpoint the most important part of the social change. It created, as it were, civil rights for the Indians equal to those enjoyed by the mestizos.

The last survival of the Indian communal organization and the inferior political status of the Indian were to be seen in the group

known as *comisionados*. The *comisionados* were Indians appointed
by the district officers to carry out orders relating to the Indians.
As late as the 1920's, these positions were filled by Indians, al-
hough by that time the function of the position had changed to one
of general messenger, and the office disappeared sometime be-
.ween 1925 and 1930.

The most overt manifestation of solidarity between the classes
s the fact that the town government is called the *comunidad indígena*. This term originally referred to the Indian community; but
oday mestizos and Indians alike have taken over the term to desig-
1ate the entire town organization.

The changes in religious organization have been described in an
earlier chapter. In general, the shift in this realm of activity involved the disappearance of fiestas which were supported by an
entire caste, the Indians' gradual loss of interest in regular re-
igious observances, and the conversion of some Indians to Protestantism. The mestizos have tended to utilize religion as a means
of establishing their class superiority by founding private religious societies and by taking the lead in regular Sunday devotion.
n religion, there are still distinctions between Indians and mes-
izos, but they are mild in comparison with those which existed in
he last century.

There is one other phase of social organization which has changed
vith the gradual alteration in the class system; this is the meaning
of the town barrios. The barrios have no formal organization but
are general territorial divisions of the town area. Originally the
area southeast of the plaza was the lower barrio and that to the
1orthwest was the upper barrio. The block-wide area to the northeast and southwest of the plaza was known as the *barrio del centro*
or the Chaupibarrio. The social significance of the barrios is to be
seen in certain religious associations and sports clubs. There
s, of course, a tendency for people to move about more within their
own neighborhood, and to the degree that a neighborhood falls within
. barrio, this also reflects more activity within the barrio. There
s a tradition, however, that at an earlier date the two major barrios, the upper and the lower, were the residential area of Indian
amilies, while the Chaupibarrio was the residential area of Span-
ards and mestizos. Strictly speaking this is no longer true, since
many more mestizos now live outside the Chaupibarrio area than
vithin it. Nevertheless, the tradition is supported by the relative
1umbers of people of each class to be found in each of the barrios
see table below); the Chaupibarrio has fewer people classed as Indian and more classed as mestizo. (Data are taken from the sam-

ple of class membership.) This residential difference seems definitely to be a survival, however, because during my stay in the
town I heard no reference to class difference in relation to residential area; rather, it was repeated that the Chaupibarrio scarcely
existed any more.

	Indian		Undecided		Mestizo	
	No. of Families	Per Cent	No. of Families	Per Cent	No. of Families	Per Cent
Lower barrio	36	55.4	17	26.2	12	18.4
Upper barrio	31	43.1	33	45.8	8	11.1
Chaupibarrio	4	26.7	5	33.3	6	40.0

Through the years the observable criteria by which one could
distinguish an Indian from a mestizo have become modified, disappeared, or become common to both groups. The greatest difference
now lies in social participation and the attitudes which the people
hold with respect to the members of the other class. On the surface, differences seem to be greater between rich and poor, educated and uneducated, more cosmopolitan and less cosmopolitan,
than between classes on the basis of specific cultural traits. Social participation itself, while providing the most important difference, is subject to variation, and with constant mobility new
class members are little by little accepted into the mestizo group
    A class system is apparently developing in Muquiyauyo which
will ultimately involve three distinct classes. The population over
which there is presently disagreement by the judges does not yet
constitute a distinct social class. However, this group now forms
approximately one-third of the population, and it may be expected
to grow as more Indians assume positions of importance and increase their wealth. One of the effects of the breakdown of the
caste system has been to make available to the Indians educa-
tional opportunities which had previously been somewhat restricted
to the mestizos. This, coupled with encouragement from certain
mestizos of the town, permitted a number of young Indians in the
early part of the century to achieve engineering, medical, and other
professional training. These young men, upon returning to Muquiyauyo, brought a new prestige factor into the class system; i
was possible for an Indian to achieve the same professional status
as a mestizo, and the prestige which went along with such positions
brought a new criteria of class membership. A person might have
been born into an Indian family, but acquisition of a professional

degree placed him considerably above many of the mestizos in the estimation of the local people.

The new class system will probably develop along the lines of the table below; with respect to these features, change is already

SOME CHARACTERISTICS OF THE EMERGENT CLASSES IN
MUQUIYAUYO*

Aspects	Emergent Upper Class	Emergent Middle Class	Emergent Lower Class
Composition Chapter 5	Composed of two groups; one of old solidly entrenched mestizo families, the other of Indians who have received professional prominence	Families of recent Indian mixture, families of Indian origin who are locally wealthy, and poorer old mestizo families	The bulk of the present Indian population together with a few mestizos who "live low as an Indian"
Agriculture Chapters 7, 8	Landowners, some of whom still do their own work; employ labor	Landowners, renters	Renters and day laborers
Commerce Chapter 9	A few may have local stores, but may have commercial ties outside of town	Some have local stores, carry the bulk of the heavy local store trade.	Some, mainly women, keep small stores in one room of their home
Mining Chapter 6	Employees and some professionals	Some employees, some laborers	Laborers
Woman's clothing Chapter 11	European urban	European urban and *centro*	*Centro*
Language	Spanish only	Spanish, some Quechua	Spanish, much Quechua still among women
Education Chapter 6	Primary and secondary school; some to university and professional schools	Primary and secondary schools, perhaps not finishing secondary	Primary school, some not finishing
Political leadership Chapter 3	District leadership and some communal offices	Community leadership, and some district offices	Only minor posts in district, somewhat more active in community organization
Religion Chapters 4, 14	Active private associations; women attend Sunday Mass; no Protestants	Active private associations; fewer attend Sunday Mass; some Protestants	Mainly active only in public fiestas; some Protestants
Residence	Many of the men live outside the town although their wives and small children may live in Muquiyauyo	Generally live in Muquiyauyo, except for those working at mines	Live in Muquiyauyo except for annual labor at the mines
Community work Chapter 13	Directors or bystanders	Foremen and workers	Workers

*The chapters in which the various aspects are discussed are indicated.

evident. It would be difficult to obtain explicit data from Muquiyau-yinos in terms of three classes today; they tend to think in terms of two extremes, which probably account for between 40 and 60 per

cent of the population. The middle group is generally considered to
be an exception to these two extremes, rather than the basis of an
entirely new formulation of the system. Thus, thinking is often in
terms of three groups, but labeling is in terms of two and exceptions to those two; there is no name or label for the developing
middle group.

An incident occurred at the mines which indicates something of
the importance of the class system. Early in the present century,
the Cerro de Pasco Copper Corporation, an extensive North American-owned mining enterprise, started operations in the central
highlands, and the people of Muquiyauyo began to look upon the
company as a regular place of work. The company began to play
such an important role in the life of the local population that some
areas, such as the Jauja Valley, regularly accounted for a sizable
proportion of the total number of workers employed. But by 1934
between seventy and ninety workers from Muquiyauyo had shifted
their employment from the Cerro de Pasco mines to a more recently established French mining concern, the Compagnie des
Mines de Huarón. This movement marked a major change in the
townspeople's preference; since that time, many more Muquiyauyinos have gone to the Huarón mines than to the Cerro de Pasco
company. In January, 1950, I visited the Huarón mines and heard
the following story.

In 1934, two Muquiyauyinos with professional training were working in Muquiyauyo, one as an accountant and one as a mining engineer. At that time, the Huarón company sent out a call for employees; and first one, then the other, of these two men went north to
take up positions with the company. Very shortly thereafter, many
Muquiyauyino miners working at the Cerro de Pasco company
started to move to the Huarón mines. In a discussion of this with
five Muquiyauyinos at Huarón, including the two men who made the
original move, seven major reasons were given to explain why the
miners had moved from Cerro de Pasco to Huarón and why the latter
place continued to be preferable in their opinion. These were: (1)
some Muquiyauyinos with good reputations went to work for the
Huarón company and other workers followed them; (2) Huarón paid
higher salaries; (3) a good worker with ambition had a chance to
rise in the company hierarchy and to achieve a better position and
salary at Huarón; in the American-owned mines, the Americans
always remained at the top and it was impossible for Peruvians
from the highlands to advance beyond a certain level; (4) the manager or assistant manager of the French mines sponsored a fiesta
each year in which all workers and employees participated; also

during Carnaval, the manager sponsored another large fiesta with certain customs common to the region included, just as they would have been in the workers' own towns (involved in this was the fact that most of the French were Catholics and many of the Americans were not); (5) in the Huarón mines, bonuses were given for years of service and for good work to miners, technicians, and office workers; (6) the working conditions were not difficult; at Morococha, one of the Cerro de Pasco mines, an eight-hour day was enforced; at Huarón, it was not mandatory to work eight hours; pay was in accordance with the amount of work done; workers at Huarón were not under contract, so that they were free to work more or less as they pleased, without being threatened with loss through violation of the contract; (7) vacations at Cerro de Pasco were granted for thirty consecutive days; at Huarón, a worker could take a few days off whenever he desired.

Such were the opinions expressed by the men with whom the problem was discussed. Time did not permit checking the validity of most of the claims either for 1934 or for today. At present, however, salaries are about the same at both companies, and fiestas are sponsored at some of the American mines as well as at the French mines. Of major concern here, however, is that what was probably the principal reason for the original movement was not mentioned by any of the 1950 informants. This was the fact that the first two men who went to work in Huarón were not only of good reputation, but were men who had come from Indian families in Muquiyauyo.

It was probably fortuitous that the Huarón company, in hiring these two men in 1934, picked two men who were of the Indian class. I have no indication that either the French or the Americans were, or are, aware of any significance attached to being a member of the Indian social class as opposed to being a mestizo. Foreigners have tended to regard most highlanders as Indian, unless a superficial judgment indicated that the person was mestizo. But to the Muquiyauyino miners, most of whom were of the Indian class, the fact that Huarón employed two Indians in high positions was of special importance. Mestizos had been given opportunities before, but this was evidently one of the first cases in which men considered by their own townspeople to be Indians had been given a chance to hold a high position in the mines.

The class system today at Muquiyauyo has meaning not only within the town; it goes with the Muquiyauyino wherever he may be. But in Lima, in the mines, or in other towns, the person of the Indian class finds opportunity for advancement somewhat easier than at home. That the system is still changing seems clear, however; the large population which is not clearly defined as either Indian or mestizo must eventually become crystallized.

In looking back over the four hundred years since Pizarro first landed in Peru, it is possible to see the general outline of the evolution of the class structure. First was the distinction between the white conquerors and the conquered Indians. Developing from this was a caste system composed of whites (divided into Spanish or peninsular-born, and creole or American-born), mestizos, and Indians. In many of the mountain rural areas the whites ceased to be a significant factor except politically and as they individually entered the region to join the general mestizo group. By the time of the establishment of independence in 1821, the upper stratum of this organization included a mixture of Spaniards, creoles, and mestizos; while there may have been distinctions within this group, all were unified in that they were superordinate to the Indians.

While in many parts of Peru this system continues in much the same form today, in the Jauja Valley, particularly at the northern end, the caste system began to dissolve under a series of changes. In Muquiyauyo specifically, the events in which Indians and mestizos had previously been separated either died out or were changed to permit joint participation. Customs, such as clothing, language, and occupations, ceased to serve as distinctive features. There began to emerge a group of people who were not consistently recognized as either mestizos or Indians, but fell somewhere between. In the years of the nineteenth century, the mestizos and Indians of Muquiyauyo were thrown together through common needs; both wanted independence from the political and religious domination of Huaripampa; both felt the increasing pressure of a growing population and the relative decrease of available arable land; and both began to go outside of the town to seek employment at the mines and in the cities. Without studies elsewhere, it is impossible to know whether the two castes were brought together in other communities through common interests, but in Muquiyauyo there is little doubt that this community of purpose facilitated the breakdown of the caste barriers. It has permitted, within the space of the last seventy-five years or so, a change from a caste to a class system.

6

INFLUENCES FROM THE OUTSIDE

THROUGHOUT postconquest history, Muquiyauyo has been affected
by the rest of the region, the country as a whole, and, indeed, by
the entire world. The Muquiyauyinos work or visit other parts of
the Jauja Valley and Peru, and some have gone as far as the United
States, Russia, and China. The "outside" has played a great role
in the local changes which have taken place. In reconstructing the
events of the past, it is not possible to track down the great major-
ty of influences which have been brought in from time to time by
men who have gone outside and returned; nor is it possible to dis-
inguish the visits and ideas brought in by strangers. We know that
most of what is called the "content" of the culture of the Muquiyau-
rinos was derived from the outside, but it is not possible, nor is
it my purpose, to trace the history of the arrival and gradual as-
imilation of each element. In this chapter will be discussed some
of the ways in which new things have entered the town and, more
pecifically, some of the sources of influences which have been of
articular importance in recent times.

Perhaps the most important of the many outside influences felt
in Muquiyauyo have been those which stemmed from contact over
many years with the mining centers. The increasing scarcity of
and and the growing population have made outside employment a
ecessity for many of the townspeople. Muquiyauyinos have gone
into various professions and trades outside the town, but only mining constantly draws a large number of residents and has done so
or at least fifty years. We do not know how important mining may
ave been in the early history of the town. It is certain that in the
colonial period the Spanish drew Indians from many parts of Peru
to exploit their mines. From the point of view of recent culture
change, however, it is the recent expansion of the highland mining
companies which has been been of particular importance.

The major mines which have been favored by the Muquiyauyinos are the Cerro de Pasco mines, in various localities, and the
French-owned mines in the area of Huarón. The first of these
started in the beginning of the twentieth century, and the second
about 1916. Before the establishment of these foreign interests,
many of the same mines were being exploited by Peruvians. In 1888
a Muquiyauyino, Manuel Quintana, bought two; one of these was
San Francisco de Morococha, which was subsequently sold to the
Cerro de Pasco company and has been one of their major centers
for many years. The small mine owners continue in Peru and some
Muquiyauyinos work at these smaller enterprises, but their number is insignificant in comparison to the number who are and have
been employed in the larger foreign-owned concerns. At the time
of this study, a lawyer from the town had opened a mine to the east
and had succeeded in interesting a number of his neighbors in the
enterprise.

The popular conceptions of the Peruvian mining conditions that
have come down to us from the colonial period are no longer accurate. Many aspects of mining continue to be dangerous, both
physically and physiologically; many mines lack modern safety de-
vices; and not all enterprises have very enlightened labor policies.
Nevertheless, the mines have been improving over the years and
from the point of view of the Muquiyauyino and many other highlanders, have provided an important source of steady income which
would have been difficult to obtain otherwise. Not only have the
mines offered work to those who had no land, but many who suf-
fered from occasional bad crops have made their way to the mine
to obtain temporary work or earn sufficient cash to live out the
year. Today, many men look upon the mines as a second home.
Thus, it must be recognized that, good or bad, the mines have
played a role of great importance in the lives of many highlanders.

The mining enterprises are complex. Since they require a large
technical personnel, they have constantly trained promising employees in mechanics, electricity, and other specialized fields.
In addition, the North American-owned mines have developed over
the years an industrial organization which has been imitated by
various other mines in Peru. The Muquiyauyinos have benefited
from these things. Some have learned trades which they later use
in other connections; others have been stimulated to seek further
education. Besides various phases of mechanics and electricity,
men working at the mines have often learned much of construction
techniques, and some have carried home miscellaneous medical
techniques that they learned while working in the dispensaries

Muquiyauyinos at the mines early organized associations of people
from the town. These organizations have two functions. They serve
to bring the home town people together in the strange surroundings
of the mining centers; they sponsor football teams, interclub games,
and occasional fiestas. They are social centers in which people
continue the social relationships established in their own towns.
The other function has been to provide positive help to the public
projects being sponsored by the Muquiyauyinos at home. Some
clubs have been formed with this specific end in view; when a project was started in Muquiyauyo, a club would be formed at a mining center to further it. The principal help that has been sent to
the town from these clubs has been money and materials for public
works projects; the groups established at Morococha and Huarón
have been the most important in supplying this kind of aid. One
Morococha group, which no longer exists, provided the wire cables
for the suspension bridge which the Muquiyauyinos built over the
Mantaro River; this group also arranged with the Cerro de Pasco
company for the loan of an engineer for the installation of the electric plant, and sent money to aid in the work. Several clubs have
been established in Morococha; in 1926 there existed the Muquiyauyo Workers' Circle; in the same year a new club was formed,
the Muquiyauyo Union; in 1936 the Muquiyauyo Park Commune was
formed with the express purpose of helping with the expenses involved in the construction of the park on the plaza; also in 1936 a
new general club, the Muquiyauyo Cultural Action, was established.

Tho club in the mining center of Huarón has had a rather more
stable existence than have some of those set up at Morococha. The
Huarón association, the Muquiyauyo Social Center-Huarón, was
founded in 1937, and in the same year the members sent S/. 300
to help the girls' school in Muquiyauyo. The following year they
sent seventeen chairs for the new school. Their most ambitious
project so far has been to collect S/. 2 monthly from each of their
members to establish a fund to aid the Muquiyauyo project to set
up a potable water system. Many of the members regularly contribute more than the quota, and in 1949 the club sent to the town nearly
S/. 8, 000 from this fund.

There is little question that the maintenance of these clubs and
their periodic efforts to aid the town are due to the activities of a
relatively few individuals in each organization. While devotion to
the home town is deeply felt by Muquiyauyinos, as it is by most
highlanders of Peru, its expression is often lost in sentimentality
when not consciously channeled into some constructive effort. The
association of Muquiyauyinos in Lima, the Muquiyauyo Center, de-

cided in 1931 to try to get a certain Muquiyauyino lawyer into the
national congress. It was agreed that a committee should be formed
to do so, but nothing more was done about it. This Lima organization was very helpful, however, when the town was dealing with an
importer to obtain the generators for the power plant; its existence
made it unnecessary to send a man to Lima every time a new problem arose.

It is difficult to estimate the total influence of the mining centers
on the changes which have occurred in Muquiyauyo during the past
half century or so; we do not know enough about the situation in
1880, nor exactly how the influences were exerted. There have
been at least three important effects of the mines. First, they were
a source of funds that enabled the Muquiyauyinos to retain family
and communal unity during a period of population expansion when
many sons of the town would otherwise have had to seek work on
the Peruvian coast; they permitted the Muquiyauyinos to obtain work
in centers not far from their homes and permitted the social organization to retain some of the same integrity which had been developing early in the century. Second, they provided many Muquiyauyinos
with knowledge of new techniques; these techniques were not merely
there to be seen and adopted if so desired, but many townspeople
actually underwent training and learned how to do new things. In
addition to teaching specific techniques, the mining population at
the American mines had constant contact with certain aspects of
contemporary western culture in its nonurban phases. For example, the people at the mines could not only see that there was electric light, but they could see daily the powerhouse which produced
the electricity. In the cities, the powerhouse often was never seen,
and only its product, the light, was visible. Consequently the Muquiyauyino in Lima would appreciate having electric light, but the
Muquiyauyino in the mines would appreciate more easily the problems involved in getting electric light. It was, in fact, men returning from the mines who brought the idea of setting up the power
plant in the town.

Third, the mines also aided in the destruction of some of the
older social and religious customs. There is little doubt that life
at the mines tended to reduce religious activities. Most religious
observances had been carried out by families, barrios, and other
groups in the town, and there were no groups to sponsor such activities at the mines. The Muquiyauyinos, however, like other highlanders, always went back to their home town for the main fiestas.

There were various cases of men who married women from other
towns at the mines; in some cases they took these women home with

them, and in others they went to live in the towns of the wives. The marriage to outsiders has been particularly evident among persons who are classed socially as Indian.

Among the men who learned trades at the mines, there has been a reluctance to return to agricultural work. .Relatively few of these specialists have returned to Muquiyauyo, since there is little for them to do in the town. Nevertheless, they return each year for the fiestas and thus constantly make their neighbors aware of the other kinds of work available outside the town. The scarcity of land regularly forces many members of the younger generation to seek. employment elsewhere, and these contacts with townsmen working outside provide channels through which work can be found. Since agriculture is carried on by both men and women in the town, this does not reduce the knowledge of agricultural techniques or fundamentally break the train of tradition in the basic economy, but it does serve to drain the town of many of the younger people.

Questionnaires were given to thirty-five of the men working in one of the mines at Huarón, and twenty-five answered them. Of this group all but one, who was working during his vacations from school, had been employed at the mines for periods varying from one to over fourteen years; the majority had been working between three and eight years. Twenty-one of the twenty-five had worked at other mines previously and all but the student were over twenty-four years of age. The age norm was twenty-six to thirty but two were over fifty.

Of the group, seventeen owned land in Muquiyauyo and three others expected to inherit some; hence the miners were by no means people entirely dispossessed of land. Four-fifths of the group were *obreros,* or workers, earning between $. 60 and $1. 00 (U. S. currency) a day; the other five were "employees" and earned between $53. 00 and $125. 00 a month. The sample group had an excessive proportion of employees, since it was easier to locate them than the workers.

Half of the men were married to women from Muquiyauyo and one-quarter to women from other towns; one-quarter were unmarried; this shows a rather high proportion of men making alliances with women from other places. Twenty of the men had relatives who also worked at the Huarón mines. All but four had houses in Muquiyauyo. In education, the amount of schooling reported among this group was quite high; all had gone to primary school, half had gone to secondary school, and one-quarter had received further education in schools or through correspondence courses. In general, answers to the questionnaire indicate that there is

considerable following of relatives to the mines, that most of the
men have families, that a significantly high percentage of them
have married outside the town, and that many work at the mines
even though they have lands and homes in Muquiyauyo.

The mines have not been the only outside influence at work. By
no means all the Muquiyauyinos who left town in search of work
went into mining. It was my impression that in recent years more
people have tended to go to the national capital on the coast than to
centers in the highlands. While people returning recently from
Lima have brought various urban coastal customs, this influence
has been felt ever since the colonial days among the mestizos of
the town. The culture of the mestizos of the last century was more
closely related to that of the people of the national capital than to
that of the Indians of the highland region. The influence of these
customs on the Indians of the town and the region in general may
be said to have come more from the local mestizos than directly
from the capital.

Some new things have been brought in directly from the capital
and other centers, however, and have been taken up by both Indians and mestizos. Among the most interesting of these are certain radical ideologies. In the 1920's, the influential Peruvian
Marxist philosopher José Carlos Mariátegui was in Lima and among
his younger followers were some Muquiyauyinos. A few of these
young men returned to Muquiyauyo and put up a red flag over the
district government building; it was promptly pulled down by the
elders, and the boys were given to understand that such behavior
was unacceptable. One of the boys started a sports club which he
called the "Lénin Athletic Club"; but the *gobernador* of the district
told him that this would not do, and so he changed the name to "Club
Román Amanzo" after the local culture hero. The effect of these
Muquiyauyo Communists was felt not so much in the town, however, as elsewhere in Peru through the reputation created for the
town. Among the students who studied under Mariátegui was the
son of a mestizo; this boy never brought his teaching back to Muquiyauyo because in the early 1930's at a public demonstration in
Lima staged by Sanchez Cerro, the president of the country, he
ran from the crowd and shouted, "Down with tyranny!" He was
promptly jailed and then deported to Mexico. He apparently worked
a while in various student Communist organizations in the Caribbean
region and then started on a trip to Russia. After visiting Russia
he made his way back across Siberia and through Japan. Today he

is a lawyer in Lima and is reported to have lost all interest in communism.

The name of Muquiyauyo was first brought to the attention of political circles in Lima before the formation of the community organization in 1930. Hildebrando Castro Pozo, a sociologist and Socialist, went to Jauja to convalesce from a case of tuberculosis in the early 1920's. While there he heard of the activities in Muquiyauyo with respect to the communal group organization and the feverish work which had produced the electric light plant. This venture was well known in Jauja because the provincial capital was receiving power from the plant. Castro Pozo visited the town and talked with some of the leading citizens. On the basis of this visit, he included a long section on Muquiyauyo in his book, *Nuestra Comunidad Indígena,* on the excellence of the communal organization in the town and its qualifications as a model to other communities. In 1931 he again visited Muquiyauyo and discovered to his delight the new twist the organization had taken. The news was spread among Socialist circles in Lima, and Sanchez Cerro, Peru's president, was quoted as having said that Muquiyauyo was the focus of communism.

At this time another left-wing movement, the APRA, or Aprista Party, was gaining support throughout Peru. During most of the 1930's and early 1940's, Aprista activities were carried out underground. In some parts of the Mantaro Valley, it took an early hold, and apparently its first members from Muquiyauyo enrolled during this period. Some of these men took part in a few of the Aprista uprisings, but it was not until 1945 when the party began operating openly that Muquiyauyo felt any pressure from its local members. There were apparently at this time eleven men in the town who professed open interest in Aprismo, and six or eight of these were enrolled in the party. Adequate data on the Apristas is not readily available, since the government had declared the party outlawed and at the time of this study very few wished to discuss any former connections they may have had with the organization. Informants held that the Muquiyauyinos were in general not much attracted by the party; they gave the names of certain other towns in the valley as places where it had been much more active.

The relative lack of success of Aprismo and communism in Muquiyauyo can probably be laid to the same reasons. Aprismo was evidently more successful and its agitators and propagandists were much more active in the Mantaro region than were the Communists.

However, compared to the poverty found always over much of Peru, the Muquiyauyinos were pretty well off. The townspeople had a communal government with a degree of local autonomy almost unknown elsewhere in the country. They had an elective system in this government, and their electric plant provided the town with a large and steady source of income. They were not rabidly interested in the national government, and since neither radical group offered to them much that they needed, they did not develop much interest. The fact that Muquiyauyo had developed a communal government has probably led some writers to believe that the government was Communistic. Findings in this study did not support this conclusion. Both communism and Aprismo were presented as revolutionary doctrines and revolution was something to which Muquiyauyinos seldom resorted. Their own communal changes had come about slowly and through a process of evolution.

While innovations brought into Muquiyauyo by returning townsmen are probably the most important kinds of outside influences, there have been other channels of some importance as well. One of these is the laws, decrees, and other orders sent down by the national government. The governmental control in Peru is so centralized that permission often must be asked of the provincial, departmental, or national government to act in matters which are manifestly local in relevance. For example, before building the new cemetery wall in 1948 and 1949, it was necessary to have the permission of the Section of Indian Affairs in Lima. In some cases local projects have wider importance as well, as in the case of the construction of the bridge across the Mantaro; this serves traffic passing from Huancayo to Lima.

Besides such approvals, the records of the district in Muquiyauyo are full of orders and requests sent down from the various levels of the national government. These vary from rendering the annual district accounts for provincial approval to the institution of the district government by decree. There are frequent cases of sudden removal by the provincial or departmental officers of an existing alcalde or *gobernador* and replacement of him with someone who had gained favor. The most flagrant of these cases occurred a few years ago. The prefect of the department established a new council, as was his responsibility under the existing laws. In the next month the provincial subprefect arrived in town with a Muquiyauyino who had obtained professional education and no longer lived in the town. The subprefect decreed a change in the formation of the district council and placed the professional in the post of alcalde. This case

was important because the individual involved was an Indian, and
only twice in the entire previous history of the council had Indians
been mayors. As it turned out, the new mayor soon lost interest
in his responsibility, and the job fell to a more responsible council
member.

The provincial subprefect has also sent orders to Muquiyauyo
from time to time to assemble people for work on public projects
being sponsored in Jauja. Even though the pattern of communal
labor is old in the valley and still somewhat common in the provincial capital these projects have not always been to the liking
of the Muquiyauyinos since so much time is required for the community work in Muquiyauyo.

Some of the governmental interventions in town life have been
with the overt intention of helping, through improvement of the
farming or livestock conditions, and these efforts have usually been
accepted with gratitude. The earliest of these in the existing records is a recommendation in 1920 by the Ministry of Development
(Ministero de Fomento) that fruit trees be planted. In 1927 bul-
letins from the Commission for the Improvement of Wheat Cultivation were distributed, and in 1930 the Agronomy Commission of
Junín and Huancavelica recommended the use of improved wheat
seed. In 1938 the Department of Livestock and Agriculture offered
to trade seven good Merino sheep for seven local sheep of poor
quality. As can be seen by the efforts listed above, most of these
acts of the government took the form of recommendations and, as
such, had little effect; they were duly recorded and forgotten.

I encountered only one attempt on the part of the national government to interfere with the development of the communal organization in Muquiyauyo. This was in March, 1927, when the departmental prefect placed a note before the national government recom-
mending the dissolution of the communal group. What reasons may
have been behind this action are not clear, but it seems likely that
one of them was financial. The various levels in the national hierarchy could, though frequently not altogether legally, call for funds
from the administrative units directly subordinate to them. The
formation of the town treasury under the communal group had removed certain funds from the Muquiyauyo district government,
placing them under the care of the communal organization. The
provincial and departmental governments had no control over community funds, although the district was under their control at all
times. Consequently, if the community government were abolished,
these funds would automatically fall into the hands of the district
government and would be at the disposal of the higher administra-

tive levels. When the communal group in Muquiyauyo heard of the prefect's action, they went immediately to the subprefect in Jauja to see what could be done to stop it. Evidently the recommendation of the prefect was never approved because nothing more is mentioned in the records concerning it.

A hierarchical governmental system such as exists in Peru works both ways; while the higher levels of administration command the lower, the lower in turn have the right to request aid from the upper. The projects carried on by the Muquiyauyinos have frequently been in need of funds. Requests to the national government for money to finance these projects have met with varying success. A most notable failure was the long-standing potable water project. It is a firm belief locally that the chemicals dumped into the river by the smelter at La Oroya are a real danger to the health of the people who drink the water and to the crops that are irrigated. Furthermore, the canal water becomes very muddy during the rainy season. For the last twenty-five years, various members of the district and community organizations have tried to achieve the installation of a potable water system. The expense of such a project would be large, since the main sources of potable water are springs on the other side of the mountain behind the town and their use would require constructing a canal of some seven kilometers. In 1929 the provincial deputy to congress reported that he had obtained S/. 4, 000 for this project, but, as with so many appropriations, it seems to have disappeared before it reached Muquiyauyo Discussion of the water problem continued through the next two decades and various other means were suggested; wells, a pipe across the river to the springs in the town of Ataura, and the utilization of the small local springs in the mountain behind the town were all presented as alternative plans, but none materialized. Individuals and whole committees of alcaldes and prominent local men from Muquiyauyo, Huaripampa, and Muqui called on various officials in the national capital but there have been no tangible results.

While orders and decrees from the higher national governmental authorities may at times cause the Muquiyauyinos some concern it is seldom that they cause startling changes in the life of the townspeople. Such acts as the termination of the elective system in the district have, of course, had important repercussions; but in general the national government is a long way off and the local people do not pay it a great deal of attention except during times of local or national crisis.

Another source of outside influence is the contact which the Muquiyauyinos have with other highlanders in the surrounding towns. Very few significant changes result from this contact, since the culture of the neighboring villages is similar to that found in Muquiyauyo. Interpersonal relationships through kinship, friendship, and business with people of other towns in the valley are very common. In addition, there are many ways in which the people of one town as a whole interact with those of another town. There has been cooperative participation by the people of Muquiyauyo and certain other centers in community work projects and in fiestas. Cooperative work is usually limited to projects carried on with the two communities immediately to the north and south, Huaripampa and Muqui. Physical proximity and common problems have made cooperative work between the neighbors valuable. With Muqui, usually under the direction of the district council, the periodic work projects of canal cleaning and road repair are accomplished. Huaripampa is a separate district, so there is no single authority to recommend and direct project work involving the two towns. The principal cooperative work carried on by Muquiyauyo and Huaripampa is the annual repair of the dikes along the river. During the months of rainy season the Mantaro River rises and threatens the lands adjacent to it. For at least the past fifty years Huaripampa officials have suggested to Muquiyauyinos that they undertake together the repair of broken dikes and the construction of new ones where necessary. Huaripampa is the initiator of these projects because it is nearer the river's entrance into the valley and has a longer river shore than does Muquiyauyo; it will incur greater loss if the river is not controlled. Muquiyauyinos would suffer too, however, if there were no dikes to hold the flood waters back, so they have never refused to aid in their repair. The dikes themselves consist of wooden pilings in double lines with a fill of rocks between them. It was once suggested that the towns obtain some abandoned railway ties to build a more permanent barrier, but the materials were never acquired.

Visiting from one town to another is most frequently done on the occasion of a fiesta, fair, or market. The biggest crowds are drawn for the annual fairs and for the major fiestas. There is a group of people who make it their business to attend fairs every week. Grand fairs, such as the opening fair in Muquiyauyo in 1931, the four-hundredth anniversary of the founding of the town of Concepción, and the annual livestock fair held at Chupaca, involve the sending of official invitations by the district concerned to the other towns.

Invitations are also sent out for particularly large public fiestas. While it would not be accurate to say that these ventures are purely commercial, they clearly have commercial importance. Both fairs and fiestas bring money to the sponsoring town, and the larger the celebration, the greater will be the income of both the local vendors and the local district.

Relationships among neighboring towns are not always as cordial and cooperative as they are at the fairs, fiestas, and work projects. The long history of rancor between Muquiyauyo and Huaripampa has already been described. Another common type of conflict which occurs is the boundary dispute. Such disputes are usually long and costly to both sides. The Jauja Valley is not a hacienda region so the encroachment of large private holdings on community lands, an occurrence common elsewhere in the highlands, has not been a particular problem to Muquiyauyo. Most of the haciendas are small, and the owners are themselves local people. Muquiyauyo has had three or four disputes with other communities for every one it has had with private landowners.

It is rare that a whole group of towns in the valley will get together to cooperate on some venture. The town of Sincos twice initiated congresses to consider problems which were of concern to a large group of towns. One of these was held in 1926, when all the mayors of the districts of the provinces of Jauja and Huancayo were invited to discuss the disposition of the *cofradía* lands. Muquiyauyo officials were undecided as to the stand they should take with respect to these lands and finally decided not to attend the congress. In late 1942 and early 1943 Sincos, together with the town of Orcotuna, called for a congress of alcaldes and communal presidents of the towns on the southwest bank of the river to meet with the deputy from the Department of Junín in an effort to promote the construction of a highway to Huancayo, on their side of the river. The old road, and the only one which is still passable for motor traffic in all weather, runs along the other bank. In the late 1930's the government began a highway on the southwest side which, had it been completed, would have drawn all the traffic from Lima away from Jauja and the towns on the northeast side; it would have increased the commercial importance of Muquiyauyo and its neighbors. The congress in Sincos was held, but the lobbying powers of the opposing Jauja group in Lima and the lack of government funds to continue the road put at least a temporary end to the project.

In spite of the fact that people visit back and forth between the towns and many have relatives living in neighboring centers, and even though there are periodic cooperative efforts between the towns, each highland town dweller tends to place great value on his own town. The concept of *mi pueblo* is important to the Muquiyauyino. The fact that things may be somewhat different in another town, that customs may vary slightly, does not mean that they should be imitated. Occasionally something happens in one town, however, which seems to be of value and is imitated elsewhere. The political organization of the communal government which crystallized in Muquiyauyo was soon imitated by other towns in the northern end of the Jauja Valley. The fact that other towns had weekly fairs spurred Muquiyauyo to start its own Saturday fair. In many such matters, however, Muquiyauyo has been the leader in the valley, rather than a follower; Huaripampa, for example, imitated Muquiyauyo's new district government building, and another town decided to set up a light plant in imitation of Muquiyauyo. Huaripampa also imitated Muquiyauyo in building another bridge across the Mantaro River.

The real influence of the other valley towns on Muquiyauyo has not been one of innovation but one of restraint. These towns share with Muquiyauyo a general culture which is peculiar to the valley. The customs of other towns perpetually provide everyone in the valley with a reminder of what is generally the correct way to behave. No town can be too divergent without becoming an obvious deviant from the general way of life recognized in the valley. A reluctance to enlarge the power-plant facilities in the early 1930's when the opportunity presented itself is in part a reflection of this conservative influence. The people in Muquiyauyo evidently did not want a big change that would make them extremely different. To the degree that the changes in Muquiyauyo have given other towns the incentive to make similar changes, such as has been the case in the creation of the communal organization, Muquiyauyo continues to make gradual alterations. But where they have not been imitated, the indication is that the general culture of the valley is not following the lead given by Muquiyauyo, and the Muquiyauyinos themselves hesitate to allow themselves to become too different from everyone else.

One way in which the Muquiyauyinos have been introduced to the ways of the outside has been through the local schools. The recent history of the development and effects of formal education in the town are of considerable importance in both the introduction of new traits and the change in the class system. Through all the years for which we have session books the Muquiyauyinos have shown interest in their schools. By the end of the last century, there was still a marked tendency for the schools to be attended by mestizos rather than by Indians. It was almost unknown at that time for Indians to seek education beyond that offered in Muqui-yauyo. During the first decade of the present century, the members of the Sociedad Pro-Indígena, all Indians themselves, led in having the school expanded from three grades to five and collected money for the purchase and installation of a school bell. In the records of the 1890's and early 1900's, there is frequent mention of such matters as giving the teachers adequate salaries, fixing the buildings in use, and so on.

In the first two decades of the twentieth century, there were evidently two teachers in the school who played an important role in promoting the education of the people of the Indian class. One of them constantly preached against the mestizo-Indian distinction and tried to get all children of both classes to come to school. He would tease both parents and children into getting the children to come regularly. His efforts had considerable success in encouraging many of the youths of the town to seek further education. The importance of education to an individual in the Indian class is revealed by the following story told by a man who was a student in that period:

> A number of the mestizos in Muquiyauyo wanted to help the Indians; but one, Don P., was not like that. One day I met Don P. on the street when I was about sixteen years old; he started to insult me; he said that I was not as good as his own sons who were going to medical school and who had better clothes; he said that I would always be like the other Indians, and serve him and the other mestizos. This made me very dissatisfied. Don P. was typical of many of the mestizos; he exploited people by lending them money at an interest of sometimes 20 per cent per month, and took the houses of the Indians when they could not pay. So I had heard of correspondence courses, and started taking courses with a correspondence school in Los Angeles. I was also teaching in the school in Muquiyauyo then, helping the director. After a few years, I decided to go to the United States. I earned some money by selling eucalyptus trees, and finally went. When I came back, I went up to Don P. and patted him on the back and called him "silly little girl."

During the 1920's, the correspondence course became an important source of education for both Indians and mestizos. It permitted many people who could not afford to leave Muquiyauyo to take courses in subjects which could be of special use to them. According to one informant there were at least twenty Muquiyauyinos between 1920 and 1925 who took correspondence courses, and a number of people were taking them in 1949-50, at the time of this study. In general, the use of the correspondence course has been among persons from the Indian class who, if they had the money, would be going to high school. Older mestizos who felt the need of more education in some particular line but could not afford it have also used these courses. The part played by the correspondence courses in the development of Muquiyauyo is difficult to measure; many people who took courses never made use of them; others took them as supplementary aids in learning subjects with which they were becoming familiar anyway through their work in the mines or in Lima.

In days when the school was completely under the control of the district, it was the custom to employ local mestizo teachers. Just when the school became the object of interest of the national Ministry of Education I do not know, but for some years now many of the teachers have been people who have taken their secondary training in the national rural normal schools. In this way, people have been sent to teach in Muquiyauyo who are natives of other towns. The teaching staff at the time of the study was composed of both Muquiyauyinos and outsiders. I detected no prejudice against teachers of Indian background, although some of the teachers, especially those who came from other towns, were said to be Indians.

The school today emphasizes practical work in carpentry, agriculture, and bee-keeping, as well as in the more usual subjects of reading, writing, arithmetic, biology, geography, and history. The textbooks are chosen by the Ministry of Education. The interest of the townspeople in the school is still lively; aside from having built all the local schools at local expense, usually through communal work projects, they do not hesitate to interfere in the running of the school when they feel that it is necessary.

An interesting sidelight on the formation of the behavior of the Muquiyauyino is the manner in which stylized histrionic gestures are taught to the children in public speaking. Oratory is still an important aspect of the curriculum as it was some years ago in schools in the United States. The young Muquiyauyino is taught a series of wooden actions and other ways to accent his speaking, making all the oratory sound identical, whether it concerns the death of a national patriot or the antics of a drunkard. These gestures are used by the adults in speeches given on public occasions. They seem to be reserved for such occasions, however, for rarely are they employed in the course of community or *cuartel* meetings. The search for education beyond the primary school level forces the Muquiyauyinos to leave the town. Consequently, higher education not only involves the formal subjects taught but familiarizes the person with other areas of his country. Some years ago the Muquiyauyinos built the structure now occupied by the boys' school and gave it to the national government to be used as a rural normal school; the government used it for a few years, but then changed its policy in rural education and reduced the number of active schools. The Muquiyauyo school was one of those which were cut from the budget. The building reverted to the townspeople and was taken over as the boys' school. There are many in the town, however, who want the government to reactivate the school and are striving toward that end. They feel that it would give the town further prestige in the valley.

Perhaps one of the more critical aspects of the nature of the secondary education is that it drains the town of its most able young men. A person who goes away to high school or professional school frequently can find no opportunity to employ his new abilities in Muquiyauyo. As a result those who want to gain a higher education are taken from the town while still in their teens and many of them never return to take up permanent residence. They form, instead, the growing body of Muquiyauyinos who revisit the town during fiestas or work sessions and take a directing interest in the conduct of the town's affairs but do not live there and do not provide the local leadership that at times is very much needed. In general, the Muquiyauyino with higher education must either return to the life of a farmer or must live elsewhere.

Of the various influences from the outside perhaps the most constructive in introducing new techniques and stimulating the Muquiyauyinos to achieve new goals have been the mines and the schools. The influences from these sources have been felt over a long period of time and, while by no means always beneficial, have played an important role in many of the changes that have made Muquiyauyo appear progressive. The least helpful influences have been the national government and the surrounding towns. The former, so far as I could discover, never really provided any serious stimulus to the town, and the latter more often acted as a restraining influence. The national capital and the highland centers also were the sources of the radical ideologies that for a time branded Muquiyauyo as a center of leftist development.

In terms of processes of culture change, the outside has both

provided solutions to problems faced by the townspeople and presented them with new ones. The population pressure found its greatest release in the migration of labor to the mines and the national
capital. The desire for education sent more out to seek further
training and professional degrees. These people, returning with
their new experiences, in turn bring new problems to their town.
Many of them can find no place for themselves in the local scene
but nevertheless bring new needs and desires to the Muquiyauyinos
who remain at home. The light plant was a product of the contact
of Muquiyauyinos with power facilities at the mines. Students returning from Lima bring new clothing styles and modes of behavior
which are fashionable among the young people with whom they associate there. They provide the residents with annual glimpses
of the developments down on the coast and elsewhere, but there
is no room in the community for the expatriots or for many of their
new manners. Those who remain at home benefit from the ideas
brought back by their friends and can take their time about de-
ciding which of these ideas will find a place in the local scene.

PART TWO

CONTEMPORARY LIFE IN MUQUIYAUYO

7

THE FARMER AND HIS LAND

FARMING is the basic occupation of the Muquiyauyino, and the land and its acquisition are an important part of his life. Land is ordinarily obtained by the Muquiyauyino through inheritance, purchase, or sometimes in lieu of the payment of a debt. Inheritance is the most common mode of acquisition, although purchase is becoming increasingly common as the plots which are divided in inheritance become so small that they cannot sustain a man and his family. Land purchase usually requires the formal change of title arranged through a notary or lawyer in Jauja. There is no such thing as an abstract for property, and disputes over land ownership entered Peru with the concept of private landed property brought in by the Spaniards. Now, after four centuries of legal practice, the Muquiyauyino is highly conscious of the tricks which can be played on the unwary by unprincipled lawyers. Property acquired prior to marriage remains in the hands of the individual, while that purchased after marriage belongs to the couple jointly. It is a fairly common practice now for a man or a couple to make out a will and have it notarized in Jauja. While the heirs to a piece of property do not legally come into possession before the death of the owner, it is frequently the practice for the children of widowed or aged parents to have usufruct of the land which will ultimately be received in inheritance. Thus it is not uncommon to hear a young man speak of "his land, " when in fact it still belongs to one or both of his parents.

The most important aspect of the inheritance system is that the land must be divided equally among all the children or otherwise legal heirs. This may be done by means of a will, or simply through agreement of the heirs after the death of the owner. Sometimes a man will divide his lands before his death and continue to live on a small section reserved for himself.

For the person who does not own enough land, there are certain kinds of usufruct which permit him to work land in and around the town; among these are rental, mortgage, sharecropping, and *remate*. In land rental, the renter simply pays the owner of the land a sum agreed upon beforehand and has the right to take one crop off the land. The renter supplies all the materials and labor and gets the entire crop. Mortgaging *(hipoteca)* is resorted to if the landowner himself needs cash; he turns over the land in question for a given sum, and at the end of an allotted period of time the land and money are returned to the original owners. In this way, a man pays interest on the loan by permitting the land to be used during the time that he has the money. If the loan cannot be repaid, then the person who made the loan simply takes title to the land. While land rental offers an advantage to the landowner in that he keeps the rent paid, mortgage offers advantages to the mortgagee since he has the use of the land and, in the end, will also have his cash.

Sharecropping *(partidario)* is usually resorted to by persons who are too poor to rent. The owner provides the land and half the seed, while the *partidario* provides the labor. The produce is split equally between the two. It is quite common for the owner to help the sharecropper with the preparation of the ground and the planting. Sharecropping is frequently used by men who have landholdings in other jurisdictions. Local people will sharecrop on the land and the owner will help during the early work.

The land usufruct known as *remate* (literally "auction" or "highest bid") is used only in the situation where the individual works municipal, church, or communal lands. Formerly it was used to work the *cofradía* lands of the church, as described above. Today the community or district, whichever happens to own the land, rents it out to the highest bidder. Payment is usually made in advance or at stated intervals. *Remate* is a traditional method of renting publicly owned properties for a year at a time in order to guarantee the community an income without having to provide the labor and materials for cultivation.

I was told before going to Muquiyauyo that it would be very difficult to discover the amount of land owned by individuals as they were very secretive for fear the information would be used ultimately as a basis for taxing the land. With this in mind, I attempted to ascertain from certain informants, who seemed willing to divulge the information, the amount of land which they had, how it was used, and so on. It developed that there was no evident reluctance among this group about giving out these facts, and a questionnaire was then distributed to a number of other people. The questionnaire failed, but only in part because of reluctance to answer. The principal reason for its lack of success was that there seemed to be a wide divergence in the comprehension of land measurements. In Muquiyauyo when one asks the size of a piece of land, the answer may be in terms of square meters, *cuadras, yugadas,* or hectares. While the meter and the hectare (ten thousand square meters) are standard units of measurement, the *cuadra* and *yugada* may vary tremendously. Also, after many discussions on the basis of the data provided on the questionnaires, I am convinced that some people were using the term *yugada* and hectare interchangeably. Theoretically, a *yugada* of land is the amount of land which a team of oxen can plow in one day (elsewhere it had other names: *fanegado, tongo,* and so forth). This, of course, is an inexact amount but is usually considered to be about one-third of a hectare, or 3,333 square meters. Since this is an awkward total, it was decided in a communal meeting some years ago that the *yugada* should be standardized in Muquiyauyo as 4,000 square meters. This decision seemed to have little effect, however, for many people tended to think of the *yugada* in terms of 3,000 square meters.

Unless a piece of land has been measured and the owner remembers how much it was, the relation of the given size in *yugadas* to any standard measure such as the hectare or square meter will vary. The *cuadra* is usually thought of as about a quarter of a *yugada,* but the variation in the use of this term is, if anything, greater than that in the *yugada.* The term *cuadra* is also frequently used simply to refer to a "plot of land which is not very big." Thus a piece of land might vary in size from less than a quarter of a *yugada* to two or three *yugadas,* and still be referred to as a *cuadra.*

Because of the variety of terms used in referring to land areas and the wide variety of concepts lying behind these terms, the results of the questionnaire were at times ludicrous. One very poor man reported that he had sixty *yugadas* (about twenty hectares), a reasonable amount for a fairly wealthy person. A woman said that she had ten *yugadas* but upon close questioning was found to have closer to one-fourth of a *yugada.*

It was not possible in the time available to make a reliable survey of the landholdings of the townspeople. A number of documents, however, provide some idea of landholdings. The 1904 document which divided the lands of the Indian community among its members listed the amount of land received by each person.[1] At that time the average amount distributed was 1,652 square meters of irrigated land and 2,910 square meters of unirrigated land, or a total of slightly under half a hectare each. In a list made up in 1943 of the irrigated properties held by 363 *cuartel* members for the purposes of calculating the amount which should be paid for the water,[2] the average landholding of this class was 4,770 square meters. I know of no specific ratio that would hold for the amount of unirrigated land which one might have with respect to the irrigated land. My impression, on the basis of discussions, is that most people have between one and a half and two times as much unirrigated land as irrigated property. However, some have none, and some have all their lands in unirrigated sections.

While these data are neither wholly reliable nor representative of the entire town, they clearly support the complaints concerning the insufficiency of land which one hears on all sides in Muquiyauyo. Approximately an acre and a quarter of irrigated land, the 4,770 square meters held per family head in 1943, and perhaps three acres of unirrigated land, is not a very generous amount of land for a family.

The value of land in Muquiyauyo is reckoned primarily by whether it is irrigated or not. In unirrigated areas the land on the valley floor is more highly valued than that in the mountains since the latter is in many places very broken or composed of poor soil. Much of the mountain land is not even very good for pasturage. In addition to this, the mountain land is some distance from the town.

The inheritance pattern of dividing the land among the heirs has made each generation increasingly aware of the scarcity. A man may have acquired sufficient land to support himself and his family, but at his death land enough for one family must be split up to take care of two, three, four, or more families. This successive sub-dividing of land through inheritance, called *minifundio*, is a major problem wherever this inheritance pattern exists. Various solutions have been devised, but none of them permanently solves the problem. A common solution in Muquiyauyo is for one heir to sell his portion to another heir and then go into a trade or mining. Another is to retain the land, work it, and make up the difference in annual work elsewhere or as an agricultural laborer in the town. Still another solution is to retain the land and to obtain more through rental or sharecropping. In general, if an heir decides to sell his land, the other heirs are usually given the first opportunity to purchase it; the land is kept in the family if possible.

The accumulation of lands in the hands of a few has not reached excessive proportions in Muquiyauyo. Three factors have tended to discourage this. First, entrepreneurs from the outside are no encouraged to purchase lands within the community. Indian community lands have traditionally been closed to outsiders, and this tradition still has a strong hold even though the lands no longer belong to the Indian community. Second, there is a strong feeling among the townspeople that the concentration of local land in the hands of one man would mean that there would not be enough for other people. This has tended to make people who wish to become wealthy in land look outside the town for many of their purchases. And finally, the fact that a small landholder can get periodic work at the mines means that it is not always necessary for him to sell his land even though it is not sufficient to live on.

It was my impression that the people who have built up large landholdings in recent years have been principally Indians. In general, town mestizos tend to turn to other forms of activity. In a sample of 160 Indian families, 17, or 10.6 per cent, did not engage in agriculture, while 13 out of 55 mestizo families, or 23.6 per cent, did not do agricultural work. Only one of the Indian families said that it profited neither directly nor indirectly from agriculture, while four mestizo families fell into this category. However, among those who were completely dependent upon agricultural work, the proportion among the two groups was practically the same: 64, or 40 per cent, of the Indian families, and 23, or 42 per cent, of the mestizo families.

Of the criticisms heard from townspeople concerning excessive land accumulation, all were leveled against families that were listed as Indian in 1904. The only criticisms leveled against mestizo families over land concerned disputes which dated back to the colonial era and were not between families but were between a family and the community.

The fact that only about 40 per cent of the families in the sample reported being entirely dependent upon farming for a living and, further, that the average landholding is so small makes it clear that it is impossible for the community as such to subsist on agriculture. This fact, of course, was first felt years ago and we have already traced many of its consequences. There is no doubt that unless some marked changes in production are made more and more Muquiyauyinos will have to leave the town in the future, and the remaining population will have to rely even more than they do today on other sources of income.

8

CULTIVATION AND LIVESTOCK

UNLIKE many other groups in the Jauja Valley, the Muquiyauyinos have no specific craft aside from farming. Only about 4 per cent of the families in town do not have at least a few *chacras*, or small fields, under cultivation of some kind. For those who live in the town, agriculture, with seasonal rests, constitutes the principal daily work. In order to understand the Muquiyauyino it is necessary to know something of this work and the techniques and implements that are used.

For breaking the fields and for some cultivation the standard implement is the old Spanish wooden plow with a metal point. It is virtually the same plow which is still found in Central America and Mexico and is not essentially different from that introduced to the New World by the Spanish. It consists of a round log base the *arado*, two to three feet long, one end of which is narrow with a metal point, or *reja;* in the other end is set a wooden stick handle *mansera*. Rising forward from the center of the base is the *timón* the shaft which is attached to the yoke of the oxen. This is supported in the base by a vertical board, the *tirira*, which passes through the *timón* and is set firmly in the base. The angle which the *timón* makes with the plow base is set by means of wedges *cuñas*, which are placed against the *tirira* in the *timón*. Hanging from the center of the yoke is a rawhide circle, the *coyunda;* the forward end of the *timón* is placed through this circle and prevented from slipping back by a nail set perpendicular to the *timón*. This nail may be set further forward or back in the *timón*, giving the plowman another means of adjusting the angle at which the plow cuts into the earth. The *coyunda* is attached to the yoke by means of rawhide ropes. The yokes are fairly uniform in Muquiyauyo and are undecorated. The yoke is padded against the neck of the ox by means of a *colchon*, a padding of sheepskin or

118

old clothing. Leather thongs are used to fasten the oxen to the yoke.

Used everywhere with the plow is a long slender stick called the *garrocha*. On one end is the *pua,* a metal point and a circle with loose pieces of metal attached to it. The oxen learn that the noise of this may be followed with a prod of the point if they do not hurry along. The other end of the *garrocha* has a small, flat, triangular blade which is used for breaking up clods of earth. It is called the *lampa* or *lampita*.

When being taken to or from the field, the plow is turned around, the heavy base is hung over the yoke between the oxen, and the shaft drags on the ground in the rear. Sometimes a man has two or three plows in his house. In general, however, one plow per man is the limit and the poorer people who have none do all their work with a pickax or a cultivator. A few men hire themselves out with their plows and oxen to work in another's fields. Both plows and yokes are usually built by the owner. A plow lasts up to ten years and a yoke even longer.

With the single possible exception of the *azadón,* cultivator or hoe, all agricultural implements in Muquiyauyo are of European origin. The *barreta,* or utility stick, is a five-foot iron bar with one end flattened and one pointed. It is used for breaking rocks, uprooting stumps, digging holes, and so forth. The sickle is used to harvest grains and alfalfa. The *azadón* is composed of two parts, the wooden handle, *lacwash,* and the blade, *lampa*. The hoe, as such, has European predecessors, but the particular hoe used in Muquiyauyo and the surrounding region seems to be of local, preconquest origin. The most common stone artifacts to be found among the ruins on the hillsides in back of Muquiyauyo are smaller stone versions of the *lampa,* and they are so called by the modern Muquiyauyinos. The modern *lampa* is set at an angle of about forty-five degrees from the handle; this requires that the worker hold the handle almost parallel to the ground to use it. The worker must plant his legs apart on either side of the row of plants and bury the blade in the ground; he then draws it back toward him and up at the same time. The metal *lampa* is usually purchased, but the farmer makes his own *lacwash.*

The most recent innovations are the pickax and the shovel. Earlier, the *barreta* was used for pick work. One of the older townsmen claims that he remembers first having used a shovel and a pickax about the turn of the century, although there were some who used it as early as 1890. Apparently the first major public use of these tools was during the construction of the district government building in the second decade of this century. At that time, men came in from Huaripampa, Paccha, and other towns, and brought their own tools with them to do the work. Information concerning the time of the introduction of the plow is conflicting; one informant claims it was as late as 1850. There are no satisfactory data on this, however.

At the time of the study, there was no agricultural power machinery used in the town. All work was done with hand tools or with the aid of the oxen and plows.

The crops cultivated around Muquiyauyo include plants of both American and European origin. Among the former are corn, carious tubers such as the *oca, olluco, mashua,* and potatoes, the hot chili pepper, *ají,* and several kinds of squash. Until only a few years ago the native Andean grain, *quinoa,* was still grown, but there was none under cultivation at the time of the study. Among the most important European crops are the broad bean *(haba),* barley, wheat, oats, peas, onions, carrots, and alfalfa for fodder. Many other plant foods are consumed by the Muquiyauyinos, but they are produced in the *montaña* to the east, or on the coast to the west.

Quinoa is said to have been a common crop as late as the last part of the nineteenth century. The reason given for its disappearance is that it was severely attacked by plant pests. *Ají* is grown as a garden plant by a few people, but it is not generally cultivated in the town; most is purchased. The most common edible squash is known as the *zapallo,* but only that known as the *calabaza* is grown locally.

Potatoes are a staple in Muquiyauyo. Almost everyone has at least a few irrigated plots under cultivation. They are planted in rows between fifty and eighty centimeters apart; as soon as the plants are a few inches high, cultivation with a hoe begins. The soil is heaped to produce a long mound along the base of the row of plants; the result is a field of long, perfectly formed, and identical waves. The history of the potato in Muquiyauyo is curious. Although it is an ancient Andean crop, it was not seeded locally until about 1860. Prior to that time, potatoes were brought as young plants from other towns, primarily from Apaicancha in the province of Tarma; or the tubers were purchased in the market. The introduction of the seed and the beginning of the modern cultivation of potatoes is attributed to the local culture hero, Román Amanzo.

Ocas, ollucos, and *mashuas* are treated in much the same manner as potatoes. They are somewhat less common, however, and

planting is usually restricted to the upper unirrigated fields since
it is said that the lower fields attract more of the insect pests to
which these plants are particularly subject.

Corn is also a major crop in Muquiyauyo. Like potatoes, it grows
much better with irrigation and careful cultivation. Rows of corn
are planted about fifty centimeters apart; while seeds are planted
between five and thirty centimeters apart within the row, the fields
are usually crowded, with the young plants anywhere from three to
ten or twenty centimeters apart. Two plowings are made to complete the planting of corn. The first breaks up the soil and provides
the furrow in which the seeds are placed. The farmer then plows
through the field again after the seeds have been placed, throwing
earth over the seeds. The resulting furrows serve to direct the
flow of irrigation water.

Alfalfa is said to have been introduced about 1860, and its introduction is also attributed to Román Amanzo, who is said to have
brought it from Lima. Today it is the most important fodder crop
in Muquiyauyo and almost every farmer has at least one field seeded
in it. For many years alfalfa also served as a cash crop and played
an important role in the accumulation of funds, enabling the community to attempt such ambitious projects as the electric light
plant. In recent years, with most of the land in private hands, less
alfalfa has been grown, and at times it has been necessary to purchase it from the outside to fulfill the feed requirements of the
livestock. Alfalfa is planted by scattering the seed *(bolear)*. A field
is divided by ridges of earth into a series of long rectangular sections two and a half to three meters in width. One informant claimed
that the purpose of these divisions is to make the cutting of the alfalfa easier; it also serves to direct the irrigation water so that
it reaches all parts of a field. An alfalfa crop may last as long as
twelve years with periodic cuttings; as a result it is important in
crop rotation.

The *haba,* or broad bean, is similar to the American lima bean
but has an extra tough covering over the bean itself. It is planted
in rows twenty to thirty centimeters apart with occasional irrigation canals cut through the field every four or five meters. Not all
haba cultivations are irrigated, however. Planting is done in the
same manner as corn planting. In connection with the *haba,* I heard
an interesting bit of local ethnobotanical speculation. One informant
claimed that except for one town in the Yanamarca Valley, *habas*
are nowhere so common in this entire region as they are in Muquiyauyo. Both these towns, he claimed, have sent forth a higher
percentage of professional persons than have any of the other com-

munities. "Could it not be," he asked, "that the progressivism
of Muquiyauyo stemmed from the fact that more *habas* were produced and consumed there?" This theory is reminiscent of that
put forward by Dr. Ralph Linton to account for the phenomenal rise
of the pueblo civilizations in the southwestern part of the United
States during the prehistoric era.

Wheat and barley are usually planted on unirrigated tracts. The
winnowing of wheat is done by both men and women; the chaff is
stamped out by three or four donkeys which move around in a circle. The places where winnowing is done are called *eras;* the principal one used today is Antosera. Oats are used for fodder, and
barley may be cut when half-grown and used for the animals. The
time of planting and harvesting depends primarily on the time of
the beginning and the duration and intensity of the rainy season.
During my visit rains were scarce and crops matured slowly.

In plowing the fields, it is a frequent practice to cross plow and
to plow in different directions each year. It is felt that this pre-
vents the soil from wearing out so quickly. Crop rotation is also a
well-established method of preserving soil fertility. Just when rotation was first used is not certain, but John Rowe, in his summary of Inca culture at the time of the conquest, [1] says that the
chroniclers hardly mentioned the subject in their descriptions. I
could not discover any preferred pattern of rotation except that
corn, potatoes, and broad beans were frequently alternated within
the same irrigated plots, while barley, wheat, and tubers other
than potatoes were usually alternated in the unirrigated sections. In
general, the period of maturation of crops in the irrigated sections is five to six months, while in the unirrigated fields it is
seven or eight months. The main planting in irrigated fields is done
in October and November, although some people plant potatoes in
July; harvest is in May. Planting in unirrigated fields is done anywhere between late August and November and the harvest takes
place around July, depending upon the intensity of the rainy season.
The rains in this highland area are not of the heavy tropical variety
and there is a good deal of sunny weather during the rainy season.

Farming in Muquiyauyo is basically a family matter. A man may
get help by exchanging labor with a friend or relation, he may work
partidario with someone else, or he may hire additional help; but
the great majority of the work is done by a man, his wife, and his
children. The division of labor between the sexes within the family
is very generalized. The only work which men almost always do
is the plowing, and under some circumstances women do this too.

Everything else, the actual seeding, cultivating, harvesting, winnowing of grains, and transporting, may be done by either men or women; and if the work is not too heavy, it may also be done by children. If a family opens a small store in the home, the wife customarily remains home to attend to the business and family while the husband and children go to the fields. Very commonly, however, when field work has to be done, the entire family goes together, taking lunch and working together on the job at hand. In plowing, if a man and wife are present, the man does the plowing while his wife first precedes him, picks up and throws away rocks, and frequently drags her foot to make a shallow furrow so that he may more readily follow the line and dig the furrow straight. The wife then turns and follows the plowman, dropping seeds in the open furrows. The whole family joins in cultivation, each with his hoe; even little girls may work in cultivation, but they are more commonly set to pasturing the livestock. Again in harvesting the whole family may work as a group. The fact that there is so little specialization in the field labor provides a certain amount of independence for widows, widowers, and younger unmarried people who must carry on the field work without the aid of a family.

There is some division of labor with respect to the handling of livestock. If a man and his sons are capable of taking care of the field work, it will fall to the women to pasture the cattle, sheep, and burros. There is regular division of labor outside of agriculture; men are miners and professionals (except in teaching, which is open to both sexes); women usually tend stores when they are of secondary importance, sell at fairs, herd animals, and carry on the usual domestic work.

The general pattern of labor in agricultural work has its origin in the Indian way of life. Rowe, in describing the Inca methods of agriculture, writes that the man uses the digging stick, while the woman drops the seeds and breaks the clods; both work in the harvest.[2] Rowe also describes the construction of small field huts as watch-houses. In Muquiyauyo during the last half-century or more, many families have taken to building small houses near their fields so that in times of intense work they can move out to the fields and live. These houses are referred to as "country homes" and vary in size from small one-room adobe structures to regular houses of three or four rooms, sometimes with a surrounding wall. One hears of the benefits to be derived from "living in the country." It is said that the present barrio of Quichuay started in this fashion; several families after building these country homes found that they preferred them to their "city homes."

The lack of specialization in agricultural activities, then, should not be interpreted as a degeneration of the importance of agriculture; it is a holdover of agricultural organization which stems from the Incan period. Furthermore, it fits in well with the division of labor in other activities. A man may start a store in Muquiyauyo and leave his wife to attend it while he works in the fields. Or, as one man did, he may move his store to another town where business is better, and leave his wife to take care of the fields.

Quite often a man has more agricultural work than his family can handle, or his wife is occupied in other tasks and has no time to help in the fields. There are various ways in which help may be obtained. One of these is through exchange labor, known as *huaji* or *huajiti*. *Huaji* is said to mean to "return a favor" and is consequently used in connection with the old form of communal housebuilding or in any other situation in which labor is exchanged. The *huaji* relationship is usually agreed upon only for particular jobs or for a limited period of time. Two men will work in the fields of first one, then the other, for an equal period of time, usually between three days and a week. The owner of the land traditionally supplies the food. Exchange labor usually takes place between friends or close relatives. Aside from the *huaji*, there is nothing approaching the agricultural work group which has been described for other parts of the highlands in Peru.[3]

Hiring labor is not uncommon in Muquiyauyo, but the complaint is often heard that it is hard to obtain *peones*, or *obreros*, as the are more commonly called now. It is necessary to contract with a man three to six days ahead of time if one wants him to come to work. So many of the laborers go to the mines that there are very few left in town. There are, nevertheless, several poor men, all of the Indian class, who can be employed for various field jobs. Before 1940 they earned S/.40 to .70 daily, but at the time of the study they were receiving S/. 4 plus food, coca, and *aguardient* (cane sugar alcohol). If a man supplied his own oxen and plow for plowing a field, he of course received considerably more.

The *partidario* or sharecropping system is also looked upon as a way to get aid in field work, but without having to pay cash for it. The sharecropper receives his profit in his share of the crop.

I found no evidence of magic used to promote the growth of crops. The nearest thing to such practices which seem of importance today is the techniques used to protect the crops against the danger of hail and frost. Muquiyauyinos can usually predict the onset of frost and are very sensitive to the damage that it can cause the crops. Ice storms are predictable in terms of the time of year and the approach of heavy clouds. To protect the crops against ice and frost, large bonfires are built, exploding rockets are sent up, and the church bells are rung to awaken people in order that they may follow these precautions. Adults, when asked about these practices, usually deprecated them and said that only the children did such things. A number of times, however, I was awakened during the night by the exploding rockets, church bells, and shouting which inevitably accompanied these efforts and I noted that men were engaged in tending the fires and yelling. Also, during one of the *cuartel* meetings, part of the discussion was devoted to the complaint that the other *cuarteles* had not been buying their share of rockets to guard against frost. It is true that the children were visibly active in these affairs, but it was explained to me that the smoke of the fires of green wood and the exploding rockets served to heat up the atmosphere and thus counteract the cold.

No other threats to crops have been dealt with as noisily as this. Theft is not uncommon, and plant pests are known but at present are not doing great damage. Wheat suffers from a rust blight which has never reached very severe proportions.

The planting of trees has been an important activity in Muquiyauyo for many years. The valley does not have a natural tree cover, so wood for fuel and construction must be cultivated. The district session books frequently record that a committee has been appointed to see to the acquisition of trees, or that a work project will be held to plant some. The earliest mention is in November, 1887, when it was decided to hold a work session *(faena)* to plant alder trees *(aliso)* in the alameda. The first record of the district's decision to buy eucalyptus trees was made in 1911, when four boxes were ordered from Tarma. In 1920 it was agreed to plant eucalyptus on the new alameda all the way to the base of the mountain, and in a 1924 record this project is mentioned as being underway. In 1928 it was suggested that eucalyptus should also be planted in the Isla area. Until this time it had been the practice to bring the young trees from Tarma, but in this session it was suggested to seed them in Muquiyauyo. In 1931 another three thousand trees were brought in from the town of Concepción.

The first introduction of the eucalyptus is attributed to Padre Guzmán, who is said to have brought them in between 1875 and 1880. At present, this tree is by far the most common in Muquiyauyo and in the rest of the valley. Its wood is employed in the construction of houses, implements, and furniture, and is used for firewood. It is recognized as not being the best wood for construction, but it is fast-growing and consequently the most available as well as the cheapest. It is also important because of the shade it affords, and it adds visibly to the beauty of the town. While few Muquiyauyinos are expert woodsmen, both men and women are handy with the ax. The men fell trees and the women break up the kindling wood.

At present two trees are planted by seed in Muquiyauyo, the eucalyptus and the *guinda (guindo,* mazard cherry tree). The *aliso, quinual, quishuar,* and a few fruit trees are planted by shoots cut from older trees. This kind of planting is an old practice in Muquiyauyo; it is usually done in September or immediately before the rainy season so that the new trees will have sufficient water.

The irrigated sections of Muquiyauyo receive their water from a canal system which is a source of local pride and the envy of other valley towns. The original canal was planned and the building was directed by the same Román Amanzo to whom is attributed the introduction of various other improvements in the town. Amanzo built two canals around 1858. An upper one leaves the Mantaro River about ten kilometers above Muquiyauyo at the town of Miraflores and runs through the town of Huaripampa, then splits into two canals which water an area above the embankment at Muquiyauyo. The uppermost of these two branches, the Acequia Usno, carries irrigation water while the other, the Acequia Alta, carries the water for the small canals that run through the streets, providing the town with water for drinking, washing, and general service. The other main canal that Amanzo built carries water from the river in Huaripampa and forms what is now the Acequia del Molino (mill canal) and waters much of the area below the embankment.

The canal system took its present form in 1920 when the electric light plant was built. For this, water was taken from the upper canal system and put through the light plant; the water which came out of this formed the canal known as the Desague (drainage canal) which then joined with the mill canal below the embankment. In order to have sufficient water for the light plant, the main upper canal had to be enlarged so that instead of carrying about one-half a cubic meter per second, it carried three cubic meters per second. Except for the major changes which took place with the construction of the light plant, the main alterations made on Amanzo's original plan have been merely the addition of more side canals for irrigation and the construction of canal gates at critical points. The town of Muqui also uses this canal system, but Huaripampa has its own system.

Except for the stone-sided canals in the streets, all the canals are dirt ditches. It is periodically necessary, therefore, to clean them. The canals in the town are the responsibility of the house- or lot-owners who have property that faces on the canals. The many field canals are also the responsibility of the owners and users of the water. The upkeep of the main canals, however, is a community responsibility, and each *cuartel* is assigned certain portions of the work. Work sessions are held by the *cuarteles* about twice annually, or whenever the canals get into such condition that it is imperative that they be cleaned. When cleaning needs to be done, this is officially decided by the district council, but as the community has taken over more and more of such strictly communal functions the council's authority in canal control has decreased. The canal system of Muquiyauyo is essentially well planned, and the main canals are deep and fast-running. The most important water problems of the town are getting water to those lands that are still unirrigated, and providing drinking water.

Besides caring for crops and keeping water running in the canals, the Muquiyauyo farmer also keeps a few animals. Keeping livestock, for the townspeople, is a distinctly secondary means of subsistence. On the average a family has two head of cattle, six or eight sheep, a few pigs, and some chickens. Most families have one or two burros which are used to transport produce and goods, and a very few of the more wealthy ones have a riding horse. All the animals are kept in a corral near the house at night and taken out to pasture during the day.

While the people of the town are not much concerned with livestock, the population of the *aldea* of Los Andes, located in the *puna* behind Muquiyauyo, is quite dependent upon animals. This village was founded some years ago by Muquiyauyinos in an area that is not very good for agriculture. As a result most families keep more cattle and sheep, and horses are much more common for travel. Muquiyauyo's meat supply comes from Los Andes and other towns located in the mountains.

The organization of herding in Muquiyauyo depends in some degree on the size of the herd. A woman usually takes the animals out to graze in a cut alfalfa field or on the weeds which have grown up in a resting field. If there are quite a few animals, the woman remains with them and spins while the man works in his fields; if there are not many, she also works in the fields and the animals are tethered nearby.

Around the house, chickens, ducks, rabbits, and guinea pigs may be kept. Rabbits are kept in the corral with other animals or

in the kitchen with the guinea pigs. Each kitchen is provided with
a special hollow bench made of adobe bricks in which the guinea
pigs live. Both guinea pigs and rabbits, but especially the former,
are prized as delicacies and are saved for special feasts.

Dogs are abundant in Muquiyauyo. Every family has at least one
and there are numerous others that seem homeless. Throughout
the district session books are orders for periodic killings and
everyone is advised to keep his pet in while the strays are poisoned.
A few dogs are used to guard the animals in the pastures, but most
are kept merely as pets. Some cats are kept, but they are not common.

9

CRAFTS AND COMMERCE

WHILE agriculture is the principal productive activity of the people of Muquiyauyo, home crafts and services, and commerce in stores, markets, and fairs, are essential parts of the economic system. Unlike some valley people, Muquiyauyinos specialize in no particular craft. The inhabitants of Sicaya specialize in sewing, those of Caja in hat-making, and those of Aco in pottery; but Muquiyauyo is primarily a town of farmers. Many of the skills are represented in Muquiyauyo by a few men or women who carry them on as a secondary form of livelihood. Not all the craftsmen in Muquiyauyo are natives of the town. There seems to be a certain tendency within some of the trades for a specialist to settle in a town in which there is a demand for his services. Harry Tschopik noted that in Chupaca and Sicaya there were many tradesmen who came from other centers, and the same is true in Muquiyauyo.[1] If a son learns shoemaking or carpentry from his father, there may not be enough business in the home town to keep both son and father occupied. As a result, there are quite a few cases of craftsmen who have gone elsewhere and frequently married into the new town.

The list on the following page snows the number of craftsmen in the town in 1932 and in 1950. The 1932 data are from a census taken by Pedro Bustamente in that year,[2] and the 1950 figures were obtained during the course of this study.

From the census taken in 1950, it was possible to distinguish for certain crafts those people who were entirely dependent, as compared to those only partially dependent, upon the skills. This distinction can be seen in the second of the two tables.

Of this group of ninety-three craftsmen, only thirteen said they were entirely dependent upon their craft for a livelihood, while seventy-three were also dependent upon agriculture and eight on another craft. This emphasizes that crafts, from the point of view of the subsistence of the family, are generally secondary to agriculture.

Craftsman	Number in 1932	Number in 1950
Baker	-	1
Barber	1	3
Blacksmith	4	5
Carpenter	13	33
Hatter	1	2
Mason	3	21
Sawmill operator	-	2
Seamstress	9	4
Shoemaker	4	13
Tailor	5	5
Tilemaker	-	3
Weaver	3	10

Craftsman	Entirely Dependent upon Craft	Also Dependent upon Other Craft	Also Dependent upon Agriculture
Blacksmith	-	1	5
Carpenter	5	1	27
Hatter	-	-	2
Mason	2	3	16
Seamstress	-	-	4
Shoemaker	4	-	9
Tailor	1	1	3
Weaver	1	2	7
Total	13	8	73

The establishment of a bakery in Muquiyauyo has not served to fill the bread requirements of the town. Most bread is still brought regularly from Jauja and some is brought in from Muqui. The increase in the number of barbers probably reflects a slight tendency for people to have their hair cut by a specialist instead of at home. The number of blacksmiths has not changed appreciably; their work has remained very much the same: making horseshoes for the few horses in town, and making hinges and other odd pieces of iron work.

The increase in the number of carpenters is probably to be explained in terms of the full-time specialists as opposed to those who work at it irregularly. It seems likely that many of the people who were listed as carpenters in 1950 would not have been so listed in 1932, since they spent very little of their time at carpentry. It is not possible, then, to tell from these two censuses whether there has been much of an increase in the number of people practicing carpentry. The carpenter in Muquiyauyo works with fairly limited tools. In spite of the fact that there is electric current in town, there were no electric carpentry tools in use in 1950. One carpenter had a wheel about five feet in diameter which was turned manually on a horizontal axis and which by means of a rope turned a circular saw. Carpentry is an important trade in Muquiyauyo; doors, chairs, tables, house beams, coffins, and various other items are produced locally. Once a carpenter even built an entire bus body for a truck chassis purchased by a man in Huaripampa.

The making of hats is a specialty of very limited importance in Muquiyauyo; almost all hats are purchased in Jauja.

The recorded increase in the number of masons can probably be interpreted in much the same manner as the increase in carpenters. Most of the masons do not spend a great deal of time in their specialty and consequently were not registered in the 1932 census. According to 1950 informants, there are fifty-one people in Muquiyauyo who practice masonry in one way or another. Masons themselves tend to specialize. Most numerous are those who make and lay adobe bricks. Fewer specialize in laying stone foundations, building stone walls, and making the *tapia* wall, a solid wall constructed within a frame, in contrast to adobe brick construction. Only about five do plastering and three regular bricklaying.

The two men who have started sawmills came to Muquiyauyo from other towns. They have married into the town and established their trades there. The mill of one typifies the utilization of machinery for diverse purposes which is to be found occasionally through the central mountain region. The mill is composed of the chassis and motor of an old car. The chassis is buried in the ground, forming a steady foundation for the motor; a belt transfers power to a large circular saw. The owner of this mill employs from one to three assistants, depending upon how heavy his work is. At the same time, he acts as a blacksmith. Both sawmill operators double as general mechanics and carpenters.

The decrease in the number of seamstresses and the increase in weavers are both reflections of the effect of the national economy on the local crafts. Seamstresses produce finished cotton and woolen clothing primarily for women. Three factors have operated in the last two decades to reduce the number of women specializing in this production. First, the spread of the sewing machine has made it possible for more women to sew their own clothes. Formerly, sewing was a time-consuming task, and a woman who had her share of work to do in the fields could not devote the time necessary to produce all her own clothes. Second, the increase of cheap factory-produced cloth, especially cotton cloth, has made it possible for more women to purchase finished garments. This applies more, however, to the women who prefer western dress than to those who use the *centro* costume. And finally, in recent years, there has been a tremendous expansion in regional trade through the establishment of many new weekly fairs. This has made it possible for specialists in other towns to sell their goods more easily throughout the neighboring region.

The increase in the number of weavers seems to be a recent recrudescence of an old skill. According to informants, the number of weavers declined some years ago as factory goods began to replace them on the market. In the past ten or fifteen years, however, the price of these commercial goods has risen to such a degree that there has been a return to weaving. Weaving, an exclusively masculine craft, is dependent upon the production of thread by the women. Most women of Muquiyauyo spend a large portion of their time spinning. When waiting at the market or herding animals, or whenever there is nothing else occupying her hands, the Muquiyauyina spins thread. The weaver seldom produces goods for sale; the usual practice is to take the finished thread to the weaver and ask that he produce such and such a piece of work. The main products of the weaver are the *bayeta,* a plain white woolen cloth which is used for underclothing for both men and women; the poncho, a heavy, tightly woven blanket used by the men as a combination overcoat and raincoat; scarves, a regular part of the man's costume; the *pullu,* or woman's carrying blanket; and the *frazadas* and *jergas,* decorated and undecorated blankets.

Two kinds of looms are used by the weavers of Muquiyauyo. Some men use the old back-strap loom which has been handed down from prehistoric time. This loom is used principally for making ponchos, which must be very tightly woven. An expert weaver with a back-strap loom can produce a woolen cloth that is almost completely waterproof; the threads are pounded into place with the help of a bone implement so that the resultant cloth is stiff and hard. Ponchos made on this loom are woven in two pieces, since the width of the loom is not sufficient to make the whole garment at once. Each piece then forms one-half of the finished poncho. A good deal of weaving is also done on the vertical hand loom of Spanish origin; this loom is used principally for the lighter cloth.

Several trends are at work which, if they continue, will gradually push the weaver out of business. Younger women are not showing the interest in spinning that is still evinced by the older generation. Factory-made cotton underclothing is slowly replacing the warmer *bayeta* material in spite of the price fluctuations. At present most of the weavers' products are used by men, and as a strong commercial woolen goods industry grows, it is likely that weaving as an art will disappear.

There seems to be no ready explanation for the increase in the number of shoemakers in the town. Some of them are transients. The local tile industry is evidently a recent development. Tiles have long been the standard roof covering in Muquiyauyo, although even today most of them are imported from tilemakers in Jauja.

Another skill, not mentioned on the list, is that of musician. There are today about sixteen musicians in the town, violinists, harpists, and woodwind and brass players. They are hired when there is a party, religious procession, or fiesta. Musicians are hired from various towns, however, and it almost seems to be the custom to get people from out of town rather than to employ the local talent.

In general, Muquiyauyo is still quite dependent upon its own and neighboring craftsmen. Houses, furniture, coffins, agricultural implements, much of the clothing, and roofing materials are all produced by individual artisans. The craftsmen are distributed proportionately between the two social classes, but the weavers are as a rule Indians, while tailoring tends to be a mestizo trade.

Commerce in recent years has become an important activity in Muquiyauyo. While the Muquiyauyino produces a great deal of the food he eats, and local specialists produce various items he uses in the course of his daily living, there has been a great increase in the number of stores and marketing facilities since the turn of the century. Before 1890 the only stores in Muquiyauyo consisted of small home outfits called *tienduchas* or *caramercheles;* the main products sold were salt, peppers, bricks of unrefined sugar *(chancaca),* matches, *aguardiente,* and locally made tallow candles. All the stores were enterprises completely secondary to the primary activity of agriculture.

The first store to be opened as a serious business venture, importing a wider range of commodities from Jauja, was owned by a mestizo. It was opened in his house on the main street leading to Huaripampa, a block off the plaza. Shortly thereafter another mestizo opened a store in the south end of town, but still on the main street. The third such store was opened by an enterprising Indian, now one of the wealthier men in town. The first two stores to be opened on the plaza were set up by mestizo women sometime between 1895 and 1900. From data available at different points in recent history, we can see a regular increase in the number of stores in the town: in 1900 there were five; in 1932, eighteen; in 1946, thirty-two; and in 1950, thirty-eight. Of the stores established by 1900, only one is still functioning today under the same ownership. Of the eighteen recorded in 1932, six are still in operation. So while it is clear that the number of stores is increasing, there is some indication that many do not last very long. An indication of their popularity is the fact that in most of the newer houses being built, one of the front rooms is called the "store," even though the family may not be certain that it will be used as such.

Very few of the stores are operated as full-time subsistence activities. There are two full-time stores on the plaza, one run by a young man and his wife and the other by a widow not yet far along in years. In the case of the first, the man's father still lives and works all his own land with sharecroppers; he gave his son the store building at a very strategic corner. The other store is in the district government building and is rented from the district by the widow. One other store which might be regarded as a full-time activity is the one that was started before 1900; the owner is now too old to work in the fields and he attends to the store. For the most part women run the stores while their husbands work in the field; the man may take care of the selling if he has nothing else to do or if the woman has pressing domestic concerns.

Among the items carried by most stores are a variety of foods such as canned fish, oils, herbs, flours, candy, sugar, spaghetti, bread, some fresh greens when a local person brings some in to sell, and fruit, bought at a market or fair; soaps; confetti for fiestas; patent medicines and popular curatives; sewing items such as safety pins and needles; writing supplies; and various liquors, beers, carbonated drinks, wines, and coca. The most completely stocked store is the one on the plaza run by the young couple; they refuse to sell coca because they feel that it is bad for people. Most of the stores have a very limited general supply and the only items common to almost all are beer, sweet vermouth, *aguardiente,* soap, cigarettes, matches, and candles. Some carry gasoline, kerosene, and a petroleum product used for preserving wooden floors. The more serious businessmen make one or two trips weekly to Jauja to order supplies, and go once or twice annually to Lima to arrange with the larger wholesale dealers for items needed.

Most of the wholesale firms have traveling representatives stationed in Jauja or Huancayo; these men visit the towns, taking orders for future deliveries. There are also traveling vendors from small home factories who walk or go by burro through the region selling stocks of packaged herbs, condiments, blankets, or whatever they have. These sources, together with a few fresh vegetables and eggs from the local producers, provide the majority of the supplies of the stores.

The stores in Muquiyauyo are somewhat similar to our "general stores," except that they have a much more limited stock. Like the general store, some also function as a clubroom, drinking establishment, and general gathering place. During fiestas the owners of stores off the plaza may move their stocks of food and drink to a temporarily rented location on the plaza or under a cloth shelter in the park to take advantage of the traffic. In general, however, the stores are now scattered around the town and people usually purchase at those nearest their home. The times of greatest buying are during the fiestas. In normal times, there is a decline in trade on Monday, with a rise on Wednesday, another decline on Thursday, then a rise to a peak on Saturday, and a drop to the following Monday. [3] Stores which try to maintain a constant trade usually open between seven and nine in the morning and close shortly after dark at night. A few will stay open if a drinking crowd is present, but most are shut by 10:00 p. m.

Two other important means of distribution are found throughout the Jauja Valley, the market *(mercado)* and the fair *(feria)*. Muquiyauyo has both. Markets and fairs deal in essentially the same kinds of goods. Whether they are large or small depends upon the size of the town, its location, its reputation, and the time of the year. The difference between the fair and market is that the latter is open daily, with each vendor in the larger towns having an appointed stand for which he pays rent to the municipality. The fair is held once or twice a week, and the vendors set up stands wherever they like in an area set aside for them. The fair is a greatly expanded market with sellers from the entire adjacent region; the market is small and is made up of permanently located vendors. In both there is a definite pattern by which different classes of goods tend to be sold within a clearly defined part of the market or fair area.

The Muquiyauyo market is a relatively small affair and usually includes no more than ten vendors; there is no special marketplace. The vendors gather early in the morning in front of a store on the plaza and remain there with their goods until about noon, when they disperse. Products and prices are equivalent to those of the weekly fair, but there is much less selection. Fruits and some vegetables are the most common products; every two or three days a meat vendor from the hills brings down fresh meat early in the morning, and once in a great while a man or woman with pottery arrives. People from nearby towns and from Muquiyauyo take advantage of the market to sell their goods. There are a few regular sellers who come until all their goods are sold. Most sellers are women and they sit leaning against the wall of the store discussing current events. The market is so small that the local district takes little cognizance of it. It has been suggested from time to time to utilize some district land immediately below the embankment in back of the church for a regular market plaza, but nothing has ever been done about this and it is doubtful at present whether there is enough business in the daily market to make such a venture worth-while.

The Saturday fair in Muquiyauyo is much larger than the market and, while small in comparison with some others in the valley, is of considerable local importance. There are usually between thirty and one hundred sellers and a few professional buyers in attendance. In two surveys, made in October and December, 1949, fifty-eight different vendors were interviewed. They came principally from four main areas and a few came from more distant towns:

Provenance of Vendor	Number of Vendors	Per Cent
Muquiyauyo	10	17.2
Towns immediately around Muquiyauyo (Huaripampa, Huamalí, Muqui, Pacamarca, Huancaní)	10	17.2
Nearby mountain towns (Huancas, Los Andes, Llacuarí)	7	12.1
Jauja, and smaller towns around Jauja (Chucliu, Julcán, Chumán, Yauli, Pancán)	29	50.0
Various distant towns in the Jauja and Yanamarca valleys (San Jerónimo, Acolla)	2	3.5
Total	58	100.0

The greatest single number of vendors came from Jauja, and, of these, ten also followed the practice of selling at other fairs in the valley. Of the forty-eight non-Muquiyauyinos, thirty-three also sold at other fairs. There is, therefore, a regular population which makes a practice of going to various fairs to sell their goods. Other fairs visited by the people who attend the Muquiyauyo fairs are at Jauja (on Wednesday and Sunday); Masma, Huancaní, Marco, Julcán (on Thursday); and Acolla and Muqui (on Friday).

I was not told of any fairs in the region held on Monday or Tuesday. Luis Valcárcel mentions that in the southern end of the valley there are no fairs held on Tuesdays, and suggests that perhaps the reason for this is that Tuesday is "reputed to be an unlucky day."[4] I encountered no such belief in Muquiyauyo. It does seem more than coincidental, however, that Mondays and Tuesdays also have the least gross traffic in the stores in Muquiyauyo. There is no expressed reluctance to buy on these days; it seems to be due to a natural economic slump following the high commercial activity of the week end.

The goods sold at the Muquiyauyo fair consist principally of foodstuffs, but there are usually a few vendors of cheap clothing and trinkets. At the fair on December 3, 1949, there were sixty-three vendors specializing as follows:

vegetables	13	drinks	2
fruit	12	alfalfa	5
fruit and vegetables	4	meat	5
grains and vegetables	1	clothing	4
grains and eggs	1	egg buyers	3
bread	5	soap	2
hot food	5	ice cream handcart	1

The vendors from Muquiyauyo usually sell their own field products, but some come regularly to sell hot lunches and breakfasts that they cook on small portable clay stoves, gasoline pressure stoves, or in old tin cans used as stoves. The alfalfa was usually sold as fodder for immediate consumption by the cargo donkeys tied near the plaza.

Travel to the fair is by foot, burro, or bus. Regular buses run from Jauja to Muquiyauyo every Saturday morning, a factor that may explain why the Jauja area supplies such a large percentage of the vendors. People from nearby towns usually come on foot with their produce on their back or on a burro. Some from the Jauja area also come with burros to save the bus fare. A few people visit the fair to buy eggs, and sometimes barley or wheat, to take to Lima to sell. Two or three Muquiyauyo widows also are engaged in this trade, making weekly trips to the national capital to sell eggs and buy coastal produce which they bring back and sell at the fairs in Muquiyauyo and in other towns.

With the exception of the soap vendors and the clothing merchants, all the sellers at the fair in Muquiyauyo are women. In a few cases a Muquiyauyino and his wife will work together in the preparation of the lunches and breakfasts, but on the whole the selling and buying is done almost entirely by women.

Of the many fairs that now take place in the Jauja Valley, many are of recent origin. The Muquiyauyo fair began in 1931, and evidently many of the fairs in nearby towns are also recent. When one informant was a child, in about 1910, the only fairs in the valley were those of Huancayo, Jauja, Concepción, Chupaca, and probably Huayucachi. Later a biannual fair at Sincos started and was followed by a weekly fair. The fairs in Muquiyauyo and San Jerónimo began about the same time, and there followed the fairs in Masma, Julcán, Acolla, Marco, Llocllapampa, and, two years ago, in Muqui. These data on the time of beginning of the fairs have not been checked in the various towns and so the precise times of beginning may be somewhat different from those stated. That the spread of the fair complex is a relatively recent occurrence seems certain. There is little doubt that the increase in population which has characterized Muquiyauyo has also occurred throughout the valley. In view of this, the growth of the fairs doubtless reflects this increase in population and the consequent increase in the need for food products. The appearance of new fairs in the smaller towns does not seem to have detracted in any way from the major fairs in Huancayo, Jauja, and Concepción. The large regional market is an old tradition in Peru, but the recent expansion of the pattern in the Jauja Valley is very likely due to the rise in population.

The increase in the number of stores likewise reflects this growth. However, the number of stores in Muquiyauyo has increased at a much faster rate than has the population of the town. This increase in commerce must also be attributed to the fact that more people today are purchasing goods from stores than was previously the case. The increase in mining activities and the numbers of Muquiyauyinos and other valley people who are working for wages instead of producing subsistence crops has introduced a good deal more money into the region and made many more people dependent upon foodstuffs grown by others. The people who work at the mines have also become more accustomed to obtaining things through stores and to depend upon various store products that are available in the mining centers. The stores have served to bring products in from the outside as well as to distribute local goods.

The increase in stores, markets, and fairs throughout the Jauja Valley, therefore, is not an isolated event, but is closely tied in with the general growth in population, the decrease in dependence upon subsistence crops, and the concomitant increase in participation in a national economy.

THE HOME AND WOMEN'S ACTIVITIES

THE HOME of a Muquiyauyino is the center of much of his life. It is a place to eat and sleep, to visit with friends, to store crops, and to take care of the animals; in an increasing number of cases it is also a place of business.

For the past few centuries the main construction material for houses and other buildings has been adobe brick. Adobe in Muquiyauyo refers solely to large sun-dried clay bricks. Until the 1920's two sizes of adobes were used; the earlier was sixty by thirty by twelve centimeters, and the later was fifty-six by thirty-six by fifteen centimeters. The time when the first of these went out of style and the latter became preferred is not known; the change occurred before any of the contemporary population had anything to do with construction methods. During the lifetime of the present population, the second of the above sizes was used until about 1925, when another size came into style: forty-six by thirty-two by fifteen centimeters. The explanation given for these reductions in size is that good adobe clay was becoming scarcer and consequently it was necessary to use less material. Adobes are placed so that the brick's longest dimension is the thickness of the wall; as a result, by reducing this dimension the total amount of clay required is reduced.

Sometime early in this century the form of construction known as *tapia* was introduced as a substitute for adobes. While adobes are made in wooden frames and then assembled one upon another to make a wall, the *tapia* construction consists of placing a large frame directly on the wall, tamping the clay into the form, and allowing it to dry in position. The frame for the *tapia* wall is first placed over a stone foundation and a first layer is made over the entire area of the proposed wall. When the first layer is finished and dried the frame is placed to make the series of blocks for the second layer, which is allowed to dry before the third layer is begun. Three or four layers are usually sufficient for a house or field wall. *Tapia* construction did not originate in this part of Peru; it first appeared in Muquiyauyo about 1908, when the technique was brought back by men returning from a trip to the mines. There is agreement among informants that *tapia* had been used at certain of the mining centers, principally at Morococha, before its introduction to Muquiyauyo. One of the first men to use it in Muquiyauyo was a man who married into the town. Until 1935 *tapia* was used only for the construction of free-standing walls. The first man to use it in a house wall had worked previously in Concepción and had probably seen it used there. Since that time it has become increasingly popular, and there are now many houses in Muquiyauyo constructed in this way. As with other kinds of construction, *tapia* construction early tended to become a specialty and there are now eight *tapia* masons in Muquiyauyo. One of the reasons for its growing popularity is that a *tapia* wall can be constructed by a single man. It does not require the skill of adobe making and laying. *Tapia*, however, is not practical for use in construction projects undertaken by the community as a whole, since each layer must be allowed to dry before the next one is put in place; it does no good to have a large number of workers together at one time to do the work. The *tapia* wall uses no less clay than does adobe, but it is cleaner when finished since there are many fewer cracks.

The foundation built under both adobe and *tapia* walls, whether for houses or free-standing walls, is usually composed of angular rocks brought down from the hillsides. For field walls the stones are frequently taken from the river area, but these stones are water-worn and round and do not hold as well as the angular rocks from the hillside. The depth of a foundation depends upon the depth of the topsoil. A trench is dug down to the mass of rocks that underlie the entire area, and the stone foundation is set on top of this. It is impossible to say, without undertaking excavations of old walls and houses, to what extent this is an old practice.

The other outstanding change in construction materials consists in the application of mud, plaster, or cement as a final coat to the outside of adobe and *tapia* walls. Before 1935 only two kinds of coating were used: regular clay, and white clay applied over a layer of regular clay. Although many of the older houses are now destroyed, it would seem from those that remain that the use of white clay was almost universal; it is still extremely popular. White clay was most commonly used on the outside of the house, particularly on the blank wall facing the street. About 1935 the first use of plaster as a coat was introduced. The mestizo who

first used it applied it only to the inside of his home. The first
building to have plaster on the outside was that belonging to the
first *cuartel*. Recently, for decorative purposes, red baked bricks
have been used, but up until 1950 they still served no structural
purpose in house building.

Roofs in Muquiyauyo are usually made of tile. Galvanized metal
roofs in the town are quite rare, and by far the greatest number
of new structures continue to use tile. The metal roof requires a
simpler set of roof supports, but the metal itself is much more
expensive than tile. Elsewhere in the valley a composition roof
has been introduced, but by 1950 it had not been brought into Mu-
quiyaúyo. Cement, occasionally employed as an outside wall plaster, has been used principally in sidewalks and in some of the
patios within a few of the wealthier homes. This material, however, is very expensive and its use is restricted.

There have been some changes in construction techniques and
some visible improvements in skills. Technically better carpentry and masonry can be seen in the newer homes; the lines are
straighter, the walls smoother, and the beams more cleanly cut.
There also seems to be a tendency toward simplification in construction. In some of the older homes a heavy wooden wedge, the
clavija, was placed through the crossbeam that rested on the top
of the adobe walls and extended for a short distance outside the
walls. This wedge was superfluous and has been omitted in recent homes. Similarly the lowest roof support, the *alar*, used
to have a carved finish called *modillón;* in recent homes this carv-
ing has been omitted, and in some of the most modern the whole
roof support system has been modified and this piece removed altogether. Superfluous beams supporting the porch roof in some
of the older homes have also been left out in recent years.

The general house plan in Muquiyauyo has undergone an interesting evolution during the last hundred years. The essential pattern of a century ago consisted of two main rectangular buildings,
one on the street presenting a long blank wall broken only by a
large double door; the second building stood parallel to and behind the first; between the two lay the patio. To one side of the
patio or behind the second house stood a separate building or shelter for the kitchen. Behind the second house was a field, a corral,
or both. The floor for the two main buildings was at ground level
or slightly above it. Facing the patio, each of the two houses had
a porch, the *corredor*. The houses of some of the wealthy people
had a low second floor and a wooden balcony which projected out
over the street. In most cases the various units of such a com-

pound were not built at one time and often the units would be constructed by different generations.

This basic pattern is still the most popular in Muquiyauyo. Familiarity with the homes in Lima and with the American cottages at the mining centers, however, has brought in a new style which was referred to by an English-speaking Muquiyauyino as "the American cottage type" house. The most interesting feature of these cottages is the manner in which they are adapted to the local materials of construction and retain certain elements of the old basic house pattern. This merger of architectural traits is occurring not only in Muquiyauyo; examples also are to be seen in homes in Jauja, Huancayo, and elsewhere in the highlands. Among the changes which the introduction of new elements has produced are the inclusion of windows on the street front, the building of a second floor, the establishment of one of the front rooms as a "store," and the movement of the front building back from the street so that there may be a yard or garden in front as well as a patio behind.

The construction of homes often covers a long period of time. A house which may appear reasonably new might have the following history: first building constructed in 1905 and roofed in 1907; additional buildings put up in 1921 and 1927; plastered with mud in 1935; a new roof put on the older building in 1938; and, at one time or another during the period, the patio would be cobblestoned, a new corral would be built, the main inside rooms would be plastered, and so forth. One of the most prominent houses on the plaza was built in 1820. At that time it covered the entire block, but through the years sections of it have been sold off and replaced by new homes or have disintegrated. Another house, a few blocks from the plaza, was built in 1838 and roofed in 1844. Other houses with the same old architectural styling have similar histories.

In general the principal changes in house patterns have been esthetic in nature and toward simplification. The adobe and *tapia* construction both demand heavy walls and simple floor plans and the rectangular buildings still serve the purpose as well as do buildings of any other shape. The porches facing the patio protect against the sun and rain and continue to provide a useful place to keep agricultural implements and other odds and ends. The double-shed roof is necessary for houses of any size; a single-shed roof is still to be seen in smaller houses which are clearly older, but they are not often constructed today. The back corral still serves the purpose of keeping the livestock at home at night. The patio is still the center of the woman's activities whether there is a front yard or not. One practical innovation has been the introduction of a chimney in some of the houses. Where this has been done, it has permitted the inclusion of the kitchen in one of the main buildings; since the kitchen is no longer filled with smoke, it does not have to be in a separate building.

The materials used in the process of living at home are relatively simple except as more industrial products enter the scene. The kitchen presents the most complex internal arrangement of any of the rooms. There is always a *bicharra*, or clay stove, which may consist simply of two raised arms of dried mud between which a fire is built and on which is placed the cooking bowl, or it may be a more complex affair, a foot and a half high with a short chimney, a special compartment for drying matches and another for drying kindling. The clay stove is evidently of early origin in this region, but since it must frequently be rebuilt, sometimes as often as once a year, none of any antiquity was found. Since it is built relatively often, it permits the builder a certain amount of freedom of design. Cooking is almost always done on top of the stove; the only oven in town is owned by the baker. There is some regional variation in Peru with respect to ovens; in the Huánuco area they are very common but are rare in the Jauja Valley.

Almost every kitchen includes a huge pile of cow dung and kindling wood stacked in one or two corners, being dried for fuel. They are usually stacked in layers, with a layer of dung alternating with a layer of wood until the pile reaches the ceiling. Also to be found everywhere is the *batán*, the grinding stone, which is ordinarily set firmly on a pile of smaller stones and fixed with a mud mortar. While it seems reasonable to assume that the *batán* is an old device, dating from preconquest days, the archeological grinding stones found in the hills back of Muquiyauyo are somewhat different. The modern *batán* is a large flat boulder; the *manisuela*, or hand stone, is rather like an American football in size and shape and is rocked over the *batán* instead of being either rolled or scraped. The archeological stones, which are much smaller, are rounded, water-worn boulders with a concave depression from the grinding. It would have been very difficult to use the archeological stones as the modern *batáns* are used; the concave surface in the older stones indicates that they have been worn by scraping.

In addition to the modern *batán*, most homes have a small stone mortar with a hand stone about the size of a man's fist. The small mortar is used to grind salt, chili, and other things in small quantities. I found no evidence of small mortars in the archeological remains. John Gillin describes the *batán* as being used at present in the coastal town of Moche, but he does not mention the mortar.[1]

Although every home still has the *batán,* a great deal of the grain is now ground by the community-owned electric mill near the plaza. The typical Muquiyauyo kitchen rings with the squeaks of guinea pigs housed in the adobe bench *(poyo* or *cuyero)* which runs along one or more walls. Each kitchen also has a small table, but it is mainly a surface for depositing things since most of the work is done on the floor. Pots and pans are hung from nails or pegs stuck in the adobe walls, or they are set in shelves composed of old wooden cartons fastened to the wall. The insides of the kitchens are usually black with soot, and few have any escape for smoke except the cracks between the roof tiles.

The main room of the house is called the *sala,* or living room, but may in fact be used for almost anything. The other rooms, the kitchen excepted, are usually referred to simply as *cuartos* or *dormitorios.* Again, their actual use may vary from sleeping to grain storage. Beds are fairly common in Muquiyauyo; the usual bed is single width and short, and as there may be only one for the entire family many family members must sleep on the floor. The equipment of the *sala* usually includes one or more tables, depending upon how much work the man does indoors, a few chairs, and a single light globe hanging from the ceiling. The *salas* of the more wealthy families and the mestizos are arranged in the typical Spanish-American pattern of a small table in the center with four or more chairs in a circle around it. The floor is earth, wood, or in a few cases cement. Wall decorations consist mainly of large prints, charts (of anatomy, arboriculture, and so forth), maps, pictures made by the children in school, and a surprising number of Japanese bamboo panels. These last are popular because the splints of bamboo run horizontally and family photographs are held between the slits. Large colored calendars, advertisement posters of whisky or laxatives, and cheap colored reproductions of paintings are found in most houses. Every *sala* has a religious picture of Christ, the Virgin, or more rarely one of the saints. This is called the *adoratorio;* the picture may be surrounded by imitation or real flowers, together with half-burned candles. So far as I could determine, the *adoratorio* was not used with any great frequency or intensity.

Most houses have a special room *(depósito)* for storing household goods or straw and grains. The storage of foodstuffs in the home varies, and most of the formal methods employed are of some antiquity. Liquids, except those which come in glass containers, are kept in large pottery jars which are bought at the local fair or in Jauja or Huancayo. Ears of corn are frequently tied together in bunches and hung over the rafters in any one of the rooms. Loose grains are usually kept within a fencelike *troja* or *pilhua*. The *troja* consists of a long mat of bundles of straw tied together as a flexible wall. Rolled up when not in use, it can be unrolled to any desired size and provides a circular bin to accommodate the amount of grain to be stored. The *troja* stands directly on the floor of a room or the porch. When full, it looks like a squat, open silo about three feet high and from two to six feet in diameter.

During the day the home is the setting for a multitude of activities. Food is prepared and eaten, clothes are washed and mended, minor garden crops are tended, repairs are made on the house, and visits for gossip are made among the women. From early morning a pot is on the stove. At least one meal in the day, either the midday meal *(almuerzo)* or the evening meal *(comida)* will have as its main dish a *caldo* or *sancochado*. These are made up of similar ingredients and both are prepared by boiling. The *caldo*, however, is basically a soup in which the various vegetables, spices, herbs, seasoning, and meat are boiled. *Sancochado* is more like a stew and can be served on a plate. Sweet potatoes, white potatoes, yuca, rice, oregano, lard, cabbage, some kind of meat, and salt all may find their way into *sancochado*. *Caldo* may be made up of some combination of cabbage, rice, yuca, carrots, noodles, peas, toasted corn, garlic, hot peppers, onions, parsley, pork or mutton, oregano, coriander, and water and salt. A *sancochado* or *caldo* seldom contains all these ingredients, however.

Breakfast in the Muquiyauyo home usually consists of coffee with hot milk, hot chocolate, or a tea of the herb *toronjil*, and some buns. Sometimes a mush of barley or toasted corn and sugar may be included. Besides a *caldo* or *sancochado* for lunch there may be *mote* (stewed corn) or boiled cabbage, boiled or toasted broad beans, and on special occasions a dish of guinea pig or rabbit cooked with rice, small white potatoes, lard, and hot peppers. Between the midday and evening meal, a *lonche*, or snack of coffee and bread, is customary. The evening meal, similar to lunch, may have a *caldo* or *sancochado*, or possibly a pottage of broad beans seasoned with onions, hot peppers, and salt. Hot boiled milk with sugar, bread, boiled rice, or some sort of stewed fruit may complete the meal.

By no means everyone in Muquiyauyo eats this well, nor is the diet so limited. The meals described are suggestive of some which may be regular in a family of middle economic status. The preparation of food is carried on in the smoke-darkened kitchen lit by candles, kerosene lamps, or occasionally electric light at night.

Except in the houses where a special room is set aside for a dining room, and frequently even there, the men come to the kitchen and sit around a table or on the *poyo* along the wall to eat their meals. The dining room, in those few houses that have one, is usually reserved for special occasions except in the wealthier mestizo homes. If a special meal is to be served, as during a fiesta, there are usually too many guests to sit around a single table; they are scattered around the *sala* and patio with the more fortunate being allowed a place at one of the tables.

A special preparation of food called the *pachamanca* is held at green corn time. The younger men and women especially sponsor *pachamancas,* in much the same way North Americans go on picnics. Preparation involves digging a pit about two and a half feet wide, setting a fire in it, and then building a cone of stones over it. After this has been burning all afternoon, some of the stones are knocked to one side and others are permitted to fall into the pit. In the meantime, the food has been prepared. Green corn has been finely ground, seasoned and wrapped in corn husks, a sheep slaughtered and the meat cut in chunks; guinea pigs have been cleaned and spread, quantities of broad beans and potatoes made ready, and herbs collected to add flavor to the entire mass. After the stones have been put to one side, the pit is lined with layers of greens, and then layer after layer of food, separated by leaves and herbs and the hot stones, are laid until there is a great mound. When the last heavy layer of leaves is placed over the top of the mound, earth is shoveled over the whole until it is airtight. Whenever steam is seen leaking out, more earth is quickly heaped on the spot. The *pachamanca* is left in this form for two or three hours, until it is fairly dark. It is then uncovered and the food is eaten with beer, soda pop, and sometimes *chicha.*

Women do the washing in the main canals. Here they sit before the flat rocks and scrub the dirty clothes. The main implement used is the *tabliadora,* a wooden mallet with a round or square head flattened on two sides. With this the clothes are beaten against the rock until either the dirt or the threads come out. Sometimes washing is done at home, with water taken from one of the street canals and poured into a stone *mortero* fashioned out of crude rock.

When the woman stays home, she may place her toddling child in a wooden box to keep him out of mischief while she goes about her work. If she is tending the store she may keep him swung on her back in the carrying blanket tied across the chest and over one shoulder. The mornings are generally a time when women visit one another on some pretext. Gossip is shared as one works in

the kitchen or sews and the others sit chatting. Visiting between
homes is most common among relatives.

During the day the school-age children are usually at school so
the mother is responsible for only the younger ones. One of the
children is frequently sent to the fields with the husband's midday
meal if he is some distance away. If there is nothing else of pressing importance to do in the afternoon, the wife goes to the fields,
taking the animals with her.

On Wednesdays and Sundays the fair takes place in nearby Jauja,
and buses line up on the plaza to carry people from Muquiyauyo.
There are two or three busloads of people, and sometimes more,
which leave between seven and nine in the morning. There is often
important business to be taken care of in Jauja. Perhaps something
must be purchased that is not available in Muquiyauyo, a lawyer
must be seen about some matter of property, a doctor visited, or
arrangements made for a baptism. Some women buy vegetables and
eggs in the town and take them to Jauja for sale at the market. The
trip to Jauja is looked upon as a pleasant outing. Many people walk
there with their products on their shoulders or follow a donkey
packed with something for sale. Much more rarely, because of
the distance and expense involved, a trip is made to the Sunday
market in Huancayo. If odd items need to be purchased on other
days, the women go to a local store or send one of the children
for a little salt, sugar, a few eggs, cornstarch, or whatever it
may be. Vegetables are bought from one of the vendors sitting in
the local market at the plaza. Early in the morning meat vendors
from the mountain towns set up a stand or two in the plaza and the
women come down to buy. The meat is usually gone by nine or ten
o'clock in the morning.

Muquiyauyo women are quite competent in endeavors other than
field and domestic work. In the 1940 census there were almost 130
women resident in Muquiyauyo for every hundred men, and a considerable portion of the excess were widows and unmarried women
who had to look after their own needs. They knew how to repair
roofs, patch walls, chop kindling wood, and carry on most of the
daily tasks that would be done by a man were he present.

In the evenings the men return from their work, fix odd things
about the house, and eat. If it is a time of heavy field work, such
as the harvest, they may eat as late as eight or nine o'clock, but
usually the evening meal is closer to seven. The younger men may
wander around to see their friends after dinner, while the head of
the family goes out on some business of the *cuartel*, the community
or the district, or on a personal errand to borrow some money or

hire a laborer to help him in his fields. Unless there is a fiesta or meeting of some kind, the family is usually in bed by ten.

11

CLOTHING AND COSTUME

A VISITOR to Jauja or elsewhere in the central highlands is often struck with the distinctive costume of the women. The men wear overalls or suits, but the women have retained an individuality in clothing that identifies them anywhere in Peru. Woman's dress in the Jauja Valley falls into one of four classes: the *cotón*, the *centro*, modern western, and mixed. The *cotón* is the oldest and at present is still found at the southern end of the valley. It was last used in Muquiyauyo sometime in the first or second decade of the present century. The *centro*, by far the most common costume to be seen today in the valley, first made its appearance sometime in the latter part of the nineteenth century; by the early 1900's it had replaced the *cotón* in Muquiyauyo. No local informant seems to know the origin, either in locale or form, of the *centro*. Modern western dress was used by some mestizos at least by 1895; it is likely that the mestizos have always followed the styles of the national capital to some degree. Mixed dress usually involves a factory-made cotton dress with underclothing and blankets the same as those used with the *centro*. It may, however, include any combination of elements of the *centro* and the western. If there are any elements of the *cotón* left in the daily dress of the Muquiyauyina, they have so blended into the newer forms that they are no longer distinctive.

The *cotón* remains for the Muquiyauyinos a symbol of Inca dress and is used today in a highly elaborated form as the *chupaquinas'* costume in the Tunantes dance groups. The *cotón*, as it appears in the southern part of the valley today and as it is preserved in the fiesta dances in Muquiyauyo, consists of a single full-length, straight, black wool dress with short sleeves; Muquiyauyinos like to compare it to the dress of a priest. Sometimes extra knitted sleeves, *mangas*, are worn from just below the shoulder to

the wrist. Around the waist is a woven belt, the *huachaca,* and on
the fiesta dress colored handkerchiefs are hung from the belt. Over
the shoulders is pinned the small rectangular blanket, the *cata* or
manta. On the old *cotón* it is unlikely that decorations were carried
so far, but on the modern fiesta costumes, dance groups have elaborated on the basic garment in various ways. The Pastores dance
group of the Christmas fiesta use a large rectangular piece of cloth,
the *anaka,* which is the same color and design as the *manta* and
hangs from the left side of the waist. The women of the Huaylijía
Christmas dance group use practically the same costume, but
wear the *anaka* on the right side. These variations, the hand em-
broidery on the *mantas* and *anakas* and the addition of a broad
band of colored cloth around the base of the *cotón* on the dress of
the Pastores and Huaylijía, represent forty to fifty years of elaboration.

The *centro* represents a marked change from the *cotón.* The
earlier *centro* costume consisted of a flaring black wool skirt, one
to three plain, colored wool underskirts, and a white cotton blouse.
The skirt was tied at the waist. The blouse has varied somewhat
during the years. The earliest, last worn in Muquiyauyo about 1905,
was the *cotilla,* a wide piece of cloth wrapped around the chest with
two straight shoulder straps. A checkerboard design of red, yellow,
and green against white is said to have been the standard design.
Around the waist was wrapped a red belt, eight inches wide, called
the *cintura* or *cinturon.* Later blouse forms have changed radically.
The *monillo,* and later still the *blusa* (the main difference being that
the former opened in the back and the latter on the side), consisted
of a full blouse with wide sleeves tight at the wrists. These are
made today of two layers of cloth, a white underlayer and an outer
layer with printed or embroidered designs. The *monillo* and the
blusa both come to the waist, leaving very little to tuck into the
skirt. The blouse is thus easily lifted for nursing. Over the shoulders the *manta,* also called the *lliclla,* a small square blanket, is
worn. For greater warmth more and larger blankets may be thrown
over the shoulders as well.

The hats used today represent a change from those still used with
the *cotón* dress in the southern end of the valley. Formerly all
women's hats were of light-colored wool with a round crown and
wide brim. In recent years the introduction of a white, wide-
brimmed panama-type hat into the northern part of the valley has
taken place, and for everyday use only the poorer people continue to
wear the old type. In the Muquiyauyo area both styles have a black
band. In the south, where the wool hat still continues as a standard

part of the costume, it may be black, brown, gray, or white, and
the cloth band is usually of the same color as the hat. The old-style
hat is known to the hatmakers of Caja as the *huancayino* (as it is
worn around Huancayo) while the newer style is the *jaujino* (worn
around Jauja).

Other changes have been gradually made in *centro* dress. Most
outstanding has been the introduction of various colored skirts.
None of these has the bright oranges, yellows, or greens of the
underskirts; they are rather a dark green, brown, or blue, or
more rarely a light violet, gray-blue, or green. The blankets worn
on the shoulder have become varied in materials and colors used.
These blankets now have a solid-color border, two to four inches
wide, of a different material from the blanket itself, usually cotton
or satin. Recently satin has been introduced into the center square
of the blanket, and for best wear some have velvet. Only old blankets are used for daily wear; the newer ones are reserved for best.
A further variation on the skirt has been the addition of decorative ribbons. On the older skirts, which were always black, it was
usual to have a few ribbons of the same color, or folds in the skirt
itself, running horizontally around the skirt below the knees. These
ribbons or folds appeared as one set or in sets of three; there are
now various combinations of ribbons and sets of different numbers.

While working in the fields women, especially the younger ones,
often omit the outer skirt and wear simply one of the colored underskirts. Among the younger women there is also a tendency to wear
the everyday *centros* slightly shorter; the older women wear them
to the ground, but now one frequently sees hems four to ten inches
off the ground. This, with the many underskirts, gives the dress
the appearance of a ballet skirt. For best, some of the young mestizo women now omit the underskirts and wear a single cotton slip;
it is fashionable for the lace border of this slip to hang an inch or
two below the bottom of the skirt.

Whether shoes and stockings are used varies with the individual.
Long cotton stockings are sometimes worn, but they are not very
common. When going to Jauja almost everyone wears shoes, but
around the town and in the fields, especially among the Indians and
the poorer people, it is common to go barefoot.

An invariable part of the woman's apparel is the carrying blanket.
This is a locally woven product, of a hard weave, with colored
stripes. Loaded with materials or a child, it is tied across the
shoulders and thrown across the back.

Modern western dress in Muquiyauyo is used mostly by some of
the school teachers and a very few of the mestizo women. In gen-

eral both mestizos and Indians prefer the *centro* or mixed dress, since these provide greater warmth. Many mestizos, however, have western dresses for use on trips to Huancayo or Lima. The changes taking place in the women's clothing seem to be following two trends. On the one hand there is a trend for the *centro* itself to change; the skirt is getting shorter and the numerous underskirts may be omitted. On the other hand, there is a tendency toward using mixed dress. The origin of the *centro* also presents an interesting problem. It is my guess, because of the approximate time of its appearance, that it developed as an imitation of the urban dress of the second half of the last century. In appearance, the full skirt, not hooped but padded with heavy underskirts, is reminiscent of that era. The blouses (the *monillo* and *blusa*) are similar to blouses which may be seen in fashion folders of the United States of that period.

The contemporary man's clothing in Muquiyauyo adheres more strictly to a single style. The most significant change occurred in the last century when most of the Indians who were still using their old dress, called the *cordillate,* finally abandoned it; with the disappearance of the *cordillate* was lost one of the more important culture traits which formerly served to distinguish the Indian from the mestizo.

Although many Indians had already dropped the Indian dress by 1890, it was still symbolic of caste status. The *cordillate* of that time consisted of a pair of wide short trousers, called the *calzón,* a long-sleeved shirt open down the front, called the *bayeta,* and a vest, the *chaleco.* The costumes used by the masked *cochinero* dancers of the Christmas fiesta are composed of an elaborate version of the old *cordillate.* In the old *cordillate* the vest and broad short trousers were always of black wool and the shirt of a lighter grade, light-colored wool. As in the case of the *cotón,* the knitted sleeves, *mangas,* were worn in cold weather. The man's hat, the *berrete,* was the classical Peruvian Indian knitted cap with a pointed top and ear flaps. The *berrete* is still frequently seen in Muquiyauyo, but today it is worn only in cold weather under a modern felt hat. Footwear consisted of a leather strip which covered the bottom of the foot and tied across the top with leather straps, the equivalent of a soft sandal. Wool socks reaching to just below the knees were also worn at times.

This costume is said to have entirely disappeared from everyday wear sometime in the first decade of the present century. One informant, born in 1878, claims that when he was a small child practically all the Indian men wore the *cordillate.* The mestizos used long trousers, but they also used *bayetas* like those of the Indians. Like the women, the men had regular suits of the period to wear in Lima or visiting elsewhere.

Today, and presumably since the disappearance of the *cordillate*, the man's attire has consisted of styles current in Lima or the mining centers. For best, all men who can afford it have a suit of wool; some wear suits daily. Old and ragged suits comprise a good percentage of everyday about-town and work clothes. Some have overalls for working in the fields. Sweaters are very common and are usually very heavy. Under his overalls, a man may have two pairs of trousers, a shirt, and two sweaters, as well as the home-spun underwear. Every man has a woven woolen poncho for use at night, in rain, and when the weather turns particularly cold.

The wardrobe of a typical, medium-well-to-do young man today consists of the following: one or two good suits, with a few colored shirts and neckties; one or two good pairs of shoes purchased in Jauja, Huancayo, or Lima, and an equal number of old ones used for field and local wear; an old suit, or pieces thereof, used for loitering and working in town; a pair of coveralls or overalls and some old shirts for field work; sweaters, mostly worn, for various occasions; a poncho for foul weather, a felt hat, and home-spun underclothing.

The changes in clothing types in Muquiyauyo are of particular interest with respect to their meaning in distinguishing the classes. The clothing which used to help distinguish Indian men from mestizos disappeared with the changes just described; it is hard to know how long the transition lasted, but from all reports, it was short, perhaps not more than two or three decades. Today in the same way that modern urban dress serves to clothe men of both classes, the *centro* evidently serves for both mestizo and Indian women. Since it has been adopted by both classes, it does not seem likely that the *centro* will disappear rapidly, as did the men's *cordillate*. If anything serves to put an end to the use of the *centro*, it will very likely be the fact that *centro* elements cost a good deal more than the cheap cotton dresses produced by factories. The only indication at present that the *centro* may be on the way out is the fact that mixed dress is worn. It also seems likely that if and when the *centro* does disappear for daily wear, it will stay on as a part of the fiesta dance costumes, as have the *cotón* and *cordillate*.

12

THE CYCLE OF LIFE

CHILDHOOD in Muquiyauyo is a happy time. In early infancy the child is carried on his mother's back and rocked gently to keep him contented, nursed at the breast whenever he is fretful, and fondled and admired by friends of the parents. Baptism, the child's formal introduction into the world of men and spirits, usually takes place between three months and two years after the child's birth. The baptism of a baby girl that I attended in the capacity of godfather was held in the afternoon. After arriving early in order to register, the father, the mother with the child, and the two godfathers went to the baptismal font in the church. The priest was hurrying through the ceremonies for eleven children, he wanted to leave before he had finished with the last three and it required some persuasion to keep him on for the few minutes necessary to get the little girl baptized.

While waiting in the church for the baptism to take place, the child began to fret. The mother immediately began to nurse her and succeeded in quieting her. When it came time for me to hold my godchild for the rite, the little girl made it perfectly clear that she was still hungry. The mother tried to continue nursing the child while I held her, but this turned out to be a highly unsatisfactory arrangement, and so the nursing was stopped. As soon as the baptism was over the mother quickly took her baby and resumed the nursing, continuing during the celebration staged at the home of the other godfather.

The standard method of quieting an infant is to give it the breast. If the mother is too occupied with other affairs, she will put the child on her back and swing it back and forth until she can spare a moment for nursing. Usually, however, she will sit with her knees up, and, resting the baby against her legs, nurse it until it is satisfied. Everyone shows affection for children, and older brothers and sisters make great efforts to keep the smaller children amused. There is considerable fondling of children even up to eleven and twelve years of age. Correction for misbehavior usually takes the form of quick verbal outbursts at the child and an occasional slap; but rancor is not harbored. Children tend to be a little shy in the presence of a stranger, but once he makes their acquaintance they approach him with considerable confidence and forwardness. They are early taught to show respect for their elders and even though they frequently give the impression of self-sufficiency, they are quick to show affection and dependence.

The term *criatura* is used for any child until it reaches the toddling stage. From then until the child begins to manifest the secondary sexual characteristics, it is referred to as *niño* or *niña*, and later in this period the terms *muchacho* and *muchacha* are common. When boys first begin to show signs of growing a beard and girls' breasts begin to develop, they enter the stage in which they are referred to as *jóvenes*. The term *joven* is applied to anyone approaching the adult status and frequently hangs on long after a man is married.

School is attended by almost all the children. The Muquiyauyinos are proud of their school system and both the community and district show considerable interest in it. Under the present system of instruction the boys are taught various techniques of agriculture as well as the more classical subjects, and the girls occasionally take special classes in sewing and dressmaking. The school years, together with the established adult habit patterns, serve also to provide the Muquiyauyino with a skill in oratory and nationalistic eloquence that characterizes periods of drunkenness and national celebrations. Plays about dramatic periods of Peruvian history, and stories pointing out the differences between the coastal, highland, and *montaña* peoples, are among the most popular put on by school children during the fiestas.

Both boys and girls are subject to military drill while in school. They are taught to march and stand at attention and, as in many Latin American countries, they are encouraged to wear uniforms. During communal and national events the children are marched out by grade and execute simple formations for the onlooking parents and visitors.

Childhood is the time when the young Muquiyauyino learns the techniques of agriculture and animal care through participating with his parents in the work. When not in school the older children are in the fields, either with their parents or by themselves doing cultivating, setting an irrigation canal to water a field, or standing guard over the livestock. By the time a Muquiyauyino has reached the stage of being a *joven*, he knows a good deal about the tradition- al ways of taking care of a field. In this way, the many widows and unmarried women who have sons get much help from their children.

Learning the ways of Muquiyauyo life from parents and relatives is, of course, not limited to the agricultural work in the town. When the father goes off for his annual work to the mines, he may take the entire family with him. The young Muquiyauyino thus becomes accustomed to the ways of mining towns, goes to school there, be- comes accustomed to shifts in teachers, and begins to look upon mining as a form of work as traditional and acceptable as agricul- ture. These periodic spells in mining centers also expose the Mu- quiyauyino to Peruvians from other highland areas, to coastal peo- ple with their different customs, and to the foreigners working at the mines. The child is consequently early aware of different ways of life, alternative ways of earning a living, and travel.

Sometime between the age of eight and ten years, each Catholic child is confirmed. This ceremony is held in the church, and each child must have a godfather and a godmother. The godparents on this occasion are not as important as the baptismal godparents. Some of the school teachers have taken over whole confirmation classes as their *ahijados,* or godchildren.

During early childhood, children of both sexes play together, but as they come of school age and are separated into different schools on the basis of sex, the play groups tend to be composed of one sex only. During adolescence, when they become *jóvenes*, the young men and women are drawn together again. Although idle hours and close friendships continue to be limited to one sex, court- ing and formalized clubs bring about more association between the sexes.

The serenade is one of the most popular forms of evening recre- ation for the *jóvenes*. If they are lucky, the young men will be able to get together a group who play guitars, mandolins, violins, and occasionally even a clarinet. A serenade is never started before 10:30 or 11:00 at night, for it is the custom to wait until the fami- lies are asleep. The village authorities frown on what is considered a public disturbance and the community night watch frequently shuts serenaders up in jail. If the authorities know who did the serenad- ing and fail to catch them in the act, they have been known to go to the school the next day and take them off to the *calabozo* until the promises of the parents, and perhaps the payment of a fine, bring their release.

A girl's birthday is a common occasion for a serenade. The boys usually arrive at the girl's house close to midnight and sing a few songs to her. If the girl and her parents are well disposed, the boys are invited in, drinks of vermouth, wine, or beer are served, and the party continues until the early hours of the morning. If there is no special occasion for the serenade, the boys usually limit themselves to three songs outside the house of the girl and then move on to some other house. There are special songs for birthdays, as well as a variety of waltzes, boleros, tangos, *paso dobles*, and the more traditional highland music of the *huayno* and *yaravís*. Some of the young men make up their own songs, full of sentimental reflections on mothers, beautiful women, and dying of love. Most of the songs contain many stanzas so that a serenade of three songs may last over an hour.

Courting begins in the middle teens, but the young men are frequently bashful about initiating sexual intercourse. Most cases of illegitimate children are the result of temporary alliances between women and older men rather than among the younger people. Since there are no scientific contraceptives known in Muquiyauyo, it is not surprising that there is a considerable lore in abortifacients. For a pregnancy recognized within the first month or two, there are various herbal drinks which are said to be effective in causing abortion. The most popular is the *yerba buena*, in water with *chancaca* or crude sugar. Mechanical abortions are evidently common also; one such method reported is for a girl in the second or third month of pregnancy to stand on a high wall and jump with her legs spread apart. If the pregnancy goes much beyond the third month, the girl may resort to one of the older townswomen who will extract the embryo with her hands. A man in town who learned various medical techniques during many years as an assistant in one of the mining clinics has done abortions with forceps. Also, some girls have gone to Jauja to have the extraction done.

Marriage is generally late. Men usually marry in their late, and women in their early, twenties. This is due in part to the fact that men frequently must go off to the mines while still in their teens to work; but even among those who remain in town, marriage is not customarily considered during the teens. It is not uncommon, however, for a couple to begin to live together some years before the actual marriage.

According to one informant, there used to be a certain amount of barrio endogamy. This evidently was on the decline at least by the beginning of the present century, for no such tendency is recognized today. Ideally it was said to be the custom not to marry a person who is closer than second or third cousin; in practice, this

is often not observed. Marriage and intercourse are generally prohibited between relatives of the first degree. One case came to my
notice of a young man and his half-sister who had a child. There
was some surprise that such a thing had occurred, but no one
seemed to feel very strongly on the matter.

It is said that some years ago parents still had quite a bit to say
in the choice of a marriage partner, and there was a general restriction to marrying within one's own caste. Today the parents
evidently do not have much to say about it, but among the older
mestizo families there is considerable feeling against marriage
with a person considered Indian.

Marriage is a civil matter by law, but most of the Catholic families follow the civil marriage with a church wedding. The civil
marriage is held in the district council house. A request must be
posted fifteen days ahead of time and a notice posted outside the
council house a week before the actual ceremony. This follows the
Catholic custom of the posting of the banns, which permits anyone
who may have objections to the marriage to bring them forward.
At a fixed time, the legal papers are completed in front of two
witnesses, one of whom also serves as best man at the ceremony.
The civil ceremony itself lasts about fifteen minutes and only a
few relatives attend it. Civil marriages are usually held in the
morning. If a couple is well known in town, the mayor may put
aside the necessity of the eight-day notice and marry them the day
after they put in the request.

Posting a notice a week ahead of time is also required for religious ceremonies. In a family affair, before the wedding, rings
may be exchanged between the couples and the time of the wedding
decided upon. The wedding ring is given to the priest with a few
silver pieces and he then gives the ring to the bride during the
ceremony. Most of the expenses of the wedding, whether civil or
religious, fall on the godfathers. Two godfathers are chosen for
the ceremony, and it is their responsibility to give the party following the wedding. A *padrino* who does not do well by the couple
is called an *alalaopadrino,* a "very cold godfather." Years ago,
it is said, the custom was to have two separate orchestras for
the wedding, one for the groom and one for the bride. The two
orchestras would meet in the plaza immediately after the ceremony and follow the couple and guests to the house of one of the
godfathers. Today only one orchestra is used.

There are a number of customs which are said to be observed
still among some of the townspeople. One of these, the *palomay,*
involves a postceremony supper in the evening at the bride's house;

after the supper, the godfather shows the couple to the bedroom and locks them in. The party then continues the better part of the night, sometimes into the morning when the godfather returns to the room and unlocks the door. Another old custom is the *palpacuy*. All the relatives bring gifts of food, money, or animals for the newly-weds. The presentation takes place right after the supper, preceding the *palomay*, and the guests dance around as they offer their gifts to the couple.

Most of the couples living together in Muquiyauyo are married, but there are some who live in common-law marriage; they are referred to as *convivientes*. For the province of Jauja as a whole according to the census of 1940, 15 per cent of the men living with women are *convivientes*, and a little over 16 per cent of the women living with men are in this class. Some informants claimed that there were no cases of common-law marriage in Muquiyauyo, but I encountered a few in my surveys.

The rate of illegitimacy is quite high. The excess number of women in town tends to encourage extramarital relations. It is not uncommon for a woman in her thirties who has no husband to have one or two children, and a widow may have children after her husband's death. The scarcity of men makes it unlikely that a widow will remarry. In the district birth records, between 20 and 30 per cent of the registered births are illegitimate. No condemnation is attached to an illegitimate child; if the father chooses to recognize the child, and if the mother permits it, the child will take the father's surname; otherwise he takes his mother's name. Because of the Spanish custom of retaining the mother's surname after the father's, considerable confusion frequently arises as to which name a child may have. If the father does not immediately recognize the child, his name may be Juan García Gómez, with the mother's name of García coming first. Later, if the father recognizes the child, the name changes in practice to Juan Gómez García. There is seldom any attempt to change a name in the birth records once it is entered.

From 1905, the date of the earliest birth records available in the town, until 1930, the percentage of illegitimate births recorded annually was slightly above 20 per cent. Since 1930, there has been a tendency for this figure to rise. In 1940 it reached 35 per cent and then declined slightly. One explanation for this increase is that in the last two decades the cost of living has risen and fathers are now more reluctant to take on the financial responsibility of their illegitimate children. The increase in the cost of living was also given as an explanation for the recent decrease in the use of old marriage ceremonies; now they cost more and people are more reluctant to maintain them. While there is no social pressure on a man to recognize an illegitimate child, the Peruvian law now states that an illegitimate child has equal rights of inheritance with a legitimate child. For this reason, there have been recent cases of women demanding that the fathers give recognition to their children so that the children will later have the right of inheritance.

A number of informants felt that there had been an increasing amount of adultery in recent years. Whether they were referring to extramarital relations between married or unmarried people was not clear. Some years ago, according to one informant, a custom called the *otrapachalun* was stopped. When someone saw a man or woman going into another's house and the visit was thought to be adulterous, some of the townspeople would get together and leave a trail of cinders between the doors of the two houses. This was supposed to scare the participants into discontinuing the relationship. Today adultery seems to be a matter of importance to the members of the families involved, but it is seldom dealt with by community sanctions.

Descent in Muquiyauyo is bilateral; that is, a person recognizes equally his relationships with members of both his mother's and his father's family. Two factors tend to confuse the actual form that a residential group takes, however. One is the extensive amount of movement of men, and sometimes parts of families, to the mines for work. The other is the relatively high incidence of illegitimacy. When a father may be completely absent from the family unit, and when the woman may be bringing up two of her own children with different fathers, together with nephews or nieces, the complexity of family relationships becomes great. Most families, however, are composed of a man, a woman, the children of their union and possibly children that either, but more commonly the wife, has had by other unions; there may also be one of their widowed parents living with them. After marriage it is customary for the couple to move into a home of their own. If they have none to move to and must wait for one to be built, they may stay with either family.

At baptism and marriage godparents play an important role in a child's life. As in many other Latin American towns the *com-padrazgo*, or cogodparenthood relationship between men, is very important. The father and godfather of a child will refer to each other as *compadre*, and the godfather accepts the responsibility of helping the child should its own parents die. The *compadre* relationship is closely tied in with the class system in Muquiyauyo. It is very common for a person who is poor or of the Indian class to look for a mestizo or more wealthy person to be godfather of his child. In this way, he feels that the child may not only be assured of some help should he need it, but the father himself, in case of need, may ask his *compadre* for help.

Both before and after marriage a great many of the young men and women of Muquiyauyo join one of the four sports clubs which are active in the town. The boys in these clubs play basketball and soccer (called *basquet* and *futbol)* while the girls play volleyball *(volibol)*. There are no team schedules arranged, but when one club wants to play another a highly formal note is sent inviting the other group to a day of sports, perhaps followed by a social dance in the evening. The most active members of these groups are the unmarried people, but the married men usually keep active for some years and continue to remain on the membership rolls even if they leave the town. The membership of different families in the clubs reflects a tendency to join both within one's barrio and within one's class.

BARRIO

Club	Lower		Upper		Chaupibarrio		No Barrio	
	No. of Families with Members	Per Cent	No. of Families with Members	Per Cent	No. of Families with Members	Per Cent	No. of Families with Members	Per Cent
Club Minerva	15	27.3	34	61.8	5	9.1	1	1.8
Club Union	15	30.5	25	51.0	6	12.5	3	6.0
Club Aurora	51	78.5	3	4.5	6	6.2	7	10.8
Club "ABC"	13	33.3	17	43.6	9	23.1	-	--

The Minerva and Union clubs have a majority of members from the upper barrio and less than a third from the lower. The Aurora Club has over three-quarters of its members from the lower barrio and not even 5 per cent from the upper. The "ABC" Club has a fairly even distribution of members in the two barrios. Over 90 per cent of the members of the Union and Aurora clubs have members from families which were judged to be of the Indian class or upon which the judges could not decide. Both the Minerva and "ABC" clubs have a more even distribution, but only the "ABC" appears to be distinctly a mestizo affair.

The "ABC," or Avalanche Basket Club, is perhaps most active of the four. In addition to the local members, it has an associate club of Muquiyauyino members in Lima. Whenever a member goes to Lima he looks up the other associates and attends the meetings there. On one occasion I was asked to attend a Lima meeting to show movies which I had taken of Muquiyauyo. Some fifty people attended the showing, some of whom I had previously met in Muquiyauyo, but the great majority of whom were strangers to me. There are fifty-five "ABC" club members in Lima; ten are university students of whom most are in the school of medicine. The others are working in the capital or in its suburbs.

CLASS MEMBERSHIP (from sample)

	Indian		Undecided		Mestizo	
Club	No. of Families with Members	Per Cent	No. of Families with Members	Per Cent	No. of Families with Members	Per Cent
Club Minerva	18	34.0	20	37.7	15	28.3
Club Union	17	41.5	21	51.7	3	7.3
Club Aurora	28	66.7	10	23.6	4	9.5
Club "ABC"	7	25.9	18	29.6	12	44.5

Besides these sports clubs there is another Muquiyauyo group, made up of students and former students of the Colegio San José, a high school in Jauja. This group is predominantly mestizo, but includes as well some members of wealthier Indian families. The sports clubs not only play with one another on days set for games, but also set games during the fiestas and invite teams from neighboring towns to come and play. The principal players of each often march with the school children in local celebrations of national holidays.

In times of illness the townspeople tend to go to doctors or local people who have worked in the mining hospitals and clinics, but there is also a considerable use of local *curanderos,* or curers. Some Muquiyauyinos are familiar with certain phases of contemporary medicine; some have studied medicine and practice it in some of the larger highland towns and on the coast. Several young people from Muquiyauyo are now studying medicine at the University in Lima. Most of these professionals are mestizos or come from the wealthier and more cosmopolitan people of the Indian class. There is no professional doctor practicing in Muquiyauyo, however, and those who wish to visit a physician must go to Jauja. In Muquiyauyo are several men who have spent some years as orderlies or assistants in the clinics and hospitals at the mining centers. These men have picked up a considerable body of practical knowledge concerning the treatment of minor troubles, and evidently some of them are fairly acute diagnosticians for illnesses that they have seen frequently in the hospitals. One of them, referred to locally as Doctor Fulano even though he has no degree, is said to have done a great deal of reading during his years of work in the clinics. His ability is respected locally and his practice in Muquiyauyo has been sufficiently profitable to enable him to build a clinic.

There are some illnesses which neither the doctors nor the skilled curers can handle, however, and which must be treated in more traditional ways. One such way is witchcraft. There are a few old men and women in town who are thought to be witches and who are known to be working witchcraft. All the cases of witchcraft that were recounted to me had to do with black magic and means of counteracting it. Witchcraft was usually said to be learned from another witch, but some claimed that it could also be learned from books which were sold by traveling vendors. Most cases of witchcraft involve physical troubles such as loss of eyesight or paralysis. If a child is born with a harelip, a clubfoot, or a twisted hand, it is the work of a witch. If a person has an unaccountable series of pains or illnesses that are difficult to diagnose, it may be attributed to witchcraft. People try to be very careful about not offending witches, since it is impossible to predict and very difficult to cure the troubles they can cause.

All the techniques used in witchcraft that were described to me involved the use of frogs or toads. One witch, a mestizo woman, supposedly blinded a number of people by wrapping a bullfrog in ribbons of different colors. She then chewed some coca and drank some *aguardiente* and put spittle on the frog. At the same time she put thorns from a cactus plant into the frog's eyes. The frog was then taken to the house of the intended victim and buried by the main door. This woman was said to have been responsible for blinding a man in 1930 and another in 1939, and for paralyzing yet another in 1932. Two other cases of blindness, within six years before the time of the study, were said to have been caused by methods similar to this. Another method of witchcraft is to blow smoke from a cigarette on a live toad, put chewed coca and some ashes on it, and wrap it in a handkerchief. Then, as in the other case, pins are stuck in the toad, and the whole thing is wrapped like an old bundle and left in a corner, not necessarily underground, of the victim's home.

Besides calling in another witch to counteract witchcraft, there are many ways of fighting it. One is to break a bit of rue into small pieces and put them in a cup of water. The cup is then placed on a table or shelf and the person waits until the rue turns yellow.

When this happens the effect of the witchcraft should disappear. Another method is to hang *savila,* a type of maguey which grows locally, in the corner of the sick person's room. Some claim that the witchcraft can be counteracted by wearing one's socks inside out or by wearing underclothes backwards.

Another very common cause of illness, particularly among children, is fright, or *susto.* *Susto,* which rarely occurs in adults except pregnant women, consists of being thoroughly frightened, losing one's soul in the place of the scare, and becoming sick through loss of the soul. To cure *susto* a *curandera,* or magical curer, is called in. The *curandera* gathers all kinds and colors of flowers and wraps them around the child. Then, filling her mouth with coca and *aguardiente,* she sucks on the child's forehead and chest, in order to get the soul back into the child, and mutters certain words in the Indian language. This ritual is usually carried on around eight or nine o'clock in the evening; at midnight she takes the flowers and coca and goes alone to the place where the child was frightened and drops them; if she is not sure where the child lost its soul, the flowers are left out on the main highway. For the next day or two people coming across the flowers on the road make a wide detour around them to avoid the sickness believed to be there. In recent years, according to an informant, less attention is paid to these flowers than was the case in years past. During the ceremony in the home most of the family members are present and other people may watch if they are interested. Another method to cure fright is to fill one's mouth with salt water, suck all over the body of the victim, and then spit out the water. This is done until most of the body has been covered. The technique of getting the soul back into the body by sucking is called *suhulachisa.*

One of the favorite methods which the *curanderos* use for diagnosing a sickness is to examine the viscera of a guinea pig which has been rubbed alive over the body of the patient. If any specific congestion is noticed in the guinea pig's body, then the *curandero* knows that the sickness is located in the same part of the patient's body. Following this, the *curandero* may put chewed coca on the body of the animal, together with some *pisco* (grape brandy), ashes, burned cigarettes, and wrap it all in cloth and bury it in the area where it is believed that the person contracted the sickness. This type of guinea pig diagnosis and therapy is also used for *susto;* the guinea pig may be buried in the road or thrown away in the river.

It is said that to cure a headache, it is necessary to tie a dead frog on the back of the patient's head while he rests for a day or so, then bury the frog in the ground some distance away. The patient must continue to rest for two days in bed, however, or his head may suddenly twist at an angle and remain that way.

Coca is considered an important curing item; if a person has a skin irritation, a leaf of coca is moistened and placed on the skin at the point of irritation. Many people use an old piece of cigarette paper if the irritation is near or in the eye. It is quite common to see a person wandering around with a coca leaf stuck to his face.

There are some *curanderos* who specialize in the treatment of fractures. Some spread the grease of a lizard over the area around the fracture, then bind up the limb with a band of cloth about four inches wide. Others will wrap a snake around the limb, put a slab of wood on each side, and bind the whole thing up with string. In one case, a man who fractured his leg had a cast put on it by the local skilled curer, but he took the cast off a week later and put a dead snake on his leg. He continued putting snakes on the leg until he felt he was well.

The local ideas of illness are not limited to *susto*, witchcraft, and the various use of frogs, snakes, and coca for curing. It is felt, for example, that if a person sleeps in the region above the town among the ruins of the old Huanca settlements, he will get sick. Also, if a person has a nightmare or seems slightly delirious in his sleep, he will fall ill. The Muquiyauyinos are becoming increasingly aware that there are some startling differences between their way of looking at some of these mental and bodily troubles and the way the medical doctors look at them. The clearer the divergence becomes, the more embarrassed some Muquiyauyinos are about the old ways, and the less they are mentioned.

Many women and some men claim to have the ability to predict death. While many stories of such predictions were related to me, I had the opportunity to check on only one. In this case, the wife of one of my informants awoke early in January, saying that she had just been visited in her sleep by the spirit of a certain mestizo in town who was sick. By the nature of the visit she guessed he would die in about a month. This was told to me in the middle of January and the man died of pneumonia on the third of February.

The most extensive description of such an ability was provided by a university-educated professional worker at one of the mines. As a boy, he said, he occasionally saw human forms, usually indistinctly, around six o'clock in the evening. Once, when he was about fifteen, while standing in the kitchen of his home in Muquiyauyo, he looked out and saw a friend, Colonel Espinoza, coming toward his house carrying his shoes in his hand. The boy called to him, but when he looked again the colonel was gone. He told his mother about this, and she said that the colonel must surely be going to die soon. A week later he did die. Shortly thereafter in the kitchen again, he looked in the patio and saw for an instant what he thought was his grandfather, but with a "fantastic" face. He told his mother again, and his grandfather died a few days later. Still later he saw his maternal grandmother, who was a rheumatic. This time he was in the street, and saw a black cloud about eleven yards above the ground, and his grandmother was above the cloud. He saw this vision three times, each time the figure and face of the grandmother clearer; then she died. One day he saw a slanting ray of light in a doorway; going down the ray was the child of his aunt; the child died shortly thereafter. The informant said that, in general, people who had a bad character appeared in dark clothes in these visions, and people with good characters were shrouded in light. The degree of clarity with which he could identify the person permitted him to calculate how soon the person would die. Most of the people he recognized were members of his own family. After various exhibitions of his ability, his family became thoroughly disturbed by the accuracy of these predictions, and his mother decided to put an end to it once and for all. She got a brand new pottery olla, poured some steaming water into it, and put her son's face over it. It evidently worked because he never had any more visions. The informant remarked that he was sorry he no longer had these visions, as they offered him a delightful diversion. He used to be able to distinguish the sex, approximate age, and general character of the person in the vision, even if he could not tell exactly who it was. Life was a little easier in the family after the cure, however.

It is customary to hold funeral ceremonies in the home. The body is laid out on a table and covered with a sheet. A little tent of cloth with lace borders called the *capilla ardiente* or *capilla catafalco* is set up over the corpse. At the head of the body are a number of small candles, and at the foot other candles, or, if they can be afforded, *cirios,* waxed sticks with a tiny kerosene lamp on top. The whole arrangement is called the *mortuorio.* On the evening before the burial, a *velorio,* or wake, is held from about nine o'clock until four or five in the morning. During the night the male relatives and male godchildren of the deceased go to the cemetery and dig the grave. The family provides coca, *aguardiente,* cigarettes, and breakfast when they are finished. Today it is more common for the wealthy to be buried in vaults built above the ground. For these a mason is hired and he works as fast as he can to prepare the vault for the funeral.

On the morning of the funeral the family breakfasts on a _caldo_, a dish called _gizo_, made of potatoes and hot peppers, and a _patasca_, a dish of large corn grains and slices of fat in a watery liquid Everyone who was present at the wake and the digging of the grave joins in the breakfast. The body is then placed in a coffin and carried to the cemetery. The whole crowd of friends and family follows along with a good deal of talk. The close women relatives of the deceased cry and wail loudly all during the procession and the actual burial. Wreaths are carried ahead of the casket and placed over the tomb after the burial. Usually after, but sometimes before or during the funeral, the clothes of the deceased are washed in a ceremony known as the _lavatorio_. All sheets and clothing which were used are washed clean. If the _lavatorio_ takes place during the burial, the rest of the mourners will go down to the river for the final phases of the ceremony.

A Mass is seldom said immediately after the death of a relative since it is too difficult to get the priest. Sometime within two or three months, however, it is customary to arrange one. On the first and second of November, the Day of All Saints and the Day of the Dead, formal respect is paid to the dead. On the first of November a table is laid in the home with food which the dead person is supposed to have liked; bread, fruit, sweets, and some flowers and candles are set out. On the following day holy water and flowers are taken to the cemetery and the family may spend four to five hours there praying. Coca, _aguardiente_, and cigarettes are brought along on this _romería_, or pilgrimage, to the cemetery. The spirits of the dead do not seem to be much of a threat to the Muquiyauyinos. One is expected to show respect at the proper time, but I encountered no reports of a person molested by the spirits. Years ago the food used to be taken to the cemetery, but today no one does this, and even the custom of setting the food out at the table is no longer strictly observed.

13

ACTIVITIES OF THE COMMUNITY

IN MOST of the towns in the Jauja Valley every adult spends some of his time in affairs of the community. Such labors, traditional in the highlands, have formed an important basis for the development of the town in recent years. The community and the district have shared in directing local affairs, and which is the more powerful depends upon a number of factors. In general, the *gobernador*, a district official, handles the maintenance of law and order; he has assistants in each of the population centers in the district. The justices of the peace, also district officers, settle minor disputes, and the district council is in charge of matters that concern the welfare of the district as a whole. The district has a room at the back of the council building which is used as a jail. When it has inmates, they are usually young men who have been caught serenading or otherwise disturbing the peace, or local boys being held for the national conscription. While many district capitals in Peru have a small detachment of the *guardia civil*, the national police force, Muquiyauyo has not had one for some years.

The community organization has authority principally over the specific property which it owns; its main interest is in public works projects for the town. The first community meeting I attended was held early in January, 1950, to elect a new president of the community organization. For this each *cuartel* had elected one of its members as a candidate and it was now in the hands of the communal meeting to decide which of the four men would become president of the entire community. When the meeting opened, there were only fifty-three men present besides the outgoing president and the district secretary. Included among those present were a few men who usually worked outside the town but were back on vacations. The scene was the large meeting room on the first floor of the district government building. This, the *sala comunal*, is long, and at one end behind a table were stationed the outgoing president, the secretary, and a secretary for the man in charge of the communal financial records. Benches lined each side wall in a single row, and a double row faced the president from the far end of the room. The main door to the plaza opened off one side of the room and a number of community members for whom there was no room on the benches inside were crowded around the door.

After the nominations were read the president reminded the members that they were permitted only one vote. After each person had written the name of his candidate, the papers were collected. At this point a member raised the objection that none of the candidates was present at the meeting. Another member replied that it had been the precedent for two years now for the nominees not to participate in the meeting, the incumbent president having made sure before the election that the various candidates were willing to serve.

The secretary counted the votes by opening each ballot and reading the name aloud while another man kept a record of how many votes each candidate received. During the counting there was very little talk or movement among the members. Just before the end of the counting the candidate from the third *cuartel* walked briskly into the room and in a loud voice announced himself absent from the meeting. This was greeted by a burst of laughter which led into spirited conversation. The president interrupted the noise by rapping on his desk a number of times to announce the outcome of the voting. The candidate of the third *cuartel* won, with twenty-one votes. The nominees from the first, second, and fourth *cuarteles* received sixteen, two, and seventeen votes, respectively.

The winner, upon hearing the results of the vote, immediately announced that he was very dissatisfied with the form the meeting had been taking and the lack of interest shown by the community More control would be necessary; he would not accept the presidency if the community would not show order, discipline, and interest. A leading mestizo of the town then arose and expressed agreement with the new president's feelings, but said that to be elected is a sacrifice and that he should take the position in order to play an important role in the forward movement of the town; this was greeted with applause from the other members. The new president replied that this was all very well, but many members were frequently absent. At this point a member from the floor interrupted, commenting that "when the father is good, the child is good [applause], but when the father is bad, the child is bad." This ended the discussion.

Then began a discussion of the preliminaries for inaugurating the new officers. There was some further confusion as the newly elected vice-president (the man who received the second highest number of votes in the election) claimed that he would not be able to take the position; he was reminded that he had had an opportunity to say this before the election.

A member from the floor stated he felt that by the constituted regulations the justice of the peace should induct the new officers; another member answered that the induction had never been done in this manner before. The first member created a state of confusion by walking out of the meeting. Other members arose and started talking, and gradually a general hubbub developed; it was stopped by the secretary's shouting above the din that the new officeholders would work for God and country; this was greeted with an ovation and gradually everyone returned to his place.

At this point, a little under an hour after the meeting had begun, the new president took over. The secretary of the accounts read the financial report for the year, listing each item. A discussion arose over some points and the former president interrupted to say that he objected to one of the participants taking so much of the time of the meeting, since that individual was usually absent from Muquiyauyo anyway. This served to warm the discussion and the issue was finally put to a vote by a show of hands. A majority was declared without a count of hands. At this point three members left the meeting.

A new topic was then introduced, and it was agreed after more discussion that holding a social dance in the communal meeting room without permission was forbidden. Gradually more people drifted out of the meeting.

The subject of a source of drinking water was introduced, and the alcalde of the district reported on a trip he had recently made to Lima on this matter. This was discussed but only twelve men actually participated in the discussion and, of these, six occupied most of the time. It developed that the members present did not want the community to pay the alcalde for his expenses on the trip to Lima since the trip was not successful. The alcalde claimed that he should be reimbursed by the community since the district council did not have sufficient funds; after all, he is the father of a family and the loss of S/. 70 goes hard with him. The meeting finally agreed to reimburse him for the trip.

During this discussion more members left the meeting, and it was growing close to midday. The subject of naming a single treasurer in place of the four existing currently was taken up. One per-

son felt that the community *administrador de rentas* should take
this responsibility because otherwise his position was little more
than a title. This proposal was talked down and the proposition to
name a single treasurer was put to a vote and passed. It was decided that the same procedure would be followed as in the selection
of other community officers. Each *cuartel* would name a candidate.
One of the people present mentioned that for this job it would be
necessary to find a person interested in the work, but that there
was no such person. A list of four names was presented, but the
president said that a person was needed who was more serious than
any of those named. The meeting was adjourned before this business could be completed.

This communal meeting reveals a good deal about the contemporary functioning of the community organization. It was not particularly well attended, and the new president's comment on the
lack of order among community members was a reflection of the
fact that this was the third time the meeting had been called before enough people got together to make it worth-while. The discussions were dominated by only a few of the people present, and
most of these were mestizos or wealthier people. An important
role was played by men who spent most of their time working in
other centers and who returned to Muquiyauyo only during their
holidays.

The meeting also brought up a number of subjects which had been
handled in many meetings before. The use of the communal meeting room for other than official purposes had evidently been a constant source of distress to certain community members. Disagreements over procedure occurred frequently, and not infrequently caused greater ill feeling than did the disagreements over
substantive issues. The approval of the idea of replacing the four
treasurers with a single treasurer was another step in the process whereby the structure of the communal organization gradually
evolves. The existence of four treasurers had first been decreed
in 1910 to handle the funds that were being taken in by the community through renting lands.

While the meetings may be filled with a certain amount of flow-
ery oratory, time may be wasted in undirected discussions, and
many subjects of seemingly little importance may be discussed
at length, nevertheless the communal organization accomplishes
a good deal and certainly reflects the opinions of the portion of the
population which is most actively interested in community affairs.
Considerable honest opinion is expressed at these meetings and
they deal with problems of some difficulty, with participation of

everyone who is interested. This indicates that the opinion of some observers as to the inability of rural Latin Americans to handle 'democratic action" should be subjected to more extensive field study.

The communal meetings are usually held on a Sunday morning, and, while all community members are supposed to attend, the meetings are in fact attended principally by men. The *cuartel* meetings, on the other hand, are often held at night, and women as well as men attend. According to the *cuartel* membership books, both men and women are members of *cuarteles* and have equal right to participate.

Before one *cuartel* meeting which I attended, there had been six attempts to get the members together. The seventh proved successful, and the secretary of the *cuartel*, who had been working late over some material with me, was called to the meeting at the last minute. It was the first he had heard of it, but he went immediately when called. The meeting started about nine o'clock in the evening in the home of the president of the *cuartel*. Some of the *cuarteles* have erected special buildings for offices and meeting places, but as yet the third *cuartel* has none. There were in attendance about twenty-five men and twenty women, many of the latter with babies. The night was chilly; the men, dressed in their regular clothes, all had on the heavy woolen ponchos and scarves wrapped around their necks. The meeting was held in the closed-in *corredor* of the house, a long space with a few benches and chairs and two small tables at one end under the single lightbulb, where the *cuartel* officers presided.

The president opened the meeting by asking the secretary to read the minutes of the previous session. The president then commented on the minutes, calling the attention of the members to some of the issues. New business was brought up first with the reading of a note from the district alcalde concerning the appointment of a new *teniente gobernador*, and a letter from the community electric light plant directorate. The president then asked the floor if there were any *pedidos* (requests) concerning matters that needed discussion or decision. One member mentioned that the *cuartel* needed to buy some rockets (to set off during hail storms); another said that the schools needed repair, and someone noted the costs involved. With no more requests from the floor, the president reminded the group that it was time to name a new *junta directiva* for the *cuartel*.

Until this time the members had been very quiet with no private conversation or undercurrent of mumbling. The mention of the

selection of a new junta started some talk, however. During a
slight interval, the president asked if any of the women present
had any requests, but there was no response. The president then
took up the business of the day. The secretary read the list of subjects, brought up in the order suggested by the president.

The letter from the electric plant requested an increase in salaries. Since the plant was partly owned by each of the *cuarteles,*
any changes in its administration had to have the approval of each
cuartel and the community as a whole. This request for salary
increase followed upon a recent decree from the national president which stated that wages should be raised. A number of the
members present felt that an increase in the salaries of the employees was not necessary since the employees themselves were
community members and benefited from the service of the light
plant. Another member arose to say that it was true that the government decree was probably directed more toward private concerns, but nevertheless a decree is a decree and it should be followed; also, that the local people who work in the light plant sacrifice a lot to do so, and they should be able to benefit by an increase in wages. To the speaker this suggested another subject,
which was that the administration of the light plant ought to be
reorganized in order to bring in more income; he suggested that
the *cuartel* bring this up at the next communal meeting. The speaker became quite heated during his discourse and finally sat down.
The president commented that the manager of the light plant did
not feel a salary increase was necessary although the employees
did. A number of other comments followed, and it was finally
decided to put off the discussion of the increase of salary until
the next meeting; this was then changed and it was decided that
it was a community matter and could not properly be handled by
the *cuartel* anyway; it should be brought up at the next communal
meeting or in a session of the community directorate. Another
point brought up in the letter from the light plant was the subject
of S/. 5,000 which had been entrusted to one of the community
members for the purchase of new equipment; he had been unable
to make the purchase because the exchange rate was too high, but
he had not returned the money. The speaker who had become heated
before rose again, saying that the manager of the light plant was
responsible for the funds and that it was part of his duty to get the
money back. Also, he added, it did not seem right to him that one
of the members of the directing council of the light plant should
have borrowed money from the enterprise. Apparently the speaker's
fellow *cuartel* members were accustomed to his long and emotional

discourses, and so settled themselves comfortably when he started. The meeting then moved on to the subject of sky rockets. The president felt that the rockets were very expensive; more than three hundred had been bought last year and were used up very quickly. At this point a number of women spoke up for the first time, saying that the president was talking too much; this did not stop the president, however, who continued his discourse. A number of people interrupted simultaneously over the rocket issue, one saying that the person from whom they were bought sold them at an exorbitant price, another that a new purchasing source should be found, and another that there should be some over-all administration of the rocket business. It was finally agreed to ask the district alcalde to name a man to be in charge of the rockets because some of the other *cuarteles* had not bought any and the heaviest burden of expense had been falling on the third *cuartel*. One member suggested that the other *cuarteles* should hold more community work sessions to make up for the difference in the amount spent by each *cuartel* for rockets. It was suggested that it might be a good idea to make the rockets in a communal work session.

With this the president moved on to the next point. Considerable dissatisfaction had been shown over the running of the school. The suggestion was made that it be removed from the national rural school system and be run as a communal school under the control of the community. Among the specific complaints mentioned was that the products of the school garden did not benefit the community; that the school carpenter had sold nothing; that four of the children had died during the school year; that the school produced no good artisans nor any good agriculturalists; and that the teaching was generally inadequate. Since the schools are a matter of communal concern, one member then suggested that the fathers of families make an official request to their *cuarteles* to take up the subject at a communal meeting. It was also decided after a little discussion to undertake the repairs necessary on the girls' school during the vacation period.

The next hour of the meeting was devoted to the nomination and election of new officers. This was accompanied by a good deal of laughter, since it soon became evident that no one really wanted any of the positions. One member commented seriously that there were so many people (over half) absent from the meeting that it was unfair to those present since absentees could not be elected to a post. Several people were named to each of the posts and each declined with the excuse that he was out of town too much, or that he was too old, and so forth. The situation was finally resolved by keeping some of the old officers and electing only a few new ones. During the discussion and voting the women became suddenly very active; a number of them suggested names, and they carried on a lively conversation among themselves.

About 11:30 the meeting officially closed, but one member then reminded the president about the electric light problem, and it was agreed to request that the management of the light plant be suspended, a careful review made of all the books, and a new set of regulations promulgated. The member then began to dictate a letter on this matter while the president, suddenly remembering that he had forgotten to call the roll, immediately began to do so. Each of the members answered present, and most of them got up and left immediately after their names were called.

This _cuartel_ meeting was dominated, as was the communal meeting, by a few men, most of them mestizos. The president, particularly during the latter part of the session, frequently asked that the women participate more in the discussion, and when the discussion of new officers came up they did. Much of the voting was carried on informally; the president would ask if the group was agreed on such and such an issue, and if the responses were affirmative grunts, the motion was passed. Only during the election of new officials was a formal vote held.

It can be seen from this _cuartel_ meeting that subjects of some significance to local life are discussed openly. The idea of taking the school out of the national rural school system would probably not have been well received by the Ministry of Education in Lima, since by law all rural schools are run by the ministry. Yet the Muquiyauyinos did not hesitate to suggest this step, for they believed that they could be better run if under communal control. Whether this was true was still an open question at the time I left the town. If as much enthusiasm could be shown in running the schools as was displayed in the discussion, they could not fail for lack of effort. But the amount of actual community participation in both the _cuartel_ and community meetings just described leaves some doubt as to whether the enthusiasm will last.

The domination of the meetings by certain mestizos and a limited number of people who have recently tended to move out of the Indian category reflects the fact that the upper-class group in the town definitely acts as the leader in community affairs. In general, women do not participate at all in the communal meetings, although they are allowed to; and, while they do attend, they do not say much at the _cuartel_ meetings. It is not that their opinions are not positive, but they seem to feel that a good deal of what is discussed

could be said in fewer words and that there is no point in adding
their voices to those of the men who are already occupying the
floor.

Enthusiasm for community affairs becomes really apparent during the major communal work projects which are carried on every
few years. As is the case with the other towns in the region, Muquiyauyo has a long history of communal works of which the townspeople are extremely proud. These community activities are of
two major types: first there are the upkeep activities, such as
fixing streets and bridges, repairing dikes, and cleaning canals,
which go on year in and year out. The second kind of work involves the large special projects in which some new addition or
alteration is made to the community's material equipment. There
are no communal agricultural activities, since all arable communal lands are rented out to community members for individual
use.

The repetitive activities are carried out by each *cuartel* at irregular intervals as needed. Before about 1900, the district council had the entire responsibility for keeping track of what work
needed to be done. The alcalde would send word to the *cuarteles*
or the particular *cuartel* concerned that a street needed repair,
that a bridge was broken, or that a canal was not running well,
and then direct the people responsible for doing the necessary
work. At present, the council technically still has this function,
but the gradual rise of the community organization has tended to
displace the council. The community organization and the *cuarteles*
have often ignored the orders of the council and have undertaken
some tasks without instructions from the district.

The large construction projects which comprise the major group
of communal works, and for which the town is known as being particularly progressive, evidently started in the last century. Sometime around the middle of the century the first canal system was
built; later, the Muquiyauyinos built the bridge over the Mantaro
which served traffic for many years until the Huaripampiños built
a parallel bridge; in the last decade of the century the town went
as a group to help rebuild part of the convent of Ocopa. The greatest activity, however, evidently did not get under way until the
twentieth century. In 1917, a large two-story district government
building, the *municipalidad*, was constructed; in 1920, the electric
light plant was erected; in 1931-33, a new bridge was put across the
Mantaro to regain the prestige lost when Huaripampa took away
the traffic some decades earlier; a second two-story government

building was also put up in this period (1919-20) but was not roofed until 1937. Over the years from 1940 to 1943, what is now the boys' school building was erected; it consisted of a large main building and six individual classroom structures, plus some outbuildings. And finally, in 1948-49, a new cemetery wall was raised. These have been among the more important and ambitious projects in recent years. It is characteristic of many of these public works that they were spread over two and sometimes three years since the work was done only during the agricultural off-season. In these projects the work was usually divided among the four *cuarteles*. During the period of work frequent *mishkipas* are held; these are a combination of recreation and rest periods during which supplies of *aguardiente, chicha,* cigarettes, coca, and sometimes beer are provided for the working forces. The *mishkipa* is said to be a descendant of a series of such customs formerly carried on during any kind of communal work project.

The only major project that I observed was the second year's work on the cemetery wall. In the first year the stone foundations had been laid for the wall; the second year involved the actual preparation of the adobe bricks and the laying of the wall. The sections of the wall were divided into four more or less equal portions and one was assigned to each *cuartel*. This permitted and promoted considerable rivalry among the four groups as to which could work better and faster. Each *cuartel* counted among its members some masons, who were assigned to direct the construction of their sections.

Before the actual construction, each *cuartel* was assigned the task of making nine thousand adobe bricks. This work was divided among the members, and each member was responsible for a certain number. Just before construction began, auxiliary canals of water were built leading into the cemetery area to provide water for mixing mud mortar. Each *cuartel* was assigned an area near the water where the mud could be mixed. Every inscribed member of the community (and consequently of its component *cuarteles)* was expected to supply his or her labor on the days of the *faena,* or work. Anyone who could not offer his own work was supposed to send a substitute of equal capacity (a man for a man or a woman for a woman), pay a fine (S/. 8 for a man and S/. 4 for a woman), or provide a *mishkipa.*

On the first day of the construction of the wall each *cuartel* president named a *jefe de obra,* or director of the work for that *cuartel.* He in turn named a *segundo jefe,* or assistant director, and a *comisionado,* an executive who acted as yet another assistant. The *cuartel* president and the *jefe de obra* together named the *albañiles*, or masons, who were to handle the technical aspect of the work, and each mason named for himself an *ayudante*, assistant. The president and the *jefe* also named two of the strongest men in the *cuartel* as *tika-maestros*; these men were responsible for rounding up a group of adobe brick carriers, or *hombreadores*. Also named were: one or two *machas*, in charge of getting together and directing the *cargadores de barro*, the group of women and younger and weaker men who carried the mud mortar; one or two *jefes de barreros*, in charge of the men *(barreros)* at the mud pit who mixed the fresh mud; and the *aguadoras*, the women who carried water in buckets from the canal to the mud pits. The number of people engaged on these tasks on the first day of the *faena* was as follows (excluding the president, the *jefe de obra*, and his two assistants for each *cuartel):*

	Cuartel 1	Cuartel 2	Cuartel 3	Cuartel 4	Total
Albañiles	15	13	13	11	52
Ayudantes	15	12	11	11	49
Tika-maestro	2	2	2	2	8
Hombreadores	18	14	18	13	63
Machas	2	2	2	1	7
Cargadores de barro	34	17	16	11	78
Jefes de Barreros	2	1	1	1	5
Barreros	7	11	9	11	38
Jefe de Aguadoras	-	-	1		1
Aguadoras	4	5	6	12	27
Total	99	77	79	73	328

The number of people working on each of the three days of the *faena* varied somewhat.

The process of building the walls was systematic: the *aguadoras* brought water from the canals to the *barreros* at the mud pits. The *hombreadores* carried the large adobe bricks on their shoulders from the long line of adobes that had been set up nearby. The *cargadores de barro* had on their backs large sacks filled with straw which provided a flat platform at the level of their shoulders; on this was placed a piece of leather, and on the leather the *barreros* put one or two shovelsful of mud which the *cargadores* then carried to the wall. When the *hombreadores* and *cargadores de barro* arrived at the wall they deposited their loads, and the *albañiles* and their *ayudantes* placed the adobes and the mud mortar on the wall. The *albañiles*, the *jefe de obra*, the *segundo jefe*, and the *comisionado* went about making sure the wall was being made in a straight line and dropping a plumb line periodically to be sure it was vertical. The *albañiles* who were most experienced in this were also called *cordeladores*.

The work, once started, went on with great rapidity. The *hombreadores* and *cargadores* trotted between the sources of their materials and the walls. There was much yelling of "Don't touch the plumb line," "Place this adobe," "Put this adobe farther over," "Square this line," and most frequently "More adobe," or "More mud!" The work was tiring and at two- or three-hour intervals there would be a *mishkipa* among the members of a *cuartel*.

Mishkipas were usually sponsored in one of four different ways some were sponsored by widows; some were given *en cambio de faena* (in place of working in the *faena*); some were given voluntarily by a more wealthy member of the *cuartel*, usually a professional man who worked away from the town and returned only for the *faena*, and some were known as *shujupe*, a rest period sponsored by the *cuartel* itself. As the work progressed the *mishkipas* became more lively. On the last day of the work, the members of the first *cuartel* to finish its share of the work were all a little stimulated by the supplies of the *mishkipas* and, having hired an orchestra, danced from the cemetery into town and around the plaza a number of times. The stores did a good business in *aguardiente*, beer, *pisco*, *chicha*, and sweet vermouth. There was much yelling and cheering for the *cuartel*, its president, the visitors, and for anyone or anything.

In a *mishkipa* held by another *cuartel* a number of the members dug out some of the *cochinero* costumes of the Christmas fiesta and danced around in them. Aside from the use of these costumes, which was something of an innovation, this *mishkipa* was rather typical of the many that were held during the three days at the cemetery. Blankets were spread out and on them were set bottles of vermouth and *aguardiente* (sometimes barrels of *aguardiente*) and jars of *chicha*. Coca was placed in little piles on white handkerchiefs, and a woman passed about replenishing the supply of coca from a bag she carried. During the *mishkipa* the workers lounged against the wall, chatting or listening to some impromptu speech thanking the donor of the *mishkipa* or extolling the virtues of the *cuartel*. Cigarettes were passed out periodically. The *shujupe*, sponsored by the *cuartel*, was generally like the other *mishkipas* except that it was held regularly at about four o'clock each afternoon of the work, while the other voluntary *mishkipas* were held at irregular times during the work.

The community-wide *faena* is therefore not merely a time to accomplish some public project but is also one of the more important celebrations within the community as a whole. It is a time when the greatest public enthusiasm is worked up over the *cuarteles* and the community itself. It is emphasized that everyone, mestizo and Indian alike, participates in the work. Class differences are to be seen in the fact that the members of the mestizo families usually hold higher positions in the labor hierarchy and frequently excuse themselves from the work itself by sponsoring a *mishkipa*. This is recognized as quite proper, and there would actually be some concern if these *mishkipas* were not held. Class differences, however, are used to advantage and there was no evidence of resentment on the part of the Indian class concerning the position of the mestizos in the work project.

Community activities in special and annual projects, community meetings, and *cuartel* meetings take up a certain amount of each individual's time. To give some idea of the number of days of the year when a person is called upon to participate in some kind of communal activity, the calendar of events of one *cuartel* for 1948 is given below.

January 14:	Session of the community
18:	Session of the *cuartel*
February 15:	Session of the community
March 4:	Clean Acequia Alta and Uono
5:	Clean Acequia Molino
12:	Repair the roof of the girls' school
17:	Session of the *cuartel*
April 1:	Session of the community
May 1:	Session of the community
June 17:	Session of the community
July 19:	Session of the community
23-24:	Collect stones for the foundation of the cemetery wall
August 2-3:	Shape stones for the foundation of the cemetery wall
5:	Carry stones to the location of the wall
7:	Excavation for the foundation of the wall
8-10:	Lay the foundations of the wall
15:	Session of the *cuartel*
24:	Session of the *cuartel*
September 25:	Session of the *cuartel*

November   5:   Work on the road to Sincos
           6:   Clean Acequia Alta and Usno
          13:   Clean Acequia Molina
December 23:   Clean park; session of the *cuartel*
          30:   Session of the community

Fines of from fifty centavos to five *soles* were levied for absences from these events. Failure to appear at the cemetery wall *faenas*, at the cleaning of the canals, and at the work on the Sincos road cost five *soles;* absence from a communal or *cuartel* session was fined one *sole*, and fifty centavos was charged for absence from the session set for repairing the roof of the girls' school. In 1948 there were 130 members of this *cuartel*, all of whom missed at least one of the sessions or work periods. The average number of events missed per person was a little under nine, about one-third of the maximum possible, twenty-four. Of the people who had missed events, 24 per cent missed less than five sessions, 60 per cent missed between five and sixteen sessions, while 16 per cent missed over sixteen sessions. The average amount owed in fines at the end of the year was S/. 17.90. Ideally, this seems to fall somewhat short of a highly developed community sense of responsibility, but, practically, a number of factors must be taken into account. When a man leaves to go and work in the mines he is expected to attend work projects and meetings just as if he were present in the community, and he is fined for his absence. A few who work permanently at the mines maintain themselves as *cuartel* members and accumulate the total possible number of fines at the end of the year. Also, it is inevitable that many will have to miss meetings and work periods because of unexpected affairs which may intervene. The only absences that are not fined are those caused by illness or the individual's employment in some community or district position.

The number of absences, therefore, is not an adequate index of community spirit or feeling of responsibility in communal affairs. The fines are not merely a way to discourage absences, but are equally important as a method to maintain the treasury of the *cuartel*. Otherwise, the incomes of the *cuarteles* would drop alarmingly. Complaints are to be heard that people do not participate in meetings and work sessions as they used to do in the "old days," but there are no comparable figures on attendance available to substantiate these claims. What is probably not taken into account in making these complaints is that the population is now larger than it ever was before, and that while meetings may not be at-

tended by as great a proportion of the population, probably more
people are participating than in previous years. The major work
projects are times for reunions of old friends, visits home, parties, and general celebration; such projects are usually attended
by quite a few people who make no real contribution to the work
under way. The periodic projects such as canal cleaning and road
repair, however, do not attract these crowds. The people from
the higher social strata do not participate so much in these work
sessions, and there are no large-scale *mishkipas* for the recreation of the workers; the *cuartel* may buy each participant a soda
pop or some other minor refreshment, but aside from this it is a
matter of work and not recreation.

The existence of a community treasury has been equally as important as the existence of a pool of manpower in the success of a
number of the advances made. Reconstruction of the financial history of the town is complicated, however, by the fact that the cash
books during the first twenty years have many arithmetical errors.

The primary source of income for the district until 1895 was the
toll collected from the Muquiyauyo bridge. In that year, the decision to build a new bridge at Huaripampa threatened to cut in on
the profits derived from the toll. The Muquiyauyinos did everything
in their power to prevent the approaching financial crisis. They
sent representatives and petitions to the national government, levy-
ing subscriptions from the town members to finance the Lima trips,
in order to prevent the construction of the Huaripampa bridge. They
did succeed in delaying the construction of the new bridge for four
years, but by the turn of the century the receipts from the Muquiyauyo bridge had dropped to practically nothing. There was no
choice, in view of the competition from the Huaripampa bridge, but
to drop the toll, and even then most people preferred to use the
new bridge since it followed a shorter route. In 1908 the Huaripampa bridge was damaged in a flood, and the Muquiyauyo district
council immediately raised the toll on their bridge to take advantage of the traffic diverted back to them. They expected to profit
only a month or so from this event, but to their delight it took the
Huaripampiños nine months to make their bridge passable again.

Through all its early years the Muquiyauyo district council annually put its bridge in *remate* to the highest bidder for a fixed
sum. In order to discourage the *rematista* from charging excessive
tolls on the bridge, the council set the rates for the various animals, and these were announced prior to the bidding for the right
to be tollkeeper. Since all Muquiyauyinos were allowed to cross
the bridge free of charge anyway, no great effort was ever made

to see whether or not the *rematista* was overcharging other travelers. *Remate* was the district council's favorite method of collecting its funds in those days. Even the collection of municipal taxes was let out to a bidder. The council set the so-called *propios arbitrios,* the tax levied on goods sold in town (liquor, wine, tobacco, coca, alfalfa seed) and on the making of *chicha,* and publicly announced the rates prior to the bidding. No one could then claim that the council had reduced the rates after the post had been bid for, and the townspeople were able to know what the rates were so that they could avoid being overtaxed. The district also put out in *remate* the right to collect the tax on the Usno canal from the people of Muqui who used the water. Further income was derived from the licenses which the district issued giving permission to hold a public dance, to set off fireworks, to hold masked dances, to have an orchestra play, and so on. All these phases of a fiesta were taxed and provided a small but constant annual income.

As described earlier, many of the *cofradía* lands were being abandoned by their *mayordomos* in the final decade of the last century. In 1895 the authorities of Muquiyauyo met to take the first steps in taking some of these *cofradía* lands in rent. It was planned that a person from the town would rent the land from the church, that the town would repay him the cash, and that the lands would be planted in alfalfa, which could be sold. While the funds from this venture were not large, they were sufficient to start a loan system. It was customary for the moneylenders of that day to charge a monthly interest of from 4 to 6 per cent, and sometimes higher. While extremely high interest rates were against the law, if one needed the money he was simply forced to accept the terms made by the lender. The town instituted a system by which the public funds could be borrowed for any period up to one year at a rate of 2 per cent monthly. Each treasurer was made responsible for lending the money and for turning over the entire cash funds of the town to his successor at the end of the year. Thus the treasurer was made responsible for outstanding debts and was expected to make good on defaults. If one of the debtors could not pay in time for this annual turnover, it was necessary for the treasurer to pay the money and have the debtor make out a new note to him. This encouraged various treasurers to carry on private usury businesses after their terms of office, but it served to keep the public funds relatively safe.

The funds from the *cofradía* lands and the interest gained from them provided the basic cash for the investment in the electric light plant at the end of the second decade of the century. There were also funds kept by each of the *cuarteles,* money received principally from the fines charged for absences from and disorder at the work sessions. In the 1887 and 1891 district session books, complaints are recorded that certain people were encouraging drunkenness at the work projects in order that fines could be collected. Funds of the Indian community, after its dissolution, were kept by the *cuarteles* and ultimately went as part of their investment in the construction of the light plant.

With the opening of the light plant in 1921, the principal contemporary source of community income became available. Even though it was necessary in the early years of the plant to place it in the hands of a *rematista,* by the early 1930's the plant was producing comfortable annual income for the community. The Muquiyauyinos planned later to install an electric mill but did not get around to it until word drifted over from Huaripampa that the neighboring community planned to put up such a mill. This stimulated the Muquiyauyinos into immediate action, and they finished their mill shortly thereafter.

In the early 1930's Muquiyauyo was presented with the opportunity of expanding its venture in the field of public utilities, but failed to take it. At this time the power plant in the town supplied current to the towns of Huaripampa, Muqui, the provincial capital, Jauja, and of course Muquiyauyo itself. In 1931 two major towns to the south, Concepción and San Jerónimo, each came to Muquiyauyo with projects whereby Muquiyauyo could gain control of the lighting of these two towns. Concepción wanted to buy power outright from the Muquiyauyo plant; San Jerónimo had its own power plant but because of unpaid bills on the equipment and strife between political factions in the town asked Muquiyauyo to become the administrator of its plant. The administrator of the Muquiyauyo power plant was very enthusiastic about the possibilities in these proposed ventures and tried his best to convince the townspeople that Muquiyauyo could utilize its experience in the power business to exercise control over the entire northern part of the valley. The venture could have brought increasing profits to Muquiyauyo and might ultimately have made it feasible for the town to install a new power plant.

Unfortunately, the townspeople did not see eye to eye with the administrator and did not take the opportunity. While it is impossible now to guess the precise reasons for this refusal, there are three factors which probably entered the issue. First, the Muquiyauyinos may not have had sufficient confidence in their plant chief; he had returned shortly before from a six-year stay in the United

States, and they may have felt that he had picked up too many expansive ideas in his travels. Second, they probably did not accurately foresee the profits which could have been made through such an expansion. Until only a short time previous all the profits from the plant had gone into the pockets of the *rematista* and few people knew the financial potentialities of the power business. They may have felt, therefore, that the undertaking would have been in the nature of a favor to other towns and not a means of profit for themselves. Third, there was probably a feeling that Muquiyauyo had diverged sufficiently from the general valley development. If other towns were uncertain of the wisdom of running their own light plants, would it be wise for Muquiyauyo to take such a chance? All three of these reasons reflect a general lack of decision when it came to carrying an innovation too far beyond the general culture of the valley.

While Muquiyauyo is in a position today to earn a good deal of money, several factors have reduced the quantity and effectiveness of its communal income. First, the accounts of not only the community and the *cuarteles* but also the electric light plant have frequently been in the hands of persons who have had little training in accounting, and because of this and occasional mishandling, monies have frequently gone unaccounted for. Second, during recent years the Peruvian unit of currency has gradually been devalued, while prices on the world market have risen to the point that even if the Muquiyauyinos had the amount of money that purchased their light plant in the early twenties, they would not be able to make the same purchase today. Consequently, the community is financially limited at present. The light plant needs a new generator and the community would like to purchase a tractor. Neither of these things is possible until an adequate accounting system is set up and might not even then be possible with the rates that are being charged by the light plant.

In comparison with other valley towns, however, Muquiyauyo is still in an enviable position; the community has a regular income, the townspeople show considerable enthusiasm for new projects within the town, and there are capable guiding hands among both old and young men of the town. Although there may not be enough funds at a particular moment, Muquiyauyo has a reasonable credit record. Few towns in the highlands can boast these things.

14

RECREATION, INDULGENCE, AND CELEBRATIONS

SPORTS, serenades, dinner parties, fairs and markets in other towns, an occasional movie in Jauja or Lima, large work projects, or just casual meetings among friends provide the Muquiyauyino with entertainment and relief from the daily run of work. Liquors such as *aguardiente de caña* (distilled cane sugar), *pisco*, or *aguardiente de uva* (the famous Peruvian grape brandy), sweet vermouth, beer, and homemade *chichas* of corn, potatoes, or peanuts provide an alcoholic lift from the problems of life. Coca, the mildly narcotic leaf from the plant that produces cocaine, is chewed by most Muquiyauyinos of the Indian class and by some mestizos as well. It is sold in most of the stores and is used by both men and women at work in the fields and homes. It is also used by men working in the mines and is always included as a part of the *mishkipa* during *faenas*. Coca chewing is a habit; like cigarette smoking it involves a whole series of overt activities but it has in addition somewhat stronger biological consequences. Among the overt activities are carrying the coca in a special woolen bag or in a loose piece of cloth, keeping powdered lime in a small gourd called the *ishcuro* (also called *iscuro* or *ishicuro*), removing the lime by means of a small piece of worked bone, and then sucking it into a wad of coca leaves already in the mouth. The lime serves to extract the full potency of the coca leaf and is always used with it. The *ishcuro* comes in two styles, one for men and one for women; both grow naturally and are from four to five inches long with a narrow stem opening. The base of the *ishcuro* for men is pointed while that for the women is rounded. In the stem is set the *chupadero*, the piece of bone that serves both as a plug for the opening in the gourd and as a stick by which the lime is conveyed into the mouth. The coca chewer wets the *chupadero* with his tongue, inserts it in the *ishcuro* and brings it out covered with lime.

A reported rule that the *cuarteles* had forbidden the use of coca and liquor at the work sessions was not in effect at the time of my visit, [1] nor was there any evidence that it ever had been. In fact, during the building of the cemetery wall a number of people pointed out that coca was an old Indian custom and was retained because the work sessions were part of the old Indian tradition. Some people, however, particularly educated mestizos, felt it was a vicious habit that should be stamped out. Nevertheless, coca chewing is so strongly entrenched that no measure short of stopping its production could restrict its use in the immediate future.

Besides the work projects and the sports, the principal large-scale recreation in the town is the series of fiestas. It will be remembered that some of the Muquiyauyo fiestas are private and of importance only to the small sponsoring and participating groups. A few, however, are large public affairs in which it is almost impossible for the townsman to escape participation of some sort. The principal fiestas are Christmas, New Year, Candelaria, Carnaval, Holy Week, and Santiago. Santiago is actually a series of private fiestas; there is little effort to make it an affair of the entire town. While many people participate in the Holy Week celebration, it is fundamentally religious and not a recreational event to be compared with the celebrations of Christmas, New Year, Candelaria, and Carnaval. These four fiestas are by far the most important recreational events of the year and all take place during the agricultural season. Of the four, Christmas and Carnaval are distinctive; the events of New Year and Candelaria are similar and can be described together.

The Christmas celebration lasted for five days in 1949, from December 24 to the twenty-ninth, although it usually stopped on the twenty-eighth. December 27 is generally considered the critical day of this fiesta; on that day more people participate and the plans for the fiesta of the next year are made. During the afternoon of the twenty-fourth, trucks and buses from La Oroya, Morococha, Huarón, Cerro de Pasco, and other mining centers bring men and families back to the town for Christmas. The mining companies usually give vacations from December 24 to 27, but some Muquiyauyinos stay an extra day since their fiesta lasts longer. While a great number of people apparently returned to Muquiyauyo for this festival, in the questionnaire answered by twenty-five men at the Huarón mine only three specifically mentioned Christmas as a time when they returned to Muquiyauyo; whether this was due to forgetfulness on the part of the men who filled in the ques-

tionnaire or indicates that most of the mine workers do not return
for the Christmas fiesta is not known.

The arrival of the people from out of town initiates the celebrations in the homes, but the first public phase does not get under way
until after dark. At this time a band is heard coming toward the
plaza and the first of the dance groups makes a brief appearance.
In 1949 the first group to arrive on the plaza was one of the Chacra
Negro groups, masked and costumed. They moved slowly to the
heavy, blaring beat of the band; the dancers, with black leather
masks, crossed the plaza and disappeared into the other side of
the town. Gradually other dance groups began to arrive, the costumed Tunantes groups, the Negro Pachawara, the formal and conservative Pastores, and the small but unique Huaylijía. There was
very little evidence of heavy drinking, and few people collected on
the plaza; there was still an air of preparation about everything on
this first night. Women and men made their way to the houses where
the various dance groups were going to be feasted, and the dance
groups were followed by a few children and older men who also
danced in time to the music.

On the first day or so of the Christmas fiesta religious devotion
is emphasized. While Masses are held on every day of the fiesta,
the most crowded are the midnight Mass of Christmas Eve, the
Misa de Gallo, and the dawn Mass, Misa de Aurora, on Christmas
morning. Whereas the regular Mass attendance is fifty or seventy-
five people, each of these Christmas Masses is attended by four
to six hundred people. The Muquiyauyo church cannot accommodate
such crowds and many stand outside on the plaza, squeezing in if
they can. Some people stay up all night, but for the most part the
town is quiet between the end of the midnight Mass and the beginning
of the dawn Mass.

After the dawn Mass, the plaza comes alive with the return of
dance groups; at eight in the morning there is another Mass, but it
is not so well attended as the earlier two. As the dance groups begin to appear with greater frequency, they occasionally stop for
special dances, for drinks at one of the plaza stores, or just for
quick rests. After performing on the plaza for a short time, the
groups move on again to visit the houses of members of their societies, returning periodically to the plaza. During the rest periods,
the bands often play dance music for a short period so that the
spectators can dance the *huayno,* the *marinera,* or another of the
traditional dances. During the morning more buses and trucks
bring people to the fiesta from the neighboring region. Some have

relatives in Muquiyauyo; others simply come to visit because of
the celebration, to sell things on the plaza, or to attend Mass in
the church.

During the entire day at least one dance group, accompanied by
its orchestra, is always present on the plaza. There is no formal
arrangement of schedules, but each of the seven groups spends
the better part of its time on the plaza. Sometimes there are as
many as five or six of the groups present simultaneously, each of
the orchestras playing different tunes. As the day wears on and
drinking increases, it begins to make little difference to which
orchestra one is dancing.

By the afternoon of Christmas day numerous stalls line the sides
of the plaza, where cakes, pastries, fruits, gelatin drinks, sand-
wiches, *chicha*, ice cream, beer, *aguardiente*, and coca are sold.
On December 26, 1949, there were over six hundred people present
on the plaza at one time, drinking, eating, dancing, and generally
enjoying themselves. At five in the afternoon a social dance was
held by one of the associations in the district council room on the
plaza, but by nine p.m. the plaza was again quiet.

December 27 opened quietly with a single orchestra on the plaza
at eight o'clock; not until 11 A.M. did the first dance group find its
way to the center. By midafternoon, however, between six and eight
hundred people had congregated. The most important events of this
day are the *cacha-cuy* ("invite me"), referring to the election of
the officers of the various associations for the fiesta of the coming
year. Each dance group meets, usually at the home of the *caporal*
or one of the members, and the various officials are selected for
the coming year.

The Christmas fiesta continues, the dance groups appearing
and reappearing on the plaza, until the night of the twenty-eighth.
Throughout these days of dancing, drinking, and general recreation,
the groups represent two distinct themes: there are many people
dancing informally in the Tunantes or the Chacra Negros, but also
appearing from time to time are the Pastores, who dance in precise steps and add an impressive note of seriousness to the affair.
Unlike the other dance groups--except for the Huaylijía, which
resembles the Pastores in this--the Pastores group manifests a
somewhat formal attitude toward the fiesta. The similarities and
differences among the groups are shown in the table on page 191.
It can be seen that while the Tunantes, Chacra Negros, and Negritos
are similar in almost all features, the Pastores are dissimilar to
all three of them in almost all features. The custom seems clearly
to be that when men dance they wear masks; when women dance

COMPARISON OF CERTAIN FEATURES OF THE VARIOUS TYPES OF CHRISTMAS
FIESTA DANCE GROUPS

Feature of Comparison	Christmas Fiesta Dance Groups				
	Pastores	Huaylijía	Negritos or Pachawara	Chacra Negros	Tunantes
Sex of members	Mainly women & some men	Both women & men	Men only	Men only	Men only
Nature of stationary dance	Formal	Informal	Informal	Informal	Informal
Nature of mobile dance	Formal	Formal & informal	Informal	Informal	Informal
Related story	Biblical & historical	Biblical & historical	Historical	Historical	Historical & modern
People repre-sented	Highland Indians	Highland Indians	Coastal Negroes	Coastal Negroes	Spanish coloni-als, mestizos, pig herders
Masks	Not used	Men are masked, women not	Used	Used	Used
Music	Special	Special	Special	Huayno	Huayno
Approxi-mate size of group	14	12-17	4-5	5-17	19-36

they wear no masks. Thus the women in neither the Pastores nor
the Huaylijía groups wear masks; however, the Pastores' custom
differs in that the men who dance with the women in this group do
not use masks either. There are usually very few such men, but
they indicate the seriousness of their dance by not wearing a face
covering.

All groups have two distinct dances; one, which can be called
the mobile dance, is used while moving down the streets and from
one part of the plaza to another; the other, the stationary dance, is
used when they remain in one spot. In the men's groups both of
these dances are informal in that each member may perform as
he chooses, providing he keeps some sort of time to the music
and does not stray too far from his group. The Pastores, however,
use a particular formation in both types of dances, and although
there is some leeway, the men who lead the dance make the decisions as to what these variations shall be; the women simply follow them. In both dances the basic pattern is to form two parallel
lines of dancers with a man at the head of each line (if there are
enough men). Individual dancers do fairly simple dance steps from
this formation in the stationary dance while the two rows face each

other. In the mobile dance the two rows weave simple patterns as they move down the street.

The representational aspects of the various groups again differ strongly. Both the Huaylijía and the Pastores groups combine the biblical Christmas tale with the colonial history of the highland Indians. The Pastores represent the Indian herdsmen who were brought out of the *puna* to attend Catholic Christmas rites in the communities and are also supposed to be symbolic of the shepherds who visited Bethlehem. The Huaylijía men represent the men of the high Andes; their masks are red to suggest the effect of the bitter winds. The women who dance with them are their wives. The women follow a dance pattern similar to that of the Pastores group, while the men of the Huaylijía (called *llamero, kumu,* and *waqui* or *mayó)* dance fairly freely around and among them. The Negritos, Chacra Negros, and Tunantes all represent basically historical or modern characters. Both Negro groups represent coastal peoples, and the Tunantes represent highland mestizos and Indians.

The music for most of the groups is the *huayno,* the typical highland dance. For the Pastores, Huaylijía, and the Negritos, there are special tunes. The Negritos are the only group which specifically does not use the *huayno;* they have a double-tempoed music, varying from a very slow step to a brisk march. The Huaylijía, in addition to the regular instruments of the orchestra, violins and clarinets, have two reed flutes *(pinkullo).*

The two Negro groups were said by informants to represent two aspects of the freeing of the slaves in Peru; the Pachawara or Negritos, dressed in stiff, long, flaring, velvet coats, were supposed to be the house slaves, while the Chacra Negros, as their name indicates, were supposed to be the field slaves. Today the fairly formal Negrito group is disappearing, but the Chacra Negros are changing with the times. Instead of representing freed slaves only, the group permits varieties of costume, providing only that the Negro mask continue to be used. At one point, a man dressed in top hat and tails appeared with a small United States flag in his buttonhole; later a "bridal couple" (both men) formed part of the same group.

The Tunantes group, or the Tunantada, includes three principal costume types, the *chonguinos, chupaquinas,* and *cochineros;* but here too variation is entering. Chongos and Chupaca are towns at the southern end of the valley; the *chonguinos* are dressed in the costume of the Spanish, and the *chupaquinas* wear the older style woman's costume, the *cotón.* The third group, the *cochineros,* is the largest. While the *chonguinos* and *chupaquinas* maintain a fairly serious demeanor in the course of their dances, the *cochineros* are frankly clowns. Besides these three, in each of the groups there appear various other costumes, usually not more than one of each. Among them are the *argentino*, suggestive of a colonial muleteer; the *jalapichi*, in a pierrot costume; the *charro* or tramp; the *mejicano*, with the tight-fitting trousers and wide-brimmed hat of the Mexican cowboy; the North American cowboy costume, which was copied from a movie character called Zorro; and various animals. Throughout the dance, whether in motion or stationary, the *chonguinos* and *chupaquinas* tend to remain in the center of the group and the others dance and jump in a circle around them.

After the Christmas fiesta there is a rest of two days when the Muquiyauyinos collect themselves and prepare for the New Year fiesta, another four-day affair beginning on the night of December 31 and lasting until the fourth of January. The excitement and expenditure of energy on Christmas seems in no way to reduce the activities of the New Year celebration.

As was mentioned earlier, the New Year fiesta can be paired with that of Candelaria, held in February. There are matching dance groups in each, and each is taken care of by members of one of the two principal barrios. In both, there are three main features: the masked and costumed dance group, known as the Corcovados (literally, the "humpbacked"), who prance around much as do the Tunantes in the Christmas fiesta; the bullfight; and the *tumbamonte*, or tree-cutting dance.

There were formerly two sets of dance groups in the New Year fiesta, and both still remain in Candelaria. The main one, the Corcovados, has three types of dancers, the *conquistadores* or *decentes*, the *jaujinas*, and the *indios de retaguardia*. The *conquistadores* use a costume which is basically the same as that of the *chonguinos* of the Christmas fiesta. As their name indicates, they represent the Spanish conquerors. The term *decentes* is a social class term which evidently was used to distinguish the Spanish from the mestizos and Indians. The *jaujinas* are men who dance in the current woman's costume of the valley. Just as the woman's costume of the Christmas fiesta is named after a town in the southern end of the valley where the older costume is still to be seen, so the costume in this dance is named after the town in the northern end of the valley where the new costume is predominant. The *jaujinas* supposedly represent the Indian wives of the Spanish conquerors. The *indios de retaguardia* behave very like the *cochineros* of the Christmas fiesta; they are the clowns, but they do not play this role with as much vigor as do the *cochineros*. The *indios* are supposed to be the guards of the Spaniards, going before them to clear the streets and protecting the rear of their procession; they are supposed to be dressed in cast-off Spanish clothing. In the 1950 New Year fiesta there were usually two *conquistadores*, five *jaujinas*, and seven *indios*.

The other dance group, which has survived only in the Candelaria fiesta, is that known as the Principales, or *latash aukish*. This is composed of a few males dressed as elderly men supposed to have served in the war for independence; probably similar to the United States Civil War veterans, they have here been perpetuated in a dance group. They wear knee-breeches and ponchos together with a large neckerchief and a broad hat. It was said that this group existed in the New Year fiesta until about 1904.

A feature attraction of the New Year fiesta is the *corrida de toros*, the bullfight. A large area of the plaza, directly in front of the *municipalidad* building, is fenced with logs, and a grandstand is erected along one side. Bulls are brought from some nearby hacienda in the *puna* above the town; arrangements are made for bullfighters with an entrepreneur from the capital, who hires young men from various parts of the country and assigns them to local communities for fiestas. The impresario supplies the costumes and in turn takes most of the gate receipts. The district government charges a 10 per cent tax. Even a local boy, as was the case with one of the *toreros* in 1950, must be hired through an impresario or he will have no costume to wear. There are two sets of bullfights, one on the second and one on the third of January. Each day, the dancing of the Corcovados continues.

On the last day of the fiesta the *cortamonte* or *tumbamonte* is held. A large tree is cut and erected in the middle of the plaza, and the members of the society and others begin to dance around it about three o'clock. Every few minutes someone, either a man or a woman, goes up to the tree, takes an ax from an *indio de retaguardia* who keeps general control over the matter, and takes a few swings at the tree. This goes on for a few hours, usually until about dark, or around 5:30, when the tree finally falls. Whoever delivers the final blow becomes the *padrino*, or person responsible for obtaining and erecting the tree for the fiesta of the following year.

Of course, New Year and Candelaria have their religious side as well. Unlike the Christmas fiesta, however, the religious events take place on the first day of the New Year fiesta. A wake is held all the night of December 31 in the home of the president of the sponsoring association, the Sociedad del Niño Jesus; the image of the Christ Child has been brought from the church for the occasion. On the following morning, the image is returned to the church and a Mass and a procession are held. The dancing of the Corcovados does not begin until after the procession ends about midday.

After Candelaria, in February, the next main fiesta of the year is Carnaval, held on the final days before Lent. For Carnaval there are no costumed dances and the principal activities are *carreras de cintas* and the *tumbamonte*. Unlike New Year and Candelaria, Carnaval is not sponsored by a single religious society aligned with a barrio, but by four distinct religious societies, Santo Cristo, San Pedro y San Pablo, San Juan Grande, and San Miguel. Formerly the San Juan Chico society also held its fiesta at this time; but since things evidently got somewhat crowded, this group changed in 1930 to the Monday after Easter Sunday.

Each of the societies holds a wake, a Mass, and a procession, and each sets up a tree for the *tumbamonte*. The three largest associations, which are also the three most important socially, place their trees in the main plaza; that of San Miguel is squeezed in on the other side of the park. All are cut down the same afternoon. Since there are so many people dancing, the members of the three main societies usually take turns so that there will be enough room for the members of each group to dance around their tree; occasionally, all three in the main plaza are going at once. As in the New Year and Candelaria fiestas, the trees begin to fall about dark, when most people have consumed a good deal of alcohol and are feeling in high spirits.

The *carrera de cintas*, evidently an old Spanish custom, is carried out today in Muquiyauyo by men riding bicycles under a frame hung with ribbons. At the end of each ribbon is a small ring; each rider carries a stick with which he tries to pull down one of the ribbons by inserting it in the ring. One of the ribbons has the word *padrino* written on it, and the man who succeeds in bringing down this one becomes responsible for setting up the *carrera de cintas* for the next year. Said to have been observed until 1931, the *jala-pata*, a slightly more dramatic game, was once included in Carnaval, Candelaria, and the New Year fiesta. A duck was hung by his feet from an overhead stand and riders on horseback would ride underneath, grabbing at the duck's head, and try to pull off either the duck or the duck's head.

Carnaval is by far the most boisterous and jovial fiesta of the entire year. Everyone is dressed in his best, all the women wearing new *centro* skirts and blouses; there are quantities of talcum powder and *chisguetes*, small flasks of ether, to squirt without warning into a person's face or on the back of his neck. By the end of a day of Carnaval dancing, with the combination of confetti, talcum powder, and ether in hair, eyes, and clothing, as well as beer, *aguardiente*, and sweet vermouth inside, one is heavily aware that it has been a full day.

The fiestas during the rest of the year are not so exciting as those of the first few months. Holy Week and Easter are purely religious, except for the celebration of San Juan Chico on the Monday after Easter. From time to time one of the private associations holds its fiesta, and the members may dance through the streets. But the principal remaining fiesta in which a good many people participate is Santiago, held from July 24 to 27.

Santiago is a fiesta sponsored simultaneously by a number of different families, called *pandillas*. The Santiago fiesta held by the Cáceres family, known as Santiago Mayor, starts on the night of July 24 with a wake in the *casa cofradía*, the Cáceres' house. The president, the treasurer, the *mayordomos*, and the *priostas* provide a *mishkipa* each, like those of the communal work sessions. On the twenty-fifth there is a Mass; immediately afterward the branding of animals begins, to continue all day and throughout the day of the twenty-sixth. On the last evening, a mock *corrida de toros* is held with some of the men acting the part of bulls, and the fiesta terminates in an all-night celebration.

The branding is the main rationale for the fiesta; the *pandilla* goes from house to house branding all the cattle in each. Three men are appointed *vaqueros*, cowboys, and they do the actual branding. A *mishkipa* is provided at each house, and usually five to ten houses are visited in the course of a day. The animals of any members of the *pandilla*, and those of anyone else who requests it, are branded free. The *mayordomos* of Santiago pay only for the orchestra; the members of the societies contribute for the Mass.

In all fiestas there are orchestras, usually hired from some other town, even though there are several musicians in Muquiyauyo. If there is dancing, the orchestras follow the dancing party around from house to house or sit in the corner and play for stationary dances. The orchestras are usually composed of violins, clarinets, the colonial harp; for a religious procession, various brasses will be included. For special dances some particular instrument may be used, such as the reed flute in the dance of the Negritos in the Christmas fiesta or the *tamboril* (a small drum) and bull's horn for Santiago.

Enjoying a fiesta depends to some degree upon one's wealth.

Only those with money can be active members of sponsoring groups. Also, there is competition for the privilege of being a *padrino* in a *cortamonte* or a *carrera de cintas,* for it carries some prestige. It is considered an honor to pay for the band or orchestra for a fiesta, and the more magnificent a private fiesta, the more it reflects credit on its sponsors. In the major public fiestas, however, even the poor can participate and enjoy the fun and the spectacle.

PART THREE

CULTURE CHANGE IN MUQUIYAUYO

15

THE PROCESS

ONE MOTIVE for undertaking the study of Muquiyauyo was to gain insight into why it had carried forward so many "progressive" changes. As I noted in the introduction, I am satisfied that it is impossible to account for such a series of unique events in any detail. Nevertheless, there are implications from this history that may be of some use to persons involved in culture-change situations. The next two chapters will be devoted to two general aspects of Muquiyauyo history that may be of some help in this respect. The first points out a sequence that seems to have been repeated time and time again in the history depicted here. An appreciation of the process implicit in this model can, I believe, act as a leavening factor in the activities of persons set upon directing culture change. The other aspect (discussed in chapter 16) is a general consideration of the characteristics of the region in which Muquiyauyo is located. These must be seen in perspective for an appreciation of what may be the necessary conditions for the "progressivism" attributed to the town. Lest there be any misunderstanding, I am claiming not that this approach explains *why* these things happened, but that it gives a better understanding of *how* they developed.

Everything that the Muquiyauyinos did, everything that happened to them, was merely a step or phase in a continuous historical process. Change was continual, but no single change was a violent contradiction to the contemporary situation. Rather, each change was a variation on some continuing characteristic and was acceptable in part because it did not appear to be too radical. Muquiyauyo history seems to suggest that such change is a fundamental part of the life of a society and that it is fundamental precisely because it is the way in which the members of a community handle the problems of daily living.

The model which I am undertaking to discuss in this chapter does not include all the variables in the social order but focuses on a restricted pattern of activity aspects that seems to be repeated frequently. Basically it is the following: a community is beset with problems. These problems are seen within the framework of known cultural patterns of the community dweller, and it is to these patterns that he turns for solutions to the problems. The solution is the introduction of some variation into the previously accepted way of doing things. The introduction of this change immediately sets the stage for a new situation which again has implicit in it new problems that must be solved. In addition to this, the solution undertaken may not, in fact, solve the original problem. Therefore, at any given point in time, the community is faced with both old and new problems, and every attempt at solution involves change. Let us now look at some of the specific phases of this model in more detail.

Every change that occurred was in itself not too great a change, but was an attempt to solve some problem that faced the community at the time. Muquiyauyo did not develop its community organization overnight; it did not appropriate the *cofradía* lands at a single blow; the Indians were not released from their caste by a single act; each of these things and the many others that seem in hindsight like major steps in a progressive movement of the town are either composed of numerous small steps or are in themselves small steps. If, when restudied, they seem of greater significance than many other changes which preceded or followed them, it is because our perspective makes them stand out.

A re-examination of chapters that discuss the growth of the community organization will make it clear that a development which in retrospect seems to be abrupt and of great significance was often at the time merely a passing step. An example of this process is the abolition of the Indian community, which was already weakened by the crumbling of caste distinctions, in itself a piecemeal process. The creation of a single town authority was stimulated by an immediately practical desire for jurisdiction over specific lands rather than by any sense of over-all political reform. Another step in the direction of stronger communal organization was the formalization of the *cuarteles* into legal entities, again arranged, for immediately practical reasons, in connection with the power plant.

Thus the general picture is one of evolutionary change. The communal organization of Muquiyauyo involved neither visionaries penetrating the future nor revolutionaries introducing radically

new ideas. The community organization functions today because
its formation was a gradual process in which each step filled some
specific need felt at the time.

This has important implications for community development.
First, it suggests that detailed long-range plans might better give
way to very general plans. At any specific point in a community's
history, the changes to take place next must be based specifically
on the situation current at that time. That any given situation is
a product of the previous changes should go without saying. Thus,
after the initiation of the first steps in a community development
project, there should be careful assessment of what the new situation is before future steps are planned. There has yet to be planned
a development program that can predict or take into account all
possible ramifications on the local scene. In the course of the
history of Muquiyauyo, it was frequently the secondary results of
some effort which proved to be critical. It was, for instance, not
the electricity made available by the light plant that produced the
new community organization but the issue of how the plant was
to be administered and paid for. Once a change has been instituted, it brings in its train unforeseen events that alter the scene;
this new scene is the basis on which the next steps must be taken.
The planner may plan, but the events decide.

That each of the steps in the development of the community organization was taken as a solution to a specific problem throws
some light on the specific dynamics behind the changes which took
place and provides answers to questions frequently asked by program planners. The human pressure toward the adoption of specific measures stemmed from the fact that the existing situation
was not entirely satisfactory and that an alternative seemed better.
It has for some time now been a cliché among workers in public
welfare that one must arrange a program in accordance with the
"needs" of the population in which change is to be instituted. There
is little doubt but that the term, although not the idea, has been
overworked. The people of Muquiyauyo, of course, never thought
in terms of doing what their "needs" told them to do; they felt a
need and they found something to do to satisfy it. In so doing, they
brought startling changes into their culture without consciously
planning them.

The essential part of recognizing a "need" is to recognize it as
the members of the population feel it. The welfare worker's ideas
of what a community needs may vary greatly from the needs as
seen by members of the community. And the particular needs that
seem most important at a particular time vary within the com-

munity itself. Some people of Muquiyauyo for many years have felt that their drinking water supply system was not satisfactory. Throughout the year the water flows through open canals and inevitably collects the debris that comes its way. In the rainy season the water in the river becomes brown with mud carried down from the higher mountains, and this muddy water comes into the canal system of the town. But even though this water system would strike a sanitary engineer as inadequate and even dangerous, the need was not, at least up until 1950, felt so strongly by the townspeople that all else was put aside to design and construct a better supply. Time, money, and effort were expended on new school buildings, a new cemetery wall, new park fixtures, district government buildings, and various other projects. The relative importance of some of these projects compared with a good supply of drinking water could be argued at length without getting to the main point, which is that at each particular time, through immediate situational circumstances, the need to do something else has appeared to be more immediate. The need for a better drinking water system is felt mainly by people who have learned something of the nature of the contamination of water and have been convinced by their experiences elsewhere that contamination can be avoided. The great bulk of the Muquiyauyinos are unhappy with the water situation only when the water gets muddy; otherwise, they are not aware that the supply is unsatisfactory; indeed, they consider themselves lucky that they have such a regular supply when they look at some other towns in the valley that are desperately in need of almost any kind of water supply. So far, the absence of sufficient funds, a workable plan, or sufficient interest on the part of the community has led to the postponing of this project; it will undoubtedly be undertaken when these three factors become simultaneously associated. So the question of needs is basically a viable element in the community's situation, not something in the mind of the welfare worker. It is something that the community feels when faced with a problem. Given this problem, the resources, and technological ability, the members of the community will try to find a way to solve the problem. But if these things are lacking, the members will regard other problems as more pressing or do nothing at all.

This brings us to the next point. *The problems that demand solution are defined in terms of the culture of the community and the experience of its members.* The general habit patterns of the community members shape their perception of events and direct them to see some things, and not others, as problems. But besides this general set of determinants, the various individuals of the community have had different experiences which make them consider certain specific things unsatisfactory, while their neighbors are not equally disturbed about those things. The community's culture and the individual's experience are two distinct, and occasionally conflicting, factors in the perception of a problem.

From the point of view of some of the mestizos and Indians at the turn of the century, the destruction of caste differences posed a great problem, and one that demanded solution. The two castes long had certain interests in common which served to draw them together. They fought the malpractices of the priests of Huaripampa together; they fought for the creation of Muquiyauyo as a separate district and undertook the rental of *cofradía* lands as a communal venture together. Nevertheless, the castes existed as a historical fact and as a social and cultural fact that was present in their daily lives. The presence of the fact disturbed many people, both Indians and mestizos, and they tried various ways to destroy it. At the same time, there were some mestizos and possibly some Indians, although history has lost their names, who believed that they stood to lose by such a change. In their experience they as individuals would be served better were the castes to remain distinct; cooperation was one thing, but convergence quite another. So while the general culture of the community swung in the direction of breaking down caste distinctions, there was a reverse trend under way to crystallize a system of distinctions on a new basis. From this was born the class system. For the same reasons that the caste divisions served certain purposes, the class system was firmly based on the fulfillment of some of these purposes. While the general community culture was pointing to a convergence of the castes, the habit pattern of numerous individuals selected certain elements, around which class distinctions were formed.

While the emergence of the class system may have been the result of efforts of individuals to put limitations on a general trend in the culture of the community, the reverse situation has also occurred. An excellent example was the refusal of Muquiyauyo to accept the opportunity to take over the direction of power facilities for the entire northern end of the Jauja Valley, as recounted in earlier pages. Traditional attitudes prevailed, the opportunity was lost, and the townspeople were satisfied. The young professional men who had favored the project shrugged their shoulders; they remained community members and continue to this day to give good service to the town when they can, but they have always felt that

this loss of the opportunity was a signal that "progress" in Muquiyauyo was coming to an end.

Actually, as will be noted in the next chapter, it was simply a
case of a prospective change too much against the traditional ways
of the community. Had it come in smaller steps, the change cham-
pioned by these young men gradually might have become an accomplished fact. Their experience in the outside world suggested that
such an effort would have been worth the trouble. In terms of the
general culture of Muquiyauyo, it not only was not worth the effort,
but was an actual threat.

In both these cases tradition and individual experience were active. They served to shape perception of the proposed changes in
slightly different ways and thus influenced the way such changes
were handled. In planning public welfare projects, both these factors must be taken into account. It cannot be said that tradition is
always a conservative force and the individual's experience a force
toward change. Tradition itself gradually changes and, as in the
breakdown of the caste system, individuals may resist it. The
important thing is that the presence of a problem is determined
by these two factors, and the handling of the problem will be a
direct result of the manner in which these two factors interact.

*Not only will the problems be set but the solutions selected will
be shaped by the culture and experience of the community members.*
Muquiyauyinos not only perceived problem situations in terms of
their prior experience, but their solutions were in most cases
suggested by prior experience. Perhaps the most outstanding instance of this is in the basic answers given to the increasingly
pressing problem of how to solve the man-land ratio issue. If a
given amount of land is not producing enough for a given population
to live on, there are three logical answers to the problem: (1) reduce the size of the population dependent upon the land; (2) increase
the size of the available land; and (3) increase the productivity of
the land.

The colonial and republican traditions of Peru in general, and
certainly of Muquiyauyo in particular, used the first two of these
solutions. Population was reduced through emigration. Muquiyauyinos have for at least fifty years, and probably for much longer,
been moving to other centers. Mining has long been a traditional
alternative form of labor in Peru, and many of these migrants have
gone into that work. Others have gone to the cities and found work
there. To increase the amount of land available, Muquiyauyinos
both individually and collectively have purchased more land. The
community bought the lands of Tunancancha at the end of the last

century, and various Muquiyauyinos have bought land in other districts. Some have even tried exploiting land in the jungle in the *montaña* to the east, but have returned defeated by the climate and inadequate road conditions. To reduce further the number of people dependent upon the land, people within the town have opened up stores to sell the outside products that people had heretofore gone to Jauja to purchase.

The Muquiyauyinos have also used another traditional method: the redistribution of existing lands. Basically, of course, this provides little more actual land surface, although it may bring under cultivation some land that had not been cultivated for some years. This method was used in the colonial days, as is witnessed by the 1742 repartitioning of land, and it was used again in 1904, with the distribution of the lands of the Indian community.

All of these solutions are semitraditional in Peru and among the people of the Mantaro Valley. The final alternative, however, the use of improved agricultural techniques to increase productivity, has never been seriously considered by a significant portion of the population. Muquiyauyo has today essentially an agricultural technology which is derived from a base of preconquest and Spanish agricultural crops and techniques of four hundred years ago. There has been combination and selection of traits, but nothing essentially new has been introduced. During the study, I frequently discussed past conditions with informants; in the course of these talks, there were no more sterile moments than those devoted to trying to ferret out changes in the agricultural activities. The planting of potatoes and alfalfa was introduced, but in general a person born 150 years ago could take up agriculture in Muquiyauyo today with little need for readjustment. The principal exception to this is the irrigation system, which, it must be noted, is an important technical advance. However, irrigation was carried on by both the preconquest Peruvian cultures and the Spanish; it could hardly be called an innovation in terms of either of the parent cultures.

Why have Muquiyauyinos who have traveled in other parts of Peru and other parts of the world not brought back new agricultural ideas? They have brought back new ideas in other spheres of living. The answer is probably that the people who wanted to be agriculturalists never wanted to leave Muquiyauyo at all. Those who did leave went to earn a living or to learn a trade or profession, not to do agriculture. As a result, we have had Muquiyauyinos working in New York and Los Angeles, but always in the city, never on the farms. These traveling Muquiyauyinos may have been impressed with large-scale agriculture elsewhere and with developing scientific methods of cultivation, but they have usually reflected that such things would be impossible with the limited resources and lands of the community.

To some degree they are correct; but their pessimistic views are conditioned by their traditional way of thinking about agriculture. While work on a community project is permissible communal activity in Muquiyauyo, farming is not. Even the fields owned by the community are not worked communally but are rented out to community members. Agriculture is a family matter, or a matter between individuals; it is not a matter for communal activity. Consequently, the Muquiyauyinos did not seriously consider working the lands in large areas or using cooperatives; these practices would probably not have appealed to the farming population of the town or to a Muquiyauyo traveler who thought of the possibility. Similarly, the tourist looked at the mechanization of agriculture and reflected that such implements were far beyond the reach of the Muquiyauyo farmer; in this he was correct. But again, few Muquiyauyinos have thought to press the idea of using some of the collected communal funds to purchase agricultural machinery instead of building a new government building, improving the appearance of the town park, or for some of the other communal work projects.

In this way, the Muquiyauyinos have continued to see the land-man ratio issue in terms of traditional solutions. It is not our argument here that improvement of the agriculture technology would solve the problem while the other solutions would not; while technological improvement would help for a while, in the long run the continuing increase in population would outstrip even the most modern production methods on the limited-lands available. The point is that this particular alternative has never been seriously considered by more than a few of the people of Muquiyauyo, and even among most of those who have thought seriously about it, the obstacles in the way have led them to refrain from promoting their ideas.

There are many other illustrations in both important and trivial matters of how tradition has shaped the selection of a solution to a problem. When the community decided to take over the unused *cofradía* lands at the end of the last century and use them as a source of income for the community rather than merely for the fiesta, the focusing was done by the traditional past. The Indian community had traditionally handled lands, and what was more reasonable than that the emergent mestizo-Indian community should also handle lands? The fact that Indians and mestizos could cooperate on such a venture reflected the cooperation between the castes

which had been established in Muquiyauyo at least as early as 1819
in the dispute with Huaripampa.

When the mestizos wanted to reaffirm the class distinctions which
were being weakened through the various efforts to "democratize"
the town, they chose a very traditional form of differentiation; they
started certain new fiestas in which participation was limited to
mestizos, and they re-established the differential participation in
religious activities which had been slipping away since late in the
nineteenth century. Here again tradition dictated how to attack the
problem.

When the electric light plant was nearing completion in the early
1920's, the problem of how it was to be run arose. One member
of the community council, according to the traditional handling of
communally owned or sponsored projects, suggested that one member of each *cuartel* be appointed to form a group to run the plant.
Fortunately for the well-being of the plant machinery, the suggestion was put aside in favor of another which stemmed from the personal experience of men who had worked around light plants in the
mining centers. They pointed out that the running of a power plant
needed a technically trained person, not just anyone from the *cuarteles*. In this case, a traditional solution was rejected for a solution
which came as part of the power-plant complex, that is, efficient
professional management; on the administrative side, however,
the governing body was formed along fairly traditional lines.

Even in those phases of their activities that gave Muquiyauyinos fame in many parts of Peru as being "progressive," the local
people showed a strong adherence to tradition. Of the many public
works projects which they undertook, almost all were in line with
the kind of community improvements that may be seen in many
of the towns of the Mantaro Valley and in other parts of the country;
better school buildings, a better park, better government buildings,
a larger cemetery, more extensive canals, and various other projects were not outside the local and regional traditions, but a part of
them. The enthusiasm which the Muquiyauyinos showed for these
projects perhaps serves to distinguish them from their neighbors
of other towns, but neither the projects themselves nor the way in
which they were done was very unusual.

In the same way that tradition has directed the selection of certain solutions and alternatives, it has served to reject certain others. The radical ideologies of Aprismo and communism were offered to the Muquiyauyinos by fairly enthusiastic converts; but these
ideologies helped solve no special problem and found nothing familiar in local traditions. Muquiyauyinos were not revolutionaries;

that some of their own children had become imbued with the new ideas made them no more attractive. They rejected these ideologies because basically they were so at variance with the local patterns of thought that they were really incomprehensible to most of the local people.

Recognition of a problem and the exertion of efforts to solve it do not necessarily bring success. One of the greatest problems in Muquiyauyo, that of the expanding population, has never been solved. Each new generation must face it again. Usually, of course, the old solution of seeking outside work is followed. For the present, a kind of stability has been achieved between the town and the mines; work is almost always available and the people in turn automatically think of mining when they need work. Presumably this stability can be maintained until either the population starts getting too large and the mines cannot employ all those seeking work, or until mining operations cut down or stop. When either one of these things happens, Muquiyauyo will be headed for further changes because of the old problem of expanding population.

While the solutions adopted by Muquiyauyinos have frequently not permanently solved the problems at hand, they have often had effects in and of themselves. *In the process of solving one problem, new problems are often created.* The problem of how to pay for the power plant brought the solution of renting it out to an individual; this brought in its turn the problem of how to get it back from the individual. The problem of how to get better education for some of the town's members brought the answer that they must go away to study; this in turn brought the problem that once away and accustomed to the culture of the city some of the most able Muquiyauyinos did not permanently return to the town to help solve its problems. This has been partially alleviated by the fact that a native Muquiyauyino's attachment to his home town is so strong that he returns for brief periods relatively often. Basically the problem remains unsolved.

The solutions arrived at by the Muquiyauyinos have in many cases been more realistic than those which have been presented by welfare workers in similar circumstances elsewhere; they have, at least, been devised in terms of the local culture. In many instances, however, they have been responsible for the creation of new problems in equal degree to solutions offered by outsiders. According to some anthropologists, this should not be the case; if a solution is reached in accordance with the nature of the culture involved, new problems should not be so likely to arise. And yet we must, in view of the history of Muquiyauyo, accept the conclusion that culturally sympathetic solutions can be quite as upsetting in the long run as those which are made with little reference to the culture. This presents us with what seems to be a dilemma: if culturally sympathetic solutions also present problems, why should we make a special effort to orient solutions in terms of the culture of the people involved?

The answer to this lies in the acceptance or rejection of a given solution, whether or not it produces problems. Solutions which are developed with little reference to the social order and way of life of the people for whom they are designed will not find easy acceptance; those which do take these circumstances into account will be more readily accepted. This says nothing about whether or not either solution will produce more or greater problems in the future. Thus the design of solutions which will avoid future problems must take into account more than merely the culture for which they are designed; they must take into account as well the consequences, both cultural and noncultural, of the solutions. This requires a much more intensive analysis of the factors involved than either the average community member or average welfare worker is interested in or capable of carrying out. It is a serious question whether it is even possible to design solutions to some problems which will avoid the creation of future problems. Perhaps one of the most obvious facts that all of history hands down to us is that nothing in human life, even the environment, remains stable and constant. The creation of new problems is merely one of the ways in which now possibilities for change are framed.

The principal events of culture change in Muquiyauyo, as outlined here, can be summarized in terms of problems, their solutions, their reappearance, and the creation of new problems. Technical aid programs inevitably enter communities when some changes are already under way. Even a brief examination of the changes which have been occurring in the past can help a great deal in both the planning and development of such programs in the future.

16

THE PARTICULAR

THE TRAVELER in the Mantaro Valley notes few outward differences among the various towns between Jauja and Huancayo. Some are larger than others and are built under different restrictions of terrain, but in general they are highly similar to one another. Within the towns, in the fiestas and daily life, the similarity goes still deeper. The same orchestras are used, the same kinds of dance groups and costumes, the same *centro* and *cotón* dresses for women; *mishkipas* are held and work sessions are carried on. In short, it is hard to find differences in the superficial culture between one town and another.

In the course of exploring Muquiyauyo's history, one finds the superficial similarity to other towns in the area even more apparent; Muquiyauyo built itself a bridge, a new municipal government building, a canal system; so, then, did Huaripampa. Muquiyauyo started taking over the usufruct of *cofradía* lands; but so did numerous other towns, and some, such as Sincos, took them over much more forcefully than did Muquiyauyo. The style of dress has been changing in Muquiyauyo, but it has been changing in all the other towns in the valley, particularly in the northern part. There has been elaboration in fiesta costumes and dance groups in Muquiyauyo, but the same elaborations are to be seen in the other towns. There are communal works in Muquiyauyo, but there are also communal works in the other towns, and the other towns also have communal pride and spirit. Indeed, some of the towns have been the subject of monographs, the acme of local enthusiasm, and patriotic fervor has not yet produced a monograph for Muquiyauyo.

It must be concluded that the special quality which has given rise to comments by outsiders on Muquiyauyo's progressiveness does not stem from a unique culture. Muquiyauyo has been the leader in a number of innovations, particularly the electric light plant and the communal government, which have been especially important. Aside from this, however, it is the general valley culture shared by Muquiyauyo with the other towns which is, itself, somewhat special. The valley customs are so distinct from those of the Indians of the southern highlands and so noticeably of Spanish derivation or influence that the inhabitants cannot be considered culturally in the same category as the Indians of Cuzco or Puno. Indeed, a number of writers who have had occasion to study phases of valley culture have referred to its inhabitants as mestizos.[1]

I am firmly convinced that basically the reason Muquiyauyo has made a name for itself is because it was a particularly active town in a particularly active region, with emphasis on the latter. We would not expect to find Muquiyauyo's counterpart in the more completely Indian departments of the country. To see the uniqueness of Muquiyauyo, then, we must look briefly at the region of which it is a part.

The Peruvian folklorist José María Arguedas has listed four characteristics of at least the past one hundred years which he believes account for the mestizo character of the culture of the Mantaro Valley.[2] These are: (1) the large-scale mining operations in the department of Junín; (2) the construction of the central railway (1903-8) which linked Huancayo and the valley to Lima; (3) the proximity of the valley to the national capital; (4) the agricultural richness of the zone and the fact that most properties were in small holdings so that development was not restricted by a pattern of large haciendas and a vast worker group. There is little doubt that all these factors have been very important. In my study of Muquiyauyo, the consequence of the mines was particularly obvious. The kinds of influence that are exerted by contact with Lima are no less important although more difficult to list, since they become effective gradually and originate not only in Lima but in other centers as well. That the Mantaro region is not a hacienda region, while not stressed in the present study, stands out in a comparison of it with other regions of Peru.

However, three of Arguedas' factors are not dynamic; the presence of the mines, the proximity to Lima, and the railway are in themselves conducive to only a limited culture change; they open the way for change if pressure toward change is felt. The pressure, as pointed out earlier, has come in the form of population growth and the resulting increased participation in the national economy; these have forced the utilization of the nondynamic factors. The mines, the railway, and Lima were visited and became influential because under the pressure of the expanding population, people were forced to leave the valley. Population growth, of course, has combined with Arguedas' fourth factor, the overwhelming presence of small landholdings, to produce the increasingly restrictive man-land ratio which was the form the population pressure took.

Division of the valley into small landholdings also played a non-dynamic role. Besides combining with population growth to produce population pressure, it gave each individual some freedom to remain in agricultural work if he inherited or could purchase enough land. Since large haciendas did not control all the land in the region, small ownership was always possible for a limited proportion of the community, and this was doubtless conducive to a rather unusual attitude toward life and labor in general. In Muquiyauyo, the ordinary citizen is an independent operator; he is not dependent upon a landlord.

Combining the fact of expanding population with small landholdings, then, people have been forced out of Muquiyauyo and the valley in general; the railway has provided the path to the mines and to Lima. It is one of the coincidences of history that the expansion of mining began early in this century at about the time when the population pressure was becoming really strong. This picture tells us how Muquiyauyinos were forced out of the town to new places to learn new things.

There are still two aspects of the picture which we must consider: what brought emigrants back to the town with the new things they had learned in the mines and cities; and what made the town accept the new things that their traveling countrymen introduced. When Muquiyauyinos go away to work, they seldom plan to remain forever. Many have or will inherit lands in Muquiyauyo, and they plan to return for at least part of the year to do agricultural work. Others, particularly those who gain professional training and those who work in the city, may live permanently away from the town, but inevitably return from time to time, usually at the time of one of the fiestas or for one of the major work sessions. It is not just a few who bring new ideas to the towns; there are such travelers in almost every family. The Muquiyauyo community has members scattered over many other regions; some of them return because they have a better living waiting for them at home, others only because they find themselves emotionally attached to their families or birthplace.

Whether he works regularly away from or in the town, the Muquiyauyino is often able to provide his town with suggestions as to how things should be done. Indeed, it is sometimes a person who works regularly outside the town who takes the lead in community discussions and carries more weight than does the permanent town-dweller.

In bringing back information on how things are done elsewhere, however, Muquiyauyinos are not very different from other valley townspeople. It is not until we come to the final factor, that of the actual adoption of the suggested innovations, that we touch on something in which Muquiyauyo may differ from its neighbors. We do not know what has made the people of Muquiyauyo more ready to adopt, and more capable of adopting, new ideas than those in other communities. One factor, however, may be especially important.

During the nineteenth century, the mestizos and Indians of Muquiyauyo were thrown together a number of times through common interest. The first mention we have of this is during the 1819-20 dispute with Huaripampa, in which we find the Indian community and the community of mestizos, creoles, and Spaniards getting together to gain the right to support only one church. The creation of the irrigation canal system just after the middle of the century very likely brought the two together again, since the land of both groups was to be irrigated. Later, as the issue of district independence became stronger, the two groups again felt common interest. Perhaps the clearest indication of this gradual growing together was the ease with which the Indian community, as an organization, was dissolved by the new district council in the early 1890's, and, following this, the goodwill with which the Indians divided up their own communal lands and thereby abolished the last vestige of the Indian community as a distinct economic or political entity. The establishment of the community group to handle the renting of the *cofradía* lands at the end of the century was another positive action taken by Indians and mestizos together; they were acting as a community, not as two conflicting caste or class groups.

This cooperation between members of the two classes brought about not only the possibility of united community action but equally important side effects. The emphasis placed on education, especially education of the Indians, opened a whole new area of activity for persons of high native ability. Most mestizos previously had stayed in the traditional professions of law and medicine; a very few had gone into engineering or the other professional lines of work. The Indians who left to study often went into accounting, engineering, or some other activity in which there was not so much mestizo competition. As a result, when the community considered the possibility of a new engineering venture or encountered an accounting problem, there were trained people available, frequently of Indian background, who could provide the technical help needed.

It seems reasonable to suppose that these related factors--that the community could act as a whole and that there were technically capable men available locally--may well have played an important part in Muquiyauyo's ability to come to decisions and act on these decisions.

Another factor worth exploring is the relative importance of the democratic process of reaching decisions, which was witnessed in the community and *cuartel* meetings described earlier. In both meetings mestizos tended to carry the main discussion; however, the persons of the Indian class were not in any way discouraged. The only person I ever saw stopped from speaking was one who had already held the floor for some time. Indeed, efforts were made to obtain participation which was not always forthcoming. The history of these meetings may be in some part a distinctive contribution of the Indian heritage of the town. The old Indian community meetings are described as being very similar to those I witnessed, with some obvious changes: in the Indian meetings there were no records kept and the meetings were held outdoors; of course, those who were considered the local leaders also made the greatest contribution to the discussions.

The breakdown of the caste system in Muquiyauyo not only brought a change in the many traits which formerly distinguished members of one group from the other, but actually encouraged a positive cooperative interaction between the mestizos and Indians. To what degree this cooperative community action is duplicated in other communities I do not know; in Muquiyauyo, however, the community is established on the basis of active participation by all members of the community, not just by people designated as representatives.

Another consideration, hard to recover from history, is the degree to which leadership has played a role in placing Muquiyauyo ahead of some of the neighboring towns. The differences among the accomplishments of the various communities is so slight that it is easy to lay the credit for Muquiyauyo's advance to the fact that it had particularly good leaders.[3] Muquiyauyo has indeed had very good leaders. Román Amanzo, to whom is attributed most of the early ventures in public works and who has assumed almost legendary proportions in the memory of the townspeople, the Padre Guzmán, Mariano Torres, Gabriel Bustamante, and Manuel Quintana, together with various others both in past and present generations, have without doubt dominated in furthering many various activities. However, leadership can break its head against unrespon-

sive groups of followers, and there is little doubt that the Muquiyauyo population has played a dynamic role in its responsiveness.
When the townspeople do not wish to do something, they make it
abundantly clear, and even excellent leadership will not sway them.

Some of Muquiyauyo's reputation must be attributed to a continued effective relationship between leaders and followers. The
development of the communal organization was a community product and, while rather random in its creation, certainly one for
which no single individual or group can take credit. It was generations in the making. The fact that it was quickly copied by other
communities in the valley indicates that the basic cultural and
social establishment was already present in the other towns, and
Muquiyauyo served as a model and catalyst. We know from the
studies of Escobar, Muelle, and Tschopik that many of the features
of the organization, such as *cuarteles*, have been present in other
communities. [4]

With respect to leadership, it is probably significant that the Muquiyauyinos with whom I talked never attributed any of the major
Muquiyauyo enterprises to any one man.

In recognizing Muquiyauyo's dependence upon the general cultural
development of the entire valley for parts of its own development,
it is necessary to recognize that it has also been limited by this
culture. The most outstanding example of this which comes to mind
is the case of the opportunity to assume charge of the power facilities for the northern end of the valley. It will be remembered that
representativos of two of the largest valley towns, Concepción and
San Jerónimo, came to Muquiyauyo at that time and presented prop-
ositions which would have given Muquiyauyo control of the power
facilities of most of the major towns of the valley. While it is not
certain, it seems likely that Muquiyauyo's refusal to take advantage of these opportunities may be due to the fact that it seemed
like too big a proposition; being so much larger than anything previously envisaged, it may have appeared as an imposition on the
part of the other towns. No one else in the valley was carrying on
such exaggerated efforts; why should Muquiyauyo?

In evaluating the accomplishments of Muquiyauyo and the leadership it has shown in public works and community organization in the
Mantaro Valley, it is necessary to remember both the process and
the particular. The process, or the development and perception of
problems, the design of solutions in accordance with the culture
and experiences of the townspeople, and the reappearance of problems are to be considered as the means by which cultural and social

change has gone on throughout history. The particular features which make the Mantaro Valley unique in Peru, and Muquiyauyo individualistic within the Mantaro region, provide us with an insight into some reasons behind the special way in which the process worked in Muquiyauyo. The principal particulars were the regional factors of population pressure, mining, open routes to the mines and the coast, and local pride and attachment, combined with Muquiyauyo's own particular social history of cooperation of the two castes.

APPENDIX

METHODS AND MATERIALS USED IN THE STUDY

THE STUDY of Muquiyauyo was planned with a methodological as well as a research goal; culture change and progressivism in Muquiyauyo were to be studied, and the major concentration would be on local historical sources. The materials of local history are not often relied upon by anthropologists in the field; their principal work is usually to study the contemporary culture rather than local documents. When anthropologists do resort to history, such research is usually carried out in the libraries of major cities, or is limited to birth, death, marriage, and court records of the community in which they are working.

The Use of Local Historical Materials

The materials of local history, that is, the documentary materials which have relevance only to a highly localized area, can be utilized to afford clues to new data, to provide a means of checking data already gathered from informants, and frequently to establish a fairly reliable chronology of events which take on special meaning when their precise time sequence is known. Even in a fairly well-documented area, however, a number of problems confront the ethnologist who tries to make use of such materials.

First, the kind of social and cultural information contained in most local records is very limited. Redfield pointed this out in validating his own methods in Yucatán (*The Folk Culture of Yucatán*, Chicago, 1941, p. 341): "There is doubt that the documents and the artifacts will ever yield decisive information on such problems as changes in the kinship system, on forms of courtship and marriage, or on the steps by which some of the saints were incorporated into the pagan pantheon while the pantheon in other respects was also changing character." Redfield, of course, listed only a

219

few of the aspects of culture that are rare or entirely absent in the usual sources of local history.

Second, while such documents do provide certain information of a type that can be obtained in no other way, locating them in a town even as small as Muquiyauyo may consume days and even weeks of valuable field research time. The value which may suddenly be attached to some heretofore forgotten document by its owner when it is discovered that someone wishes to use it is an aspect of human psychology which has long irritated the historian, but which has seldom troubled the ethnologist. And, of course, the careless loss and mislaying of such documents is commonplace.

Third, from the point of view of quantitative accumulation of data, the use of such materials is more time-consuming with less result than can be shown from more traditional ethnographic work. On the other hand, it must be looked upon as a specialized method and, as such, must be judged on the basis of results as well as economy of time.

All in all, the difficulties do not overbalance some of the excellent results to be gained from utilizing documentary materials from the local community. These materials, from the point of view of access and use, may be divided into two categories: the systematic and the scattered. The scattered documents are usually separate papers, occasionally in sets, which may or may not be useful in some particular problem confronting the student. These frequently come to light quite by accident, although the student may have knowledge of their existence long before they can be located. An example of this in the present study is the list of Indians who received land in the 1904 repartition of lands, together with the amount of land they received and where it was located (Document A-20). This list gave the names and allotments of land that had formerly been the property of the Indian community and provided an almost certain list of those family heads who were considered to be members of the Indian caste or class at the turn of the century. I was told of the existence of this paper shortly after beginning the inquiry into the social composition of the social class system. Ultimately a copy was provided from the papers preserved by Pedro Bustamante, who had made a copy by hand before the original was lost.

The second kind of document, the systematic, includes all those records kept by various offices and organizations because they form a systematic part of their operations. These papers, in the kind of research being carried on in Muquiyauyo, must be considered as wholes. That is, one does not approach them with the state of mind of the biographer searching for data on a certain person, or the historian who wants material only on a certain topic; rather, they must be approached from the point of view of the general ethnographer dealing with an informant. Almost anything in the records may ultimately be of value, and consequently all of them must be read with great care and copious notes taken. The degree to which one generalizes in notes will be the degree to which data is obscured later because of lack of detail. Each volume examined must be considered an informant; the ethnographer must note digressions, innuendoes, excessive emphasis, corrections, and so forth. Only cumulative experience helps the student learn which short-cuts are safe, which tasks may be bypassed.

It might be well to describe a few of the kinds of information utilized in the present study which were derived from the study of these documentary sources. The termination dates for fiestas could in many cases be narrowed down through verbal reports concerning their continued use. In others, the references to the abandoning of the *cofradía* land served to give quite an accurate dating for the end of the celebration of a fiesta. Informants knew that at one time there was fighting between the barrios in fiestas; I had no way of ascertaining when this stopped except by the fact that there were references to it in the books. The entire history of such things as the construction of the new church building, the appropriation of the *cofradía* lands, the development of the community organization, the decline of older organizations and surviving elements, the work projects, relations with other towns, differential treatment of Indians and mestizos, and the parts played by individuals in all these and numerous other events were taken almost entirely from the documents.

Perhaps one of the most useful, and frequently disturbing, results of using the papers was that they provided a check on the accuracy of informants. They permitted the verification of specific data and a general evaluation of a particular informant as a source of information. This latter was disturbing because it led the writer to be very skeptical of the memory of perhaps two-thirds of his informants. In some cases, however, consistent accuracy of the informants forced the writer to change his attitude toward information which, on some other basis, he originally doubted.

The use of documents obviously cuts in considerably on time that might otherwise be used to gain information through questioning, observing, or carrying on systematic studies on specific topics. There were, when I left Muquiyauyo, some townspeople who did not know that I had been living there, much less the manner of thing I might have been doing. Ethnography suffers, of course, in direct proportion to the amount of time devoted to the historical material.

The specific documents that provided the basic data on which the present study is based were handled in two ways. One group was systematically summarized; the other was copied.

The summarized documents included the following:

1. Session books of the district of Muquiyauyo, 1887 to 1949, except for the years 1898 to 1903, which were lost. This loss was very unfortunate since it covered the years in which so much occurred in the rental of *cofradía* lands and the repartitioning of the Indian communal lands. The volumes used consisted of six legal-sized volumes of between two hundred and five hundred leaves each.

2. Session books of the Junta Comunal and the Comunidad, 1895 to 1938. The books after 1938 were not available. Nine volumes of the same general size as the district session books.

3. Miscellaneous community records: cash books, papers on litigations, land listings, and so forth.

4. District statistical records: birth, marriage, and death records kept by the district from about 1900.

5. *Cuartel* papers: comprising session books, cash books, land rental books, lists of fines and work projects, and so forth, which in general parallel the books kept by the community and date from the same period. The records from only one *cuartel* were summarized.

6. Records of the sessions of the religious Sociedad de Santo Cristo, dating irregularly from 1811. This group of papers was summarized by Edward Bernard.

The other kinds of documents were those which were, for the most part, copied word for word. In general, the documents that were copied in this manner were those in which the wording was of some importance, those of which I felt I could not know the full significance until after I had completed most of the field work and turned to analysis, and those whose owners did not wish to relinquish them for too long. They include what we have referred to as scattered papers. It is only to these papers that particular reference has been made in the notes throughout the book. They are divided up into series, each of which is assigned a letter; the papers in each series are numbered consecutively.

1. Document Series A, papers 1 to 21. Historical documents, copies of which have been preserved by Pedro Bustamante; dates are 1662, 1728, 1735, 1742, 1879, 1886, 1904; this series also

includes a summary of events related in district acts, 1886 to 1901.

2. Document Series B, kept in notebooks. Birth, death, and marriage records.

3. Document Series C, papers 1 to 49. Copies and summaries of the papers of the Sociedad de Santo Cristo; the originals are in the possession of Don Gaspar Vilca and Jesús Quintana.

4. Document Series D. Miscellaneous documents of a political nature, most of which are of little consequence.

5. Document Series E, papers 1 to 75. Historical papers covering the dispute between Muquiyauyo on the one hand and Huaripampa and the parish priest on the other, in the years 1819-20.

6. Document Series F, papers 1 to 8. Miscellaneous documents relating to the purchasing and receiving of land by the community, 1879 to 1938.

7. Document Series G. Copies of the land ownership lists made out for irrigated properties for the purpose of calculating water rents, 1943.

Before leaving the subject of documentation in local history studies, it would be well to mention some of the papers which the writer never had the opportunity to examine, not only to let the reader know the limitations of the present study, but to give him an idea of the vast amount of material that is still available for the study of even a single highland community like Muquiyauyo. These sources include:

Records of the numerous religious associations

Records of the Justices of the Peace

Records of the *gobernador* (many of these papers are lost in Muquiyauyo because the *gobernador* has never had an official office in which to store his papers)

Tax records in the Caja de Depositos y Consignaciones y Departamento de Recaudacion in Jauja

Records of the short stay of the Guardia Civil post in Muquiyauyo, kept in the office of the Comandancia de Policía in the departmental capital, Huancayo

Records of the Dirección de Agricultura del Ministerio de Fomento in Huancayo

Pertinent references in newspapers, such as *La Voz de Huancayo*, *Porvenir* (Jauja), *El Comercio* (Lima), *El Jaujino* (Jauja, but no longer published), and various others, both regional and national

The many documents that may reveal some phase of local his-

torical development can, from the point of view of the ethnographer
or historian, be considered infinite. In Peru, for example, there
are an increasing number of theses being written in the normal
schools concerning folklore and economic and social conditions.
Various monographic histories of particular towns, fiestas, or
regions are written by local and professional students. The national capital, of course, has many unexplored documentary materials
which, approached from the point of view of the local community,
can provide even more information.

It should be clear that the problems of historical research into
cultural and sociological data on a local community or region will
frequently suffer not from lack of material but from the extreme
variations in the quality of information which can be taken there-
from. In general, the data that can be taken from these sources
provide an important complement to information that is to be found
in the ordinary course of anthropological field research.

Ethnographical and Sociological Study Techniques

My field work followed the fairly usual pattern of going to the
fields with the farmers, visiting in stores with storekeepers, traveling to market, pacing off land areas with landowners, recording
techniques of doing things, ways of saying things, and so on. Of
my principal informants, seven were generally regarded as mestizo, five as Indian; ten were men, two were women; three were
under thirty years of age, six were between thirty and fifty, and
three were over fifty. The bias, as can easily be seen, is toward
the mestizo and the male. The data on the feminine culture is particularly sparse, and the point of view expressed in much of the
study is that of the mestizo.

In the course of the study, two systematic surveys were made,
the census and the judgments placing *cuartel* members in social
classes. Since most of the numerical data are taken from either
one or a combination of these two studies, they will be described
here.

I learned of the existence of the social classes soon after arriving
in the town. I had not yet taken a census to get a name list, nor did
I wish to do so until I had been there a much longer time. Fortunately, the *cuarteles* each kept a list of their members, the total
of which at the time came to 459. I then received from each of four
men judgments as to whether each member was Indian or mestizo.
Judging was done privately, with separate lists of the names. It
was made clear that we were concerned with the social placement

of these people, not with their racial characteristics. From the final judgments it was possible to divide the names on the list into five categories: those which all judges agreed were mestizo (64, or 14 per cent); those which one judge thought to be Indian and three mestizo (31, or 7 per cent); those which two judges thought to be Indian and two mestizo (46, or 10 per cent); those which three judges thought to be Indian and one mestizo (92, or 20 per cent); and those which all judges agreed were Indian (224, or 49 per cent). Since the three groups over which the judges disagreed were small and there were few judges actually giving opinions, it was decided to consider three groups only for the present study: those whom all judges agreed were Indian (224, 49 per cent); those over whom the judges disagreed (169, 37 per cent); and those whom all judges agreed were mestizo (64, 14 per cent). These three groups are referred to in the text as Indian, undecided, and mestizo. It must be remembered that these judgments were concerning individual persons. In the census about to be described residential units and family heads were noted specifically, so there are names which occur in the above class sample but which do not occur in the census. Also, since there are various families which do not belong to a *cuartel,* there are many in the census which did not appear in the class sample.

The class sample is biased toward a mestizo viewpoint. At the time the study was made, I could not be sure just where the four judges would fit in the system. It developed that three of the four were mestizos. It was originally arranged to have the judgments given by eight people, four Indians and four mestizos. Only four, however, three mestizos and one Indian, returned the lists with the information.

The census was taken in March and April, 1950. It was designed principally to get data on certain aspects of the culture and social participation of the townspeople, not to get a complete list of names of the population. It could not, because of insufficient personnel, be a *de facto* census, nor could it be done all on one day. The collecting of the data was done over a period of six weeks, so that by the time it was finished, whole families had changed their residences or gone to the mines for temporary work.

A form was prepared and printed in Jauja. I found three men in the town to help gather the data. Since they had their own regular work to do, they could not put in full time on the census. The subjects covered in the form were:

Name of owner or family head

Location of residence

Names and relationships of others in the house
Occupations, primary and secondary
Civil status
Number of cattle, horses, donkeys, sheep, pigs, guinea pigs,
    chickens, ducks, and so on
Languages spoken by the parents
Languages spoken by the children
Religion professed
Religious societies to which the family head belonged
Religious societies to which his spouse belonged
Cuartel membership
Number of eucalyptus, aliso, guindo trees
Method of cultivating fields: (alone, with help of family, with
    huajiti, partidario, paid labor)
Places visited by the head of the family (Jauja, Huancayo, Huan-
    cavelica, Huarón, Ayacucho, Oroya, Cerro de Pasco, the
    northern highlands, the southern highlands, Lima, the north
    coast, the south coast)
Extent of education of the head of the family (primary, second-
    ary, other)
Sports club membership

The census finally included data on 515 residential units. I estimate that there were probably 25 residential units which were
occupied but which were not included in the census. Using the figure
of 4.2 people per family, which comes from the 1940 census, we
get an approximate population of 2,268 people for 1950.

For the purpose of analysis, the data from the census forms
and from the sample class survey were punched on keysort cards.

NOTES

Introduction
1. Hildebrando Castro Pozo, *Nuestra comunidad indígena* (Lima: Editorial "El Lucero," 1924), pp. 63-68; J. Merle Davis, "The Economic and Social Setting," in *Indians of the High Andes*, ed. W. Stanley Rycroft (New York, 1946), pp. 43-45; Harry Tschopik, Jr., *Highland Communities of Central Peru* (Institute of Social Anthropology, Publication No. 5 [Washington, D.C.: Smithsonian Institution, 1947]), pp. 46-48. Of these three accounts, Castro Pozo's was the pioneering report and Tschopik's perhaps closest to being accurate. Concerning Muquiyauyo, the report edited by Rycroft is extremely erroneous, and the reader is cautioned to place no faith in it.
2. Richard N. Adams, Muquiyauyo: A Study, with the Utilization of Ethnographic and Local History Materials, of Culture Change and Progressivism in the Central Sierra of Peru (Ph.D. thesis, Yale University, 1950).
3. See Richard N. Adams, "Personnel in Culture Change: A Test of a Hypothesis," *Social Forces*, XXX (1951), 185-89.

Chapter 1
1. William H. Prescott, *History of the Conquest of Peru* (New York: Harper and Brothers, 1847), I, 505.
2. The appended glossary includes most of the foreign words that appear in the text.

Chapter 2
1. Figures for the population of Huanca province for 1525 and 1571 are given by John H. Rowe, "Inca Culture at the Time of the Spanish Conquest," in *Handbook of South American Indians*, ed. Julian Steward (Bureau of American Ethnology, Bulletin 143 [Washington: Smithsonian Institution, 1947]), II, 184.

2. *Ibid.*

3. Population data for 1628 and 1754 are given by George Kubler, "The Quechua in the Colonial World," in *Handbook of South American Indians,* II, 338.

4. Document A-17, author's collection. The document numbering system is explained in the appendix.

5. George Kubler, *The Indian Caste of Peru, 1795-1940* (Institute of Social Anthropology, Publication No. 14 [Washington: Smithsonian Institution, 1952]), Table 2, p. 21.

6. Document A-20.

7. Kubler, *The Indian Caste of Peru,* p. 21.

8. Document A-18.

9. *Censo nacional de población de 1940: Departamentos Huánuco, Junín* (Lima: Dirección Nacional de Estadistica, n. d.), IV.

10. These colonial land claims comprise Documents A-1 through A-16.

11. Antonio Vázquez de Espinosa, *Compendio y descripción de las Indias Occidentales* (Smithsonian Miscellaneous Collections, Vol. CVIII [Washington: Smithsonian Institution, 1948]).

12. Document A-17.

13. José Varallanos, *Legislación indiana republicana* (Lima: C. I. P., 1947), p. 47.

14. Estimated from two maps made by Teofilo Moreno in 1937.

Chapter 3

1. Data on the Inca and the Inca organization are drawn principally from Rowe, "Inca Culture," pp. 183-330.

2. The term *"curaca"* was gradually replaced by the term *"cacique"* brought in by the Spanish from the Antilles.

3. Rowe, "Inca Culture," p. 255.

4. Kubler, "The Quechua in the Colonial World," p. 364.

5. *Ibid.*

6. *Ibid.,* p. 376.

7. Rowe uses the terms: *Hanan wañka, Horin wañka,* and *Sawsa.* This is fairly standard except for the last. Eliseo Sanabria Santiváñez in his *Historia de Urin Wanca ó San Jerónimo de Tunan* (Cerro de Pasco, Peru: Imprenta "Kipus," 1943) uses the term *Hatun Wanka.*

8. Vázquez de Espinosa, *Compendio y descripción de las Indias Occidentales,* p. 442.

9. Documents A-1 to A-9. See chapter 2 for further discussion of the Martínez claim.

10. Documents A-10 to A-16.

11. Documents E-1 to E-75.

12. Justino M. Tarazona S., *Demarcación política del Perú: Recopilación de leyes y decretos (1821-1946)* (Lima: Ministerio de Hacienda y Comercio, 1946), pp. 15-18.

13. Document A-18, a history of the efforts to make Muquiyauyo a district, written by Pedro Bustamante.

14. Tarazona S., *Demarcación política del Perú,* pp. 1005-6.

15. Moisés Sáenz, *The Peruvian Indian* (Washington, D.C.: 1944), p. 3.

16. S/. is the symbol for the *sol,* the Peruvian unit of currency. At the time of study, the *sol* fluctuated around fifteen to the dollar.

17. In 1824 Bolívar officially prohibited communally owned lands. The decree was not very effective in many parts of the highlands.

18. Castro Pozo, "Social and Economico-Political Evolution of the Communities of Central Peru," p. 491.

Chapter 4

1. In Muquiyauyo the term *cofradía* has been reserved for religious brotherhoods that were financed by the *cofradía* lands; the term *sociedad* has, in recent years, been used for brotherhoods that were otherwise financed.

2. George M. Foster, "Cofradía and Compadrazgo in Spain and South America," *Southwestern Journal of Anthropology,* IX (1953), 1-28. This source gives some of the background of the *cofradía.*

3. Document E-29.

4. Document A-21.

5. Documents C-1 to C-49.

6. The author's census is described in the appendix.

7. Sergio Quijada Jara, *Estampas huancavelicanas: Temas folkloricos* (Lima: Empresa Tipografica "Salas é Hijos," 1944), p. 61.

Chapter 5

1. Some of the material in this chapter originally appeared in my articles "A Study of Labor Preference in Peru," *Human Organization,* I (1951), 37-38; and "A Change from Caste to Class in a Peruvian Sierra Town," *Social Forces,* XXXI (1953), 238-44.

Chapter 7

1. Document A-20.

2. Document G-1.

Chapter 8

1. Rowe, "Inca Culture," p. 216.

2. *Ibid.*, p. 212.

3. Such as Bernard Mishkin describes for the Quechua community of Kauri in "The Contemporary Quechua" in *Handbook of South American Indians,* II, 418.

Chapter 9

1. Tschopik, *Highland Communities of Central Peru,* p. 45.

2. This was a *de jure* census, that is, it included names of Muquiyauyinos who were not actually resident in the town at the time.

3. Data on the weekly variation in store trade are taken from a record of the gross income over a period of a year and a half kept by Tobias Torres in his plaza store.

4. Luis E. Valcárcel, "Indian Markets and Fairs in Peru," in *Handbook of South American Indians,* II, 479.

Chapter 10

1. John Gillin, *Moche: A Peruvian Coastal Community* (Institute of Social Anthropology, Publication No. 3 [Washington: Smithsonian Institution, 1945]), p. 49 and Plate XIII (middle, center).

Chapter 14

1. Tschopik, *Highland Communities of Central Peru,* p. 47, footnote 9.

Chapter 16

1. Tschopik, *Highland Communities of Central Peru,* pp. 38 and 46; José María Arguedas, "Cuentos mágico-realistas y canciones de fiestas tradicionales del valle del Mantaro; Provincias de Jauja y Concepción. Archivo del Instituto de Estudios Etnológicos," *Folklore Americano* (Lima), I (1953), 111-24.

2. Arguedas, "Cuentos . . . del valle del Mantaro," p. 118.

3. Davis, "The Economic and Social Setting," p. 45.

4. Tschopik, *Highland Communities of Central Peru,* pp. 37-45.

GLOSSARY

THE GLOSSARY includes most of the foreign words used in this volume. Some are Spanish; some are words of Spanish or other European origin which, over the years, have taken on special significance in the town of Muquiyauyo. There are also words of local Indian origin. In this last group it was not possible to distinguish those which might be Quechua from those which might be of Huanca origin. Muquiyauyinos insist that the Indian language spoken there is Huanca.

The words in the following list have been classified as of Spanish origin (S) if they came to Peru from the Old World with the Spaniards; of aboriginal origin (A) if they were used somewhere in the New World prior to the conquest; and of English origin (E) if derived from English-speaking peoples. If a word is aboriginal but its provenance is not Peruvian, it is listed as (AO). At least one aboriginal word (cacique) is neither Quechua nor Huanca but of Antillean origin. A question mark indicates uncertain provenance.

Some words are listed as mixtures: *cuyero,* for example, is a combination of *cuy* (A) and the Spanish suffix *-ero* and is therefore classified as (A-S); *volibol* is a Spanish transliteration of the English volleyball and is therefore classified as (S-E).

In determining the etiology of some of the words, the *Diccionario de la lengua española,* issued by the Real Academia Española (17th edition), has been considered the final authority wherever possible; if a word has not appeared there, I have exercised my own judgment.

For the identification of plants and trees I am indebted to Dr. Volney Jones; I also used Carl O. Sauer's "Cultivated Plants of South and Central America," in Julian Steward's *Handbook of South American Indians,* Volume VI, and "El mundo vegetal de los antiguos peruanos," by Eugenio Yacovleff and Fortunato Herrera.

231

accionista (S)--shareholder.

acequia (S)--canal; specifically an irrigation canal.

adobe (S)--sun-dried clay bricks.

adoratorio (S)--the home altar.

agente municipal (S)--a municipal official of the turn of the century.

aguador (S)--water carrier.

aguardiente (S)--a nationally produced liquor made of sugar cane; the term is also used occasionally in Peru to refer to the cheaper *piscos*.

ahijado (S)--godchild.

ají (AO)--chili pepper; *Capsicum sp.*

alalaopadrino (A-S?)--a *padrino* who does not provide well for his godchildren.

alar (S)--the bottommost roof support in a house.

albañil (S)--mason.

alcalde (S)--mayor; the leading authority in the district; also one of various colonial and republican authorities.

alcalde auxiliar (S)--an official of the Indian community.

alcalde de campo (S)--an official of the Indian community.

alcalde ordinario (S)--an official of the Indian community.

alcalde vara (S)--an official of the Indian community.

aldea (S)--village.

alférez (S)--a minor official in the sponsorship of a fiesta.

alguacil (S)--a minor official of the Indian community.

aliso (S)--alder tree.

almuerzo (S)--midday meal.

anaka (A)--a rectangular piece of cloth hanging from the waist in the fiesta versions of the *cotón*.

arado (S)--plow; also the heavy wooden base of the plow.

argentino (S)--a man from Argentina; specifically one of the costume types in the Tunantes dance group.

arroba (S)--unit of weight; twenty-five pounds.

ayllu (A)--the principal unit of Inca social organization above the level of the family.

ayudante (S)--helper, assistant.

azadón (S)--hoe, composed of the *lampa* and *lacwash*.

barrero (S)--mud mixer.

barreta (S)--long iron bar used as utility stick.

barrio (S)--one of the three major territorial divisions of the town; also refers to the section known as Quichuay on the edge of town.

basquet (S-E)--basketball.

batán (S)--grinding stone.

bayeta (S)--plain white woolen cloth woven locally by hand; also a long-sleeved shirt, open down the front, which formed part of the old Indian male costume.

berrete (A?)--the classical Peruvian Indian's knitted hat.

bicharra (A?)--clay stove.

blusa (S)--the contemporary blouse used with the *centro* costume.

bolear (S)--to sow by scattering the seed.

cabildo (S)--municipal council.

cacha cuy (A)--the time at which officers for the Christmas fiesta are selected; literally, "invite me."

cacique (AO)--the head of an *ayllu;* this Arawakan word was brought from the Antilles by the Spanish and was gradually substituted for the term *curaca.*

cacique principal (S)--a leader of a group of caciques.

calabaza (S)--a squash or pumpkin.

calabozo (S)--jail.

caldo (S)--a souplike dish with various ingredients.

calzón (S)--the wide short trousers which were part of the Indian male costume.

campo (S)--a minor official of the Indian community; literally, "field."

capilla ardiente (S)--a cloth tent placed over a corpse during a wake.

capilla catafalco (S)--same as *capilla ardiente.*

capitán (S)--a fiesta official.

caporal (S)--a fiesta official

caramanchel (S)--small home store.

cargador de barro (O)--mud carrier.

carrera de cintas (S)--a fiesta game in which ribbons are pulled down from a framework by people on horseback or bicycles.

casa cofradía (S)--the house in which the headman of a *cofradía* lives, and in which the wake for a saint is held.

casta (S)--the upper social class in Muquiyauyo.

cata (A?)--the small rectangular blanket worn over a woman's shoulders.

centro (S)--the contemporary women's dress in the Jauja region.

centurión (S)--officer in Holy Week.

chacra (A)--small cultivated field.

Chacra Negros (S-A)--a dance group of the Christmas fiesta.

chaleco (S)--the vest which was part of the Indian male costume.

chancaca (AO)--block of crude sugar, brown in color.

charro (S)--tramp; one of the costume types in the Tunantes dance group.

Chaupibarrio (A-S)--the barrio in the center of town, a block wide, running between the Upper and the Lower barrios.

chicha (AO)--native American drink, made usually of corn, but can also be made of peanuts or other agricultural products. It may be sweet or strong, that is, nonfermented or fermented.

chisguete (S)--a device that shoots ether or water used in the fiesta of Carnaval.

chonguino (S-A)--a man from Chongo; specifically one of the costume types in the Tunantes dance group.

chupadero (S)--the bone stopper for the *ishcuro;* also used as the means by which the lime is removed.

chupaquina (S-A)--a woman from Chupaca; specifically one of the costume types in the Tunantes dance group.

cintura (S)--a belt used with the *cotilla* blouse for earlier type of *centro.*

cirio (S)--a large imitation candle on the top of which burns a kerosene lamp.

clavija (S)--a heavy wedge formerly used in building construction.

coca (A)--the narcotic leaf chewed by the Andean Indians; *Erythroxylon coca.*

cochinero (S)--pig herder; specifically, one of the costume types in the Tunantes dance group.

cofradía (S)--religious brotherhood.

colchón (S)--padding used to protect an ox's neck from a yoke; more generally a crude blanket.

comida (S)--evening meal.

comisionado (S)--a person who is commissioned to do something; a poet in the older communal-district structure; also a person in the work projects who acts as executive.

compadrazgo (S)--the *compadre* relationship.

compadre (S)--cogodparent; the father and godparent of a child are *compadres.*

comunidad indígena (S)--the Indian community.

conquistador (S)--conqueror; specifically, one of the costume types of the Corcovados dance group.

consejo (S)--council, specifically the district council made up of the alcalde, *regidores,* and so forth.

convivientes (S)--persons living together in common-law marriage.

convocatorio (S)--meeting of the nineteenth-century Indian community members.

Corcovados (S)--humpbacks; specifically the principal dance group of the New Year and Candelaria fiestas.

cordelador (S)--a man who checks the alignment of some piece of construction, using a cord to do so.

cordillate (S)--Indian male costume, which has now disappeared.

corredor (S)--a porch running along one long side of a house.

corregidor (S)--a crown official in colonial government after about 1570.

corregimiento (S)--the Spanish official territorial unit which replaced the *encomienda* for purposes of government; the *corregidor*, in charge of the *corregimiento*, was a paid official, not a grantee like the *encomendero*.

corrida de toros (S)--bullfight; in Muquiyauyo, it is bullbaiting.

cortamonte (S)--a fiesta game; same as the *tumbamonte*.

cotilla (S)--an early type of blouse worn with the *centro* costume.

cotón (S)--the old style woman's dress, composed of a single-piece black woolen frock; still used in the southern end of the valley and in fiesta costumes in Muquiyauyo.

coyunda (S)--the rawhide loop used to attach the *timón* to the yoke.

cuadra (S)--a unit of land measure; theoretically a quarter of a *yugada*.

cuadrilla (S)--a dance group.

cuartel (S)--one of the four subdivisions of the modern community of Muquiyauyo.

cuña (S)--wedge.

curaca (A)--a local official under the Inca and early colonial regimes; a *curaca* was usually in charge of an *ayllu*. The term was replaced in the colonial period by cacique.

curandero (S)--a lay curer; sometimes a magician who cures.

cuyero (S-A)--literally, the place of the *cuyes* or guinea pigs; hence, same as the *poyo*, the bench in the kitchen where guinea pigs are kept.

decenté (S)--same as conquistador; literally, "decent ones."

departamento (S)--the principal republican territorial subdivision of Peru.

depósito (S)--storeroom.

Día del Pascua de Reyes (S)--Day of the Kings.

distrito (S)--the smallest territorial unit in the Peruvian Republic; the original districts were created in accordance with the existing parishes at the time of the independence.

doctrina (S)--Catholic doctrine, catechism.

dormitorio (S)--bedroom.

encomienda (S)--the Spanish colonial grant of the sixteenth century of the right of exploitation of a given piece of territory; the *encomendero* is the person who received such a grant.

era (S)--a place where winnowing is done.

faena (S)--work; used specifically in Muquiyauyo for the communal work sessions.

feria (S)--fair; a weekly or periodic market.

frazada (S)--blanket.

futbol (S-E)--football.

garrocha (S)--a stick used to prod oxen.

gizo (S)--a special *caldo* (stew) used at funerals.

gobernador (S)--the district officer responsible for law and order.

guardia civil (S)--civil guard; i.e., the national police.

Guaripampa (A)--an earlier spelling of Huaripampa.

guindo (S)--the mazard cherry tree. The word *guinda* is supposed to refer to the fruit, but is used interchangeably with *guindo* in Muquiyauyo.

haba (S)--the broad bean; *Vicia faba* I.

hermandad (S)--brotherhood.

hipoteca (S)--mortgage.

hombreador (S)--carrier of adobes.

huachaca (A)--a woven belt for the *cotón*.

huaji, huajiti (A)--exchange labor.

Huanca (A)--the pre-Inca tribe which occupied the present Mantaro Valley.

Huaylijía (A)--a dance group of the Christmas fiesta.

huayno (A)--a Peruvian highland music and dance.

indígena (S)--indigene, native.

indio (S)--Indian, or a member of the Indian social class.

indio de retaguardia (S)--one of the costume types of the Corcovados dance group.

indio principal del pueblo y mandón del pueblo (S)--the leading Indian of a colonial Indian town.

intendencia (S)--a major territorial subdivision of Peru in the late colonial period; itself subdivided into *partidos*.

ishcuro (A)--the small gourd in which the lime for coca chewing is kept; also spelled *iscuro* and *ishicuro*.

jalapata (S)--an old fiesta game, no longer used.

jalapichi (A)--one of the costume types in the Tunantes dance group.

jaujina (S)--a woman from Jauja; one of the costume types in the Corcovados dance group; also used to refer to the type of white panama hat worn by women in the Jauja region.

jefe be barreros (S)--the man in charge of mud mixers in a community work session.

jefe de obra (S)--the director of a *cuartel's* work in a community work session.

jerga (S)--blanket.

junta directiva (S)--a directing council or group; directorate.

kumu (A)--one of the costume types of the Huaylijía.

lacwash (A)--the wooden handle made for the hoe.

lampa (or *lampita*) (A)--the metal blade on the hoe; also the stone artifacts of the same shape found near the town.

latash aukish (A)--same as *principal*. one of the dancers in the group of Principales in the fiesta of Candelaria.

lavatorio (S)--the ceremony of washing the clothing of the deceased.

llamero (S-A)--one of the costume types in the Huaylijía dance group.

lliclla (A)--small rectangular shoulder blanket; same as the *cata,. manta.*

lonche (S-E)--a between-meal snack; from "lunch."

macha (S)--a woman in charge of *cargadores de barro.*

mandón (S)--a minor official of the Indian community.

manga (S)--sleeve.

manisuela (S)--a hand stone used on the *batán.*

mansera (S)--the wooden handle of a plow.

manta (S)--a small rectangular shoulder blanket; same as *cata* and *lliclla.*

marinera (S)--a Peruvian dance of mestizo origin.

mashua (A)--a native Andean tuber; *Tropaelum tuberosum* R. & Pav.

mayó (A?)--one of the costume types of the Huaylijía dance group.

mayoral (S)--a secondary official in the sponsorship of a fiesta.

mayordomo (S)--a man who is in charge of a fiesta; he may either collect funds for the sponsoring or pay the cost himself.

mejicano (S)--a man from Mexico; specifically, one of the costume types in the Tunantes dance group.

mercado (S)--daily market.

mestizo (S)--a person of mixed Indian and Spanish ancestry; today the term also refers to the upper social class in the highland villages, regardless of ancestry.

minifundio (S)--the successive splitting up of land through inheritance over various generations.

mishkipa (A)--the traditional rest and relaxation period during a work session.

mitimaes (A)--populations moved by the Incas as a means of consolidating their conquest.

modillón (S)--a carved finish on an *alar.*

monillo. (S)--a blouse worn with the *centro,* not often seen today.

montaña (S)--the jungle and eastern slope of the Andes in Peru.

mortero (S)--a stone mortar used for grinding.

mortuorio (S)--the entire material arrangement for the corpse during a wake.

mote (A)--stewed corn.

municipalidad (S)--the headquarters building of the district government.

natural (S)--used in two senses: an Indian, as in the sense of "native"; a child born out of wedlock.

obrero (S)--worker.

oca (A)--a native Andean tuber; *Oxalis tuberosa* Mol.

olla (S)--a low, round pottery bowl.

olluco (A)--a native Andean tuber; *Ullucus tuberosus* Losan.

otrapachalun (A)--the custom of publicly accusing a couple of adulterous relations.

pachamanca (A)--a special meal cooked in a preheated pit.

Pachawara (A)--a dance group of the Christmas fiesta; same as Negritos.

padrino (S)--godfather; also the person responsible for the *tumbamonte* or a *carrera de cintas*.

palomay (A?)--the practice of locking a newly married couple in their room on the wedding night.

palpacuy (A)--a ceremony connected with marriage.

pandilla (S)--a dance group; a fiesta sponsoring group.

partidario (S)--sharecropper; sharecropping.

partido (S)--a territorial subdivision of the late colonial *intendencia*; Jauja was a *partido*.

paso doble (S)--a dance; also the music used for bullfights.

Pastores (S)--shepherds; specifically, a dance group and a member of the dance group of the same name; also the women dancers in the Huaylijía dance group.

patasca (S)--a special dish of pork and corn served at funerals.

patio (S)--the open space between two houses on which faces the *corredores* of each house; a patio may be surrounded on more than two sides, but few houses in Muquiyauyo are so large.

pedido (S)--request.

personero (S)--an important person in the Indian community; one of those who divided up the Indian communal lands in 1904.

peso (S)--colonial unit of currency.

pilhua (A)--indoor granary *(troja)* of bundles of straw tied together.

pinkullo (A)--reed flute.

pisco (A)--the national Peruvian grape brandy; the term is also used in Peru for *aguardiente*, but the two are usually distinguished as *aguardiente de uva* and *aguardiente de caña*.

poncho (A)--the woolen rectangular cape with a split in the middle which serves as the opening for the head; it is the standard male Muquiyauyino's overcoat.

poyo (S)--an adobe bench against the wall in the kitchen that serves as a shelter for the guinea pigs and rabbits; also called *cuyero*.

primacías (S)--a traditional gift of agricultural products to the local priest.

principal (S)--a leading person; an elder; also a member of the Principales, one of the dance groups of the Candelaria fiesta.

priosta (S)--one of those responsible for sponsoring a fiesta; usually a woman in Muquiyauyo.

propios arbitrios (S)--taxes levied by the district on the sale of goods in the town.

pro-secretario (S)--assistant secretary.

pua (S)--the metal point of a *garrocha*.

pullu (A?)--the woman's carrying blanket.

puna (A)--high Andean plateau, usually used only as pasturage area.

quebrada (S)--an erosive cut in the side of a hill; a gully.

Quechua (A)--a language, and the population speaking that language, found in highland Peru; the Inca language.

quinoa (A)--a native Andean grain; *Chenpodium quinoa* Willd.

quinual (A)--a tree, probably the *Polylepis incana* H.B.K.

quishuar (A)--a tree, probably the *Buddleia longifolia* H.B.K.

real (S)--colonial unit of currency.

reducción (S)--the Spanish colonial policy of removing Indians from scattered dwellings and establishing them in towns.

regidor (S)--an alderman on the district council; also an official in the earlier Indian community.

reja (S)--the metal point of a plow.

remate (S)--a system in which some object or right is let out to the highest bidder; the person who gets the right is the *rematista*.

repartimiento (S)--the resident Indians on an *encomienda*; the *encomienda* grant included the right to exploit the labor of certain *repartimientos* of Indians.

riegos (S)--irrigated lands.

romería (S)--pilgrimage; specifically the visit to the cemetery on the Day of All Saints.

sala (S)--the main room of a house.

sala comunal (S)--the communal meeting room.

sancochado (S)--a dish made up of various ingredients.

savila (A?)--a local type of maguey.

segundo jefe (S)--second to the *jefe de obra*.

shujupe (A)--a *mishkipa* sponsored by the *cuartel* during a *faena* or work session.

sindico de gastos (S)--district officer in charge of outgoing funds.

sindico de rentas (S)--district officer in charge of incoming funds.

sociedad (S)--society; as used in the text it refers to a religious brotherhood or association.

sol (S)--the Peruvian unit of currency.

suhulachisa (A)--a technique for restoring the soul to the body when it has been lost through *susto.*

surco (S)--furrow.

susto (S)--fright; particularly an illness which results from having been frightened.

suyu (A)--a section of land assigned to Indians in colonial Muqui-yauyo; probably from the Quechua term, *suyu,* for the major sub-divisions of the Inca Empire; in Muquiyauyo the *suyus* were assigned to each *ayllu.*

tabliadora (S)--a wooden mallet used for washing clothes.

tamboril (S)--a drum used in the fiesta of Santiago.

tapia (S)--a clay wall of rammed earth.

temporales (S)--unirrigated lands.

teniente alcalde (S)--lieutenant mayor, or assistant mayor of the district.

teniente gobernador (S)--assistant to the *gobernador;* there is usually one in the district capital and in other populated centers of a district.

tienducha (S)--a small home store carrying only a few items of daily necessity.

tierra blanca (S)--white earth; a special clay used for plastering the outside of houses.

tika-maestro (S)--the man in charge of *hombreadores* in a community work session.

timón (S)--a shaft for harnessing oxen to plow.

tirira (S)--part of a plow.

topo (A)--the Inca unit of land measurement; precise value uncertain.

torero (S)--bullfighter.

toronjil (S)--an herb, used in a tea, which serves both as a food and a medicine.

tributarios (S)--tributaries; specifically Indians in colonial Peru who paid tribute to the Spanish.

troje (S)--an indoor granary of bundles of straw tied together.

tumbamonte (S)--a fiesta game which involves setting up a tree and then chopping it down; also called *cortamonte.*

Tunantes (S)--a dance group in the Christmas fiesta, and the members of the same group.

turno (S)--a list of nominations for some appointive post.

vaquero (S)--cowboy.

vara (S)--the Spanish yard, with a value of approximately 2.8 feet; in this study the square *vara* is given the value of .697 square meters.

velorio (S)--a wake, held both for the dead and for a saint on the night before his Mass.

víspera (S)--vesper.

vocal (S)--a regular member (as opposed to an officer) of an administrative group.

volibol (S-E)--volleyball.

waqui (A)--one of the costume types of the Huaylijía dance group.

yaravís (A)--sad, native Peruvian music.

Yauyus (A)--an earlier spelling of Yauyos.

yugada (S)--a unit of land measure; theoretically the amount of land which can be plowed by a yoke of oxen in a day.

zapallo (A)--a squash; *Cucurbita maxima* Duch.

BIBLIOGRAPHY

Adams, Richard N. "A Change from Caste to Class in a Peruvian Sierra Town," *Social Forces*, XXXI (1953), 238-44.

--------. Muquiyauyo: A Study, with the Utilization of Ethnographic and Local History Materials, of Culture Change and Progressivism in the Central Sierra of Peru. Ph. D. thesis, Yale University, 1950.

--------. "Personnel in Culture Change: A Test of a Hypothesis," *Social Forces*, XXX (1951), 185-89.

--------. "A Study of Labor Preference in Peru." *Human Organization*, X (1951), 37-38.

Arguedas, José María. "Cuentos mágico-realistas y cancionco do fiestas tradicionales del valle del Mantaro: Provincias de Jauja y Concepción. Archivo del Instituto de Estudios Etnológicos," *Folklore Americano* (Lima), I (1953), 101-293.

Castro Pozo, Hildebrando. *Nuestra comunidad indígena.* Lima: Editorial "El Lucero," 1924.

--------. "Social and Economico-Political Evolution of the Communities of Central Peru," in *Handbook of South American Indians,* II (1947), 483-99. See Steward, Julian H. (ed.).

Censo nacional de población de 1940: Departamentos: Huánuco, Junín. Vol. IV. Lima: Dirección Nacional de Estadistica, n. d.

Davis, J. Merle. "The Economic and Social Setting," in *Indians of the High Andes,* ed. W. S. Rycroft. New York, 1946, pp. 13-93.

Foster, George M. "Cofradía and Compadrazgo in Spain and South America," *Southwestern Journal of Anthropology,* IX (1953), 1-28.

Gillin, John. *Moche: A Peruvian Coastal Community.* (Institute of Social Anthropology, Publication No. 3.) Washington, D.C.: Smithsonian Institution, 1945.

Kubler, George. *The Indian Caste of Peru, 1795-1940.* (Institute

of Social Anthropology, Publication No. 14.) Washington, D.C.:
Smithsonian Institution, 1952.

-------. "The Quechua in the Colonial World," in *Handbook of
South American Indians*, II (1947), 331-410. See Steward, Julian
H. (ed.).

Mishkin, Bernard. "The Contemporary Quechua," in *Handbook
of South American Indians*, II (1947), 411-70. See Steward, Julian
H. (ed.).

Prescott, William H. *History of the Conquest of Peru*. 2 vols.
New York: Harper and Brothers, 1847.

Quijada Jara, Sergio. *Estampas huancavelicanas: Temas folkloricos*. Lima: Empresa Tipografica "Salas é Hijos," 1944.

Real Academia Española. *Diccionario de la lengua española*. 17th
ed. Madrid, 1947.

Redfield, Robert. *The Folk Cultures of Yucatán*. Chicago: The
University of Chicago Press, 1941.

Rowe, John H. "Inca Culture at the Time of the Spanish Conquest,"
in *Handbook of the South American Indians*, II (1947), 183-330.
See Steward, Julian H. (ed.).

Sáenz, Moisés. *The Peruvian Indian*. Mimeographed; Washington,
D.C., 1944. Translated by the staff of the Strategic Index of the
Americas from *Sobre el indio peruano y su incorporación al medio
nacional*. Mexico: Publicaciones de la Secretaria de Educación
Publica, 1933.

Sanabria Santiváñez, Eliseo. *Historia de Urin Wanca ó San Jerónimo de Tunan*. Cerro de Pasco, Peru: Imprenta "Kipus," 1943.

Sauer, Carl O. "Cultivated Plants of South and Central America,"
in *Handbook of South American Indians*, VI (1950), 487-543. See
Steward, Julian H. (ed.).

Steward, Julian H. (ed.) *Handbook of South American Indians*. (Bureau of American Ethnology, Bulletin 143.) 6 vols. Washington,
D.C.: Smithsonian Institution, 1946-50.

Tarazona S., Justino M. *Demarcación política del Peru: Recopilación de leyes y decretos (1821-1946)*. Lima: Ministerio de Hacienda y Comercio, 1946.

Tschopik, Harry, Jr. *Highland Communities of Central Peru*. (Institute of Social Anthropology, Publication No. 5.) Washington,
D.C.: Smithsonian Institution, 1947.

Valcárcel, Luis E. "Indian Markets and Fairs in Peru," in *Handbook of South American Indians*, II (1947), 477-82. See Steward,
Julian H. (ed.).

Varallanos, José. *Legislación indiana republicana*. Lima: C.I.P.,
1947.

Vázquez de Espinosa, Antonio. *Compendio y descripción de las Indias Occidentales*. (Smithsonian Miscellaneous Collections, Vol. 108.) Washington, D.C.: Smithsonian Institution, 1948.

Yacovleff, Eugenio, and Fortunato L. Herrera. "El mundo vegetal de los antiguos peruanos," *Revista del Museo Nacional de Lima*, III (1934), 241-322; IV (1935), 29-102.

INDEX

Aco, 4, 129
Acolla, 137, 138
Adobe construction: description of, 140, 141, 143
Adolescence, 157
Adultery, 161
Agriculture: and land tenure, 113-15; implements of, 118-20, 208; crops in, 120-22, 125; cultivation practices in, 122; Inca methods of, 122, 123, 124; labor in, 122-24; magic in, 124-25; and tree planting, 125-26; technological improvements in, 207; in Mantaro Valley, 214
Amanzo, Román, 8, 120, 121, 126, 216
Animal husbandry, 127-28
Apaicancha, 120
Apata, 4
Aprismo, 209
Aprista Party, 99, 100
Architecture: in Jauja Valley, 4
Arguedas, José María, quoted, 213-14
Associations. See Cofradía lands: and fiestas; Sociedad de San Juan Chico; Sociedad de San Juan Grande; Sociedad de San Miguel; Sociedad de San Pedro y San Pablo; Sociedad de Santo Cristo
Ataura, 4, 46, 102
Atunjauja, 26, 31, 34
Atunxauxa (Jauja), 3
Aurora Club, 162
Avalanche Basket Club, 78, 162, 163
Ayllus: and reducción movement, 14; Spanish taking of, 22; description of, 24; in the eighteenth century, 27, 28; in conquest period, 47; in late colonial period, 47; breakdown of, 29, 33, 34, 47; mentioned, 25, 26, 48, 51

Barrios: significance of, 87-88; origin of

Quichuay, 123; endogamy in, 158; and sports clubs, 163
Bernard, Edward, 222
Bolívar, Simon, 18, 40
Book of Agreements of General Interest Between the Authorities and the Comunidad, 38
Bullfighting, 194
Bustamante, Gabriel, 73, 216
Bustamante, Pedro, 13, 129, 220, 222

Caja, 129, 152
Canal system, 126-27
Canchaillo, 31
Canchapunco, 31
Candelaria, 61, 62, 188; celebration of, 193-95
Carnaval: general description of, 63-65, 71-72, 195-96; at mines, 90-91; mentioned, 56, 61, 188
Caste system, 34; breakdown of, 38, 71, 86-87, 88-89, 92, 202, 205, 206, 216; and population growth, 71; and fiestas, 71-73 passim, 83; in late nineteenth century, 82-83; and differentiation, 85-86, 88, 153; and marriage, 86
Castro Pozo, Hildebrando, quoted, 40, 99
Catholic church: and land ownership, 16-17, 21, 22; and Huaripampa dispute, 51-55; and Muquiyauyo and Indians, 52, 76-78, 80-81; and duties of priest, 54-55; and relationship with Muquiyauyo, 75-77, 78, 205; and mestizos, 76-78, 79-80
Cerro, Sanchez: and revolt, 45-46, 98, 99
Cerro de Pasco Copper Corporation, 90, 91, 94, 95, 188
Childhood, 155-57

247